Inventing the American Woman

ARTHUR S. LINK

Princeton University

GENERAL EDITOR FOR HISTORY

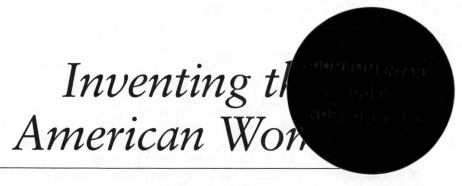

Inventing the American Woman

A PERSPECTIVE
ON WOMEN'S HISTORY

G LENDA R ILEY
University of Northern Iowa

Generously Donated to
The Frederick Douglass Institute
By Professor Jesse Moore
Fall 2000

HARLAN DAVIDSON, INC.
Arlington Heights, Illinois 60004

Library of Congress Cataloging-in-Publication Data

Riley, Glenda, 1938–
Inventing the American woman.

Includes bibliographies and index.
1. Women—United States—History.   I. Title.
HQ1410.R55   1987   305.4'0973   86-29208
ISBN 0-88295-846-1

*For the generations
of students and colleagues
who contributed
to my understanding of
and commitment to
the history of women
in the United States*

Contents

Acknowledgments

So many people have contributed to the genesis of this book over the years that it is impossible to name them all. Two historians of women who have been particularly supportive of the project are D'Ann Campbell and Sandra L. Myres. Two of my colleagues who have encouraged the writing of the work and offered help with details are Harold B. Wohl and William H. Graves. One who deserves special mention for his perceptive critiques and insightful suggestions is Richard S. Kirkendall, Henry A. Wallace Professor of Agricultural History at Iowa State University.

The project was supported in part by a professional development leave from the University of Northern Iowa. The staff of the UNI Library contributed greatly to its progress, always with unflagging good humor. Patricia Murphy proved to be an accurate and willing typist. And Karmen Berger served as an energetic and often creative research assistant and "gopher."

The work finally reached completion through the warm and enthusiastic support of the late Harlan Davidson; the press's general editor for history, Arthur S. Link; and its executive editor, Maureen Gilgore Hewitt. The style of the manuscript improved notably through the efforts of Susannah H. Jones and Lori Elizabeth Winters.

To all of these people, as well as those who remain unnamed, I am grateful.

Inventing the American Woman

This 1831 illustration entitled The Wife *shows a woman who is expected to do little to occupy herself except sit idly, resting and fanning, as her husband intently reads.* From Godey's Lady's Book, *Philadelphia, Pennsylvania.*

Prescription and Protest

Y OU may be asking yourself why you have not encountered a number of texts on women's history during your high school and college careers. You may be wondering why the story of American women has seemed to come to light only so recently. Actually, interest in the history of women is not a recent development. Americans of many eras have considered women's experiences worthy of record.

In the early 1830s, for example, *Godey's Lady's Book,* the largest selling periodical of its day, offered its readers historical sketches of women as a regular feature. An early book-length study analyzing women in the American past appeared in 1848. Elizabeth Fries Lummis Ellet, a well-known author, published a two-volume work entitled *The Women of the American Revolution,* which used oral history to recount the contributions of women to the Revolutionary War. In 1854, writer Lydia Maria Child also wrote a two-volume history of women. Entitled *History of the Condition of Women,* it spanned ancient to modern times. In 1898, yet another two-volume work, Sydney Fisher's *Men, Women, and Manners in Colonial Times,* stressed the contributions of women to American agriculture. Many other similar books and articles written by both women and men appeared throughout the nineteenth century.

By the turn of the twentieth century, many historians who had received formal training in the new American graduate schools began to join these lay historians in recording and analyzing the course of historical events. Because they usually concentrated on political and economic events such as wars, depressions, acts of Congress, and presidential policies, groups of people such as women, blacks, American Indians, immigrants, and "common" men were generally overlooked. A group of reform-minded historians known as Progressives, however, soon began to attack this view of history. During the 1920s, Arthur M. Schlesinger, Sr., in particular, raised serious questions about the virtual absence of women in most history textbooks. He called upon historians to expand their outlook to include females as well as males.

Although Schlesinger's words often fell on deaf ears, several historians took his challenge seriously. In 1938, Julia Cherry Spruill wrote a detailed survey of women's lives and labors in the southern colonies. In 1946, Mary Ritter Beard published *Women as Force in History* to demonstrate that women indeed deserved inclusion in the historical record. Beard's thoughtful and well-reasoned study presented an important argument for increased recognition of women's history. A few others followed Beard's lead. During the next few decades, some fine women's history was written yet did not receive widespread attention.

The emergence of the contemporary feminist movement in the 1960s dramatically revised this situation. No longer willing to accept historical "invisibility," feminist leaders called for exposure of women's historical heritage. They demanded that women's lives and experiences receive attention from all types of scholars, and especially from historians. No longer, they warned, would women tolerate being denied a sense of value and identity by near omission from the historical record.

Possessing an increased social consciousness as a result of the various reform crusades of the 1960s, many historians responded enthusiastically to the call to retrieve women's history. They undertook a sincere attempt to remedy the omissions, usually by adding unusual or important women to historical studies and textbooks. But change was slow and difficult to effect. In 1976, I conducted a survey of American history textbooks that revealed a discouraging picture. In a textbook written in 1972, one that offered a 409-page survey of the "complicated story" of "our national history" before 1877, only 5 women appeared as opposed to 278 men. Four of these women were covered in the only three paragraphs on women's history in the entire text. A 478-page work published in 1975 included 13 women and 406 men. Out of almost ninety illustrations, only four pictured women. Here, the topic of women's history was dealt with in less than four pages. These were typical of the large number of American history textbooks examined.

In addition, these volumes concentrated on famous women and those who participated in the woman suffrage movement. Black, American Indian, Mexican-American, and other racial and ethnic groups of women were seldom mentioned. Working, frontier, southern, and other types of women were similarly ignored. Most historians still used the pronouns "he," "him," and "his" as generic terms that subsumed women. And they continued to refer to women condescendingly as "the gentler sex" while characterizing suffragists with such phrases as "petticoats in revolt" and "a belligerent bevy of female agitators."

Despite these problems, both historians and the public began to realize that women had been given short shrift in history. More encouraging yet was the willingness of many historians to try to correct the situation. A new breed of historians, women's historians, began to emerge in the late 1960s and early 1970s to aid in the development of this "remedial history," as it soon came to be known. At first they concentrated on correcting the traditional omission of women, primarily by writing famous women into historical accounts. They quickly turned their attention to more sophisticated analysis. Both female and male historians of women began to explore questions relating to the oppression of women, their political activities, involvements with home and family, participation in reform movements, and changing roles in different eras. At the same time, they began to call for an integration of women's history into all history courses. They often naively believed that, once they had established the validity of women's history and integrated it into historical knowledge as a whole, their task would be finished.

As the study of women's history progressed and grew throughout the 1970s and 1980s, its complexity and vast scope became increasingly apparent. It also became obvious that women's history could not be dealt with simply by establishing a "compensatory" history that would interject women's contributions into a male-oriented past. The story of women's lives through time was so intricate that it clearly demanded ongoing study by many scholars who would be willing to devote entire careers to its pursuit. Consequently, women's history and the larger field of women's studies became well-established areas of research, study, and instruction. Many specialized journals, such as *Women's Studies, Signs,* and *Women's History,* now exist. The American Historical Association and the Organization of American Historians recognize women's "conference groups" within their organizations, important steps in legitimizing the field of women's history. Since 1973, six Berkshire Conferences on the history of women have been held. Numerous other conferences and scholarly sessions are now held every year. And thousands of women's history and women's studies courses and programs are now offered in American schools, colleges, and universities. Still, experts agree that the surface of the study of women has just been scratched.

Despite this trend toward specialization, historians interested in women are still dedicated to integrating knowledge about them into other history courses. A movement often called "mainstreaming" is currently afoot to encourage instructors and students alike to focus on the history of their collective past rather than on only segments of it. Like the early feminists, proponents of mainstreaming argue that women should not be denied their historical heritage. But they also add that inadequate coverage of women is unfair to men as well because it produces a biased view of the past. Reaching these women and men with a more balanced version of history requires efforts that range beyond specialized courses. Advocates of mainstreaming firmly believe that it is the function of the introductory history course to present students with a comprehensive and inclusive approach to the past.

This book, *Inventing the American Woman,* presents an introduction to the history of women in the United States that combines factual knowledge with a specific thesis intended to provoke discussion and further thought. It is my hope that it will inform, enlighten, and expand the thinking of all who read it.

In an attempt to achieve these goals, this book necessarily emphasizes what historian Kathryn Kish Sklar terms "gender specific" experiences. It focuses on those historical episodes that are more germane to one gender than the other. Specifically, women's work, socialization, roles, activities, and cultural values are of primary concern. Due to limitations of time and space, "human specific" occurrences, or those that involve both men and women, often receive little attention. As Sklar argues, it is often necessary to divide and reduce complicated reality in order to analyze its various components. In this case, women's history is separated from human history to make it manageable and understandable.

More specifically, this volume compares the model that was to direct American women's behavior with women's reactions to it. The model was created by generations of both women and men who accepted certain enduring "truths" regarding women. To them a real American woman intrinsically was, among other things, a devoted mother, an unusually virtuous person who had to remain aloof from the corruption of politics, a domestic individual who labored most happily and productively within her own home, and a weak-minded, physically inferior being who needed guidance from stronger and wiser people—men. Once accepted as truths, these ideas were embodied in a series of intricate images and stereotypes that defined and limited women's roles. In other words, people invented the American woman.

All cultures invent roles to achieve certain objectives. A variety of scholars and commentators have offered their ideas concerning the purpose served by the model American woman. Some argue that a narrow, domestic image was the creation of selfish men who conspired to keep power and privilege for themselves. Others suggest that a limited sphere for women assured the continuing consolidation of political power in the hands of an elite, prevented disquieting shifts in the nation's labor force, and forestalled anxiety-producing changes in such areas as the family, education, and social life. Yet others point out that confining women to certain activities was a logical outcome of most earlier periods of world history in which men were usually dominant.

It is not the purpose of this book to endorse any of these views. It does argue that the model was confining, tension-producing, and, at most times, outmoded, despite the fact that generations of American women and men clung tenaciously to it. These people apparently found stereotypes of women helpful or comforting. Perhaps the idealization of women seemed to ensure the continuation of a customary and thus comfortable way of life. In other words, the idea of women's separate sphere was familiar and known, like an old shoe. Never mind that the shoe's broken last and outmoded heel prevented it from functioning properly. A new shoe might create new, unknown problems.

As a result of this kind of thinking, untold numbers of women were compelled to accept the dictates of the invented image and attempted to fulfill its many precepts. If they had misgivings, questions, or doubts as they strove to develop their domesticity and accept their imputed weaknesses, many managed to keep them to themselves. Perhaps at such times they even convinced themselves that they were in grievous error to question societal prescriptions regarding their feminine nature.

Yet in addition to thousands of such seemingly quiet and accepting women, there were thousands throughout America's history who resisted the model. They openly exhibited and fervently discussed the tensions that they felt. Their feelings of conflict resulted from trying to function as unique individuals while fitting themselves, however torturously, into prescribed patterns. Although these women had distinct hopes, desires, and talents, they found it necessary to adapt their lives to the stereotypes. They accepted the idea that they had to emulate the model in order to be "true" American women. Thus, they valiantly grappled with a demand that they live up to stereotypes rather than develop their own talents and desires.

These women were often displeased that molds had been cast for them rather than opportunities offered. Societal expectations determined almost every aspect of their lives and directed most of their actions. These prescriptions caused women's education to be distinct, segregated, and of inferior quality. They forced women's literature to be narrow, often puerile, and limiting to the mind. And they encouraged women's clothing to be impractical, sexually enhancing, and limiting to the body.

The many women who disliked having to cope with such restrictions on their lives seemed to have split personalities. They continually tried both to achieve the prescribed image and to develop their own personalities. It is on this type of woman that this book concentrates. It maintains that their experience represents the lives of American women to a far greater degree than does that of the docile and supposedly happy women who, at least on the surface, shaped themselves into a facsimile of the accepted model. The primary object here is to examine from a historical perspective the lives and activities of women who lived uneasily with the invented American woman. Black, American Indian, and Oriental women, for whom the model American woman was a meaningless construct, are also considered. This book deals, as all women's history must, with both the image of the ways women should act and with the manner in which women actually did think and feel. Rather than accepting conventional and largely unfounded descriptions of women's lives, it refers to women's own words and actions as well as to recent analyses by women's history scholars.

The book proceeds through the major eras of early American history by determining the prescriptions for women and examining women's protests against them. It begins with the traditional date of 1607, the year of the first successful English settlement at Jamestown, and concludes in our own era of the 1980s. The first centuries witnessed the painful growth, progress, and unification of the American nation. For women, they also brought change, development, and a growing awareness of the benefits of solidarity. During the last century, the United States underwent gigantic changes, including industrialization, urbanization, and development as a world power. For women, the image of the model American woman was restructured but not destroyed by crucial developments including their mass entry into the labor force, the granting of woman suffrage, and the emergence of the contemporary feminist movement.

The suggested readings at the end of each chapter are designed to lead the interested reader into further study of women's issues and themes for particular periods. It is hoped that the information offered here will lend insight into the reshaping of the model of American women from simply that of "Adam's rib," restricted to a "separate sphere," to a more dynamic and attractive image of a full participant in all aspects of the modern world.

SUGGESTIONS FOR FURTHER READING

Beard, Mary R. *Women as Force in History.* New York: Collier Books, 1946.

Carroll, Berenice A., ed. *Liberating Women's History: Theoretical and Critical Essays.* Urbana: University of Illinois Press, 1976.

DuBois, Ellen. "Politics and Culture in Women's History." *Feminist Studies* 6 (Spring 1980): 28–36.

Filene, Peter G. "Integrating Women's History and Regular History." *The History Teacher* 8 (August 1980): 483–492.

George, Carol V. R., ed. *"Remember the Ladies": New Perspectives on Women in American History.* Syracuse, NY: Syracuse University Press, 1975.

Gordon, Ann D., Mari Jo Buhle, and Nancy E. Schrom. "Women in American Society: An Historical Contribution." *Radical America* 5 (1971): 3–66.

Gordon, Linda, Elizabeth Pleck, Persis Hunt, Marcia Scott, and Rochelle Ziegler. "A Review of Sexism in American Historical Writing." *Women's Studies* 1 (1972): 133–158.

Hartman, Mary and Lois Banner, eds. *Clio's Consciousness Raised: New Perspectives on the History of Women.* New York: Harper and Row, 1974.

Lerner, Gerda. *The Majority Finds Its Past.* New York: Oxford University Press, 1979.

————. "New Approaches to the Study of Women in American History." *Journal of Social History* 3 (1959): 53–62.

————. "Placing Women in History: Definitions and Challenges." *Feminist Studies* 3 (1975): 5–14.

Moseley, Eva S. "Sources for the 'New Women's History.'" *American Archivist* 43 (Spring 1980): 180–190.

Riley, Glenda. "Is Clio Still Sexist? Women's History in Recent American History Texts." *Teaching History: A Journal of Methods* 1 (Spring 1976): 15–24.

————. "Integrating Women's History into Existing Course Structures." *The History Teacher* 12 (August 1979): 493–499.

Sklar, Kathryn Kish. "American Female Historians in Context, 1770–1930." *Feminist Studies,* 3 (1975): 171–184.

————. "A Conceptual Framework for the Teaching of U.S. Women's History." *The History Teacher* 13 (August 1980): 471–481.

Smith, Bonnie. "The Contribution of Women to Modern Historiography in Great Britain, France, and the United States, 1750–1940." *American Historical Review* 89 (June 1984): 709–732.

Ætatis suæ 21. Aº. 1616.

Matoaks als Rebecka daughter to the mighty Prince Powhatan Emperour of Attanoughkomouck als Virginia converted and baptized in the Christian faith, and Wife to the wor.ll Mr Tho: Rolff.

This portrait of Pocahontas was painted by an unknown English artist after the 1616 engraving of her by Simon van de Passe. It presents her as a Euro-American woman in appearance and dress rather than as an American Indian. Courtesy of the National Portrait Gallery, Smithsonian Institution, Washington, D.C.

CHAPTER I

A Golden Age? Colonial America
1607–1776

THE year was 1607. The English, eager to enter the race for colonies in the new world, had already failed in their attempt to settle the island of Roanoke off the coast of North Carolina. Now they sent a shipload of men to settle in Virginia. Hopeful that they would find rich natural resources similar to those discovered by Spanish colonizers in South America and French colonizers in Canada, these Englishmen looked toward the new land with optimism in their hearts.

Their hopes were soon shattered. After almost destroying themselves in their futile attempts to discover precious metals and other riches, these first English colonists at Jamestown turned to agriculture. They began to grow crops to feed themselves and then tobacco to export to England. It was soon apparent to both them and the mother country that colonization in Virginia would succeed only if it were based on long-term settlement by families that could provide a market for English goods.

This policy depended on the presence of women—a critical factor in English colonization. Not only were their childbearing abilities essential to the success of colonies in North America, but their contributions as laborers, religious and social forces, and wives and mothers were also crucial. Despite the importance of women to the development of early America, however, traditional conceptions of women, transplanted from Europe and surviving the demands of the colonial environment, continued to shape women's lives. Yet the raw new world and the resistance of numerous female colonists modified customary ideas of women's roles and behaviors.

There is evidence that a few women entered the colonial scene in North America very early. Records indicate that a woman named Anne Forest and her maid, Anne Buras, arrived in Virginia in 1608. A few other women probably completed the hazardous journey as well. But the first significant number of women landed in Virginia in 1619 to be sold by their own consent as wives. The London Company of Virginia recognized the need to send women to Virginia if colonial markets and social stability were to develop in the near future. Yet despite their efforts, by the mid-1600s, men in Virginia still outnumbered women by six to one.

In 1620, a group of religious dissenters against the English Anglican Church landed at Plymouth, whose numbers included both males and females. Eighteen women and eleven girls were listed among the passengers of the *Mayflower*. Only four of the women lived until the following spring, while all eleven of the girls survived the first harsh winter. More women followed as a result of their defection from the church and of the Plymouth Company's interest in promoting the increase of families in their colony. But it was not until 1700 that the sex ratio began to equalize in Massachusetts.

As other colonies gradually established themselves, their founders recognized that women constituted an important group of settlers, both economically and socially. Lord Baltimore of Maryland encouraged the immigration of women because he believed that, "when the plantation grows to strength, then it is time to plant with women as well as with men; that the plantation may spread into generations, and not ever be pierced from without." This policy seemed particularly useful for Maryland, which by the 1650s had approximately 600 males and less than 200 females.

The shortage of women in colonial America created an urgent demand for their importation. While some women came to the colonies as wives and daughters, many others came as potential wives. Between 1620 and 1622, Virginia auctioned off 150 "pure and spotless" women for eighty pounds of tobacco. Other women came as kidnap victims of agents who saw potential gain in selling them as wives. And hundreds of others arrived as petty criminals sentenced to deportation by governments eager to decrease the population of their prisons while increasing that of their colonies.

A large number of women came to America as indentured servants. These were single women between the ages of eighteen and twenty-five who sold their labor for four to seven years in return for their passage, support during their indentures, and a small amount of cash and clothing at the end of their terms. It has been estimated that as many as half of female colonists came as indentured servants, going first to the southern colonies, and later to the middle and New England colonies. During the 1600s, approximately one third of colonial families employed an indentured servant, who was considered part of the household. Although these servants were engaged primarily in domestic tasks, they were occasionally employed in field work as well.

Violations of the indenture were punished severely. Both running away and pregnancy merited an extension of service. The latter crime was common since indentured women were not allowed to marry until the end of their terms. In Maryland alone, one fifth of indentured women were charged with "bastardy." A punitive Virginia law passed in 1692, however, indicated that such pregnancies were due to "some dissolute masters" who had "gotten their maids with child." Despite this problem, virtually all female indentures married at the end of their terms, and often married well because of the continuing demand for women.

Despite the pressure to migrate to America, women remained outnumbered by men, often by as much as five or six men to one woman throughout the South. Some historians argue that the relative scarcity of women often gave them some choice of marriage partners as well as a limited degree of independence and power. Although the family was patriarchal in structure, women were valued and protected within it. In 1712, Benjamin Wadsworth, a Puritan minister, stated that a wife, along with the house and rest of the family, "aught to be under the husband's government." On the other hand, colonial husbands were compelled by law to support their wives and to be faithful to them. Both failure to provide and adultery were punishable offenses. Physical punishment of wives was also controlled by law. In 1641, for example, Massachusetts prohibited a husband from abusing his wife "unless it be in his own defense upon her assault." Divorces and separations were also granted to women with grievances.

A good deal of the consideration extended to colonial women derived from their economic contributions, both as domestic artisans in the home and laborers in the barn and sometimes in the fields. Governor William Bradford of Plymouth observed that, when the Pilgrims landed, the women "went willingly into the fields and took their little ones with them to set corn."

Throughout the colonial period ending in the 1770s, women continued to work in the fields during periods of labor shortage. Although they often performed such male-defined tasks, males only infrequently reciprocated by performing women's domestic chores. As a region became more settled, women's work increasingly focused on the house and garden. Their duties in these areas were extensive and often performed under difficult conditions. It was the women's responsibility to translate into usable goods the raw materials generated by the men through planting or hunting. They were the key links in manufacturing raw materials into finished products. In this capacity, they were the equivalent to their families of factories to industrialized societies.

Of all the goods that women produced, food required the most continuous attention. Food production involved processing, preserving, and cooking, all tasks that demanded a great deal of time and expertise. Pickling, preserving, smoking, salting, and drying foods were a few of their many talents in this area. In addition, women manufactured soap from grease and lye, as well as candles from tallow. They cooked and washed over open fires. They milked cows, raised chickens, and tended vegetable gardens.

Women did many other jobs as well. They combed wool and hackled the flax that they spun into thread, wove into cloth, colored with their own homemade dyes, and sewed by hand into clothing. They spent untold hours at their spinning wheels and with their knitting needles. They served as nurses, apothecaries, doctors, and morticians for their families, friends, and neighbors. They were accomplished herbalists who produced a large variety of efficacious medicines. They bore a large number of children during the eighteenth century—the average is thought to have been seven to eight children per woman. Mothers taught their children early school lessons and trained them as laborers. On the "side," these women brought in cash by selling butter, eggs, beeswax, thread, and other goods that they produced. And they assisted in the family business, whether it be farm, plantation, or shop.

This brief description of colonial women's work does not begin to do justice to the breadth and complexity of their duties. Even when New England towns sprang up with shops that sold various kinds of goods, women's work continued to be extremely taxing. And in the South, the romanticized grand dame of the plantation was in reality a hardworking manager, supervisor, hostess, accountant, teacher, and medical practitioner who was responsible for a large plantation community. Thus, despite her locale, the colonial woman was a domestic artisan and economic partner whose labor was a crucial contribution to the settlement and development of the American colonies.

Some scholars argue that it was not only their scarcity but also these economic contributions which gave colonial women a measure of equality with men. Certainly, women and men were comparable in economic function and importance. But the degree of independence that early American women achieved as a result is not easily ascertained. Historian Mary Beth Norton convincingly argues that the colonial years between 1607 and 1776 were not a "Golden Age" for women. She notes that women's economic contributions to the household were not enough to give them a voice in matters deemed to be male prerogatives in a patriarchal system.

Many people of the colonial period firmly believe, however, that women in America had the best possible lives. They often pointed out that colonial women lived in a "Paradise on earth for women" because they could marry if they so desired. George Alsop of Maryland exclaimed: "The women that go over into this province as servants, have the best luck as in any place of the world, for no sooner are they on shore, but they are courted into matrimony, which some of them had they not come to such a market with their virginity, might have kept it until it had been mouldy." Alsop, like most people of that day, assumed that all women desired marriage and would be fulfilled once they entered it.

During the colonial period, marriage was indeed viewed as an ideal life for women. During the seventeenth century, the unbalanced ratio between men and women put pressure on women to marry while yet in their teens. During the eighteenth century, women usually married between the ages of twenty and twenty-three. Throughout this era, nine out of ten women did marry at least once. In his 1692 guidebook for women, entitled *Ornaments for the Daughters of Zion,* Puritan minister Cotton Mather wrote that "for a woman to be praised, is for her to be married."

Single women were often discriminated against because they were considered unproductive. Those women who did not marry were expected to become part of their nearest male relative's household. Here they became unpaid household help. One of their main duties was spinning—thus the term spinster. Single women did, however, enjoy a legal status known as *femes sole.* This meant that they could exercise a few legal rights such as controlling their personal property.

Once married, a colonial woman entered a legal state known as Civil Death or marital unity. This philosophy was derived from English common law and religious tradition. It denied legal existence to a married woman. The tenets of marital unity were summed up in Sir William Blackstone's *Commentaries on the Laws of England in 1765.* By marriage, the husband and wife are one person in law; that is, during the marriage, the very being or legal existence of the woman is suspended or at least incorporated and consolidated into that of the husband, under whose wing, protection, and cover, she performs everything.

In theory, then, a married woman had no legal existence apart from her husband. She could not sign contracts, had no right to her own earnings, was not able to own property, could not vote on civil or religious matters, and automatically lost her children in case of separation or divorce. All of a married couple's property, including their children, belonged to the husband and was controlled by him. This restricted legal status of women was known as *femes covert.* It was based on the widespread belief that women were best represented by their fathers, brothers, or husbands, who had superior knowledge of the world and would speak for the women's best interests.

It should be noted that the legal status of colonial men also changed when they married. Men, who married on the average between the ages of twenty-five and twenty-eight, became legally liable for the support of their wives and children, were responsible for their wives' crimes and debts, and had to leave two thirds of their estates to their families. One story tells of a wife who was fined by the local court for physically abusing her husband; yet he had to pay the fine imposed upon her. In another very different case, that of Hannah Duston of Massachusetts in 1697, her husband collected her reward when she killed ten Indians in a daring escape from captivity.

These provisions were initially easy for women of European, and primarily Christian, background to tolerate; they so closely paralleled the situation to which these women were accustomed. But such strict legal codes soon became awkward in a society in which women were important economically and socially. Women, whose skills were critical to family survival, who could often handle a rifle as well as men, and who effectively ran the family farm or business during men's frequent absences on business, often were not enthusiastic about the legal limitations imposed on them.

Many local courts recognized that men did not in practice always represent women's needs fairly. Consequently, many local courts of equity modified legal codes and laws through their decisions, granting American women a number of rights not enjoyed by English women. Some married women in colonial America could thus own property, enter contracts, and control their own earnings. They could also protect their property through prenuptial agreements if their husbands accepted the provisions. Moreover, widows often took over the family business or trade after their husbands' deaths. During the 1600s and 1700s, widows ran farms and plantations and worked as shopkeepers, merchants, blacksmiths, gunsmiths, and tavernkeepers. As a single woman, or *femes sole,* a widow was allowed to own property, sign contracts, and conduct her own business affairs.

Daily practice also allowed both single and married women more freedom of action than appeared possible in codes of law. Early American women actually exercised a wide variety of rights and were engaged in a large number of nondomestic activities and enterprises. They also ran away from fathers or husbands whom they found abusive or overly restrictive. Colonial newspapers carried many advertisements for runaway women, and church records included many orders for their return. Because of the labor shortage, women could easily find employment in other towns, where they were guaranteed anonymity by the rudimentary communication system of the time. Few seem to have responded to either the advertisements in the newspapers or the church orders by returning to their fathers or husbands.

In addition, women achieved a modicum of independence through employment. In the labor-scarce economy, many women could work at other jobs besides their domestic duties. Research shows that women labored as butchers, gunsmiths, jailkeepers, journalists, midwives, millers, nurses, printers, proprietors and managers of taverns and boarding-houses, shipbuilders, silversmiths, tanners, teachers, and upholsterers. Margaret Philipse of New York became a merchant and shipper of furs in the 1660s. Betsy Ross was an upholsterer in Philadelphia who employed several young men at the time that she is supposed to have designed the American flag.

Women such as Ross often learned their trades through apprenticeships. Like young men, they served apprenticeships with local craftspersons or tradespersons. A young colonial woman would be apprenticed at the ages of eleven to thirteen for a term of service as much as ten years in length. They were cared for, trained in such domestic tasks as spinning and sewing, and were taught to read and sometimes to write. In other cases, women learned their skills through their fathers, brothers, or husbands who practiced a trade in or near the family home. These men frequently sought the aid of the women of the family, who then acquired proficiency through the process of helping. Other trades and professions, such as the practice of midwifery, were passed down from woman to woman. There were thus many means by which a colonial woman could expand her competency beyond the domestic realm.

Many types of source materials offer evidence that a large number of women actually pursued the trades and professions. Records from King Philip's War (1675–1676) indicate that a Mrs. Allen served as an army physician. Some years later, another woman doctor advertised in a New England newspaper that she "follows the midwife and doctress business; cures burns, salt rheum, canker, scald-head, fever sores, rheumatism, and the piles."

The existence of female merchants is demonstrated by another type of advertisement. Registering the protest of several women merchants against local taxes, this advertisement appeared in a New York newspaper in 1733: "We, widows of this city, have had a meeting as our case is something deplorable. We are house keepers, pay our taxes, carry on trade and most of us are she-merchants, and as we in some measure contribute to the support of the government, we ought to be entitled to some of the sweets of it."

Business records indicate that women were involved in a variety of commercial enterprises. For instance, Quaker women on Nantucket Island developed into shrewd traders. With their husbands away a good deal of the time on whaling or trading voyages, they not only ran their family farms but also began to sell dry goods produced from their own flax and wool to the many trade ships passing through the area. Next, they began a profitable enterprise to provision those ships. A French visitor to Nantucket in the 1770s wrote that "the men at their return, weary with the fatigues of the sea, full of confidence and love, cheerfully give their consent to every transaction that has happened during their absence, and all is joy and peace." When the British blockaded the coastline during the Revolutionary War (1776–1783), the women of Nantucket reportedly ran the blockade in order to continue their trade, now at inflated wartime prices.

Land records show that women also exercised property rights that legal codes declared they did not possess. In 1643, Deborah Moody of Long Island received a colonial land grant. Cornelia Schuyler, also of New Netherland, later acquired a holding of 1,300 acres. In the South, Elizabeth Digges possessed a large plantation, 108 slaves, and a lavishly furnished mansion. And in the colony of Maryland, Margaret Brent owned over 1,000 acres of land. Brent was such a powerful and esteemed landholder that she was appointed the executor of Governor Leonard Calvert's will after his death in 1647. Although she thought that her request for two votes in the colonial legislature—one for herself as a freeholder and one as the governor's representative—was justified, the legislators denied it.

These cases of working, professional, and entrepreneurial women are not consistent with the customary image of docile colonial women in their prim white caps and serviceable dresses quietly caring for their homes and families. Yet many colonial writers and speakers exerted a good deal of energy promoting this image of the passive and domestic woman. In the 1660s, Cotton Mather wrote at great length about the domestic talents that a woman should acquire to "enable her to do the man whom she may hereafter have, good and not Evil, all the days of her life." He added that women were more godly and religious than men. "Truly, though a woman may not speak in the church," he observed, "yet she may humbly repeat unto her husband at home what the minister spoke in the church that may be pertinent unto his condition." Clearly, in his view, woman was the spiritual caretaker of her husband. He explained that this was the case partly because "most women have more time to employ in the more immediate service of their souls than the other sex is the owner of." He also emphasized that "the curse in difficulties both of subjection and child-bearing, which the female sex is doomed into, has been turned into a blessing," for "God sanctifies the chains, the pains, the deaths."

Although Mather and others supported a model for women that emphasized virtue, passivity, domesticity, religiousness, and other similar charcteristics, evidence suggests that many colonial women did not take this advice totally to heart. Mather's own secret diary is purported to include a passage explaining his tortured inner struggle over how to respond to the sexual advances of a woman who approached him in his study late one night. Another diary, that of William Byrd, a southern planter, also contradicted the customary image of colonial women. In describing a woman whom he greatly admired, Byrd wrote that she was "a very civil woman who showed nothing of ruggedness or immodesty in her carriage, yet she will carry a gun in the woods and kill deer, turkeys, and shoot down wild cattle, catch and tye hogs, and perform the most manful exercises as well as most men in these parts."

A recent study of women in colonial North Carolina also brings to light some interesting aspects of female behavior that clash with the image. Court and church records indicate many unexpected deeds. Two young women were called into court for swimming nude with two young men in the Chowan River. The most common crime to appear in the records was fornication, or engaging in sexual relations before marriage. Runaway women and illegitimate children were not unusual. Single women often chose their own mates and did not hesitate to elope when thwarted by their parents. Premarital contracts were frequently employed to protect women's property. Once wed, dissatisfied women sought sexual alliances outside of marriage. And when widowed, many women chose to remain single rather than to remarry. These are hardly the lovely southern belles who are customarily portrayed in their hoop skirts gracing the lawns of stately colonial homes.

Clearly, evidence indicates that there was a discrepancy between the model established for colonial women and the reality that many of them achieved. It might even be argued that the ideal was preached so frequently and forcefully precisely because many women fell short of its standards. After all, guides to behavior are not necessary when everyone in the social group understands the rules and abides by them. Perhaps colonial women understood, and even approved of, the rules but did not always find them easy to follow.

Several examples of well-known women suggest that this was indeed the case. Although they sought to become ideal women, factors in their own lives and characteristics of their own personalities led them in other directions. The colonial poet, Anne Bradstreet, is an outstanding illustration of the conflict between the image and the personal reality with which many women grappled. After immigrating to Massachusetts Bay with her husband, Simon, in 1630, she pursued her household duties, bore eight children, and demonstrated her talent as a poet and writer.

Bradstreet was not unaware of women's accepted roles and duties. There were many sermons, statements, and books that clearly spelled them out. Two books published in 1620, *A Good Wife, God's Gift* and *Marriage Duties,* were only a few of the many guidebooks available. And if women deviated from the accepted rules, they were quickly held up to public scorn. The venerable and respected governor of the Massachusetts Bay Colony, John Winthrop, declared in 1645 that Anne Hopkins, the wife of the governor of Connecticut, had "fallen into a sad infirmity, the loss of her understanding and reason, by occasion of her giving herself wholly to reading and writing many books." He explained that "if she had attended her household affairs, and such things as belong to women, and not gone out of her way and calling to meddle in such things as are proper for men, whose minds are stronger, she had kept her wits, and might have improved them usefully and honorably in the place God had set for her."

Yet Bradstreet felt compelled to go on with her writing, often after a long day's work during which she attempted to be the ideal wife and mother. In 1642, she expressed her bitterness regarding the censure that her work drew. "I am obnoxious to each carping tongue," she wrote, "who says my hand a needle better fits." She concluded: "If what I do prove well, it won't advance/ they'll say its stolen, or else it was by chance."

In 1650, a book of her poems, *The Tenth Muse Lately Sprung Up in America,* appeared anonymously in London. Bradstreet was soon identified as its author. Her brother minced no words when offering his opinion of her activities. "Your printing of a book, beyond the custom of your sex, doth rankly smell," he stated in a public letter to her published in London. Despite her discouragement over this episode and her increasing acceptance of the idea that "men can do best, and women know it well," she continued to write.

Six years after Bradstreet's death in 1672, her works were published under the title *Several Poems Compiled by a Gentlewoman in New England.* Present-day poet Adrienne Rich has eulogized her appropriately: "To have written these, the first good poems in America, while rearing eight children, lying frequently sick, keeping house at the edge of wilderness, was to have managed a poet's range and extension within confines as severe as any American poet has confronted."

Bradstreet was not the only New England woman to defy these limitations. The well-known religious dissident, Anne Hutchinson, also contributed jarring notes to the ongoing debate regarding the nature of women. Like Bradstreet, she was cognizant of the type of behavior that the model prescribed for women. Hutchinson, a Biblical scholar, was also fully conversant with the admonition of St. Paul that women should "keep silent in the churches." Yet after her arrival in Boston with her husband, William, in 1634, she increasingly became the center of a religious controversy.

Hutchinson believed that individuals could communicate with the spirit of Christ and interpret Biblical teachings and sermons on their own. Such beliefs were problematic because they threatened the power of the authoritarian Puritan ministers in Massachusetts. Her ideas were termed antinomian, meaning antiauthority. Her beliefs were a social problem as well as a religious one because they provided a way for women to express their frustrations with their limited roles. Antinomians stressed the individual's ability to feel God's grace within, a tenet that minimized the guidance and teachings of ministers. This encouraged women to think and question rather than simply to accept ministerial pronouncements.

Governor Winthrop, fearing the disruption she was causing, denounced Hutchinson as a woman of "a nimble wit and active spirit, and a very voluble tongue, more bold than a man, though in understanding and judgement, inferior to many women." But she would not be quieted and, in direct opposition to the Pauline doctrine of silence, defended her beliefs both in the community and in church. Her charisma and teachings attracted many followers, both women and men. Prominent and affluent merchants and craftspeople who felt constrained in their businesses by church rules supported her. Her views also appealed to a number of women who seemed to be restive and looking for a way to express themselves. Yet Hutchinson was not just a rebel and an agitator. She was also exemplary in fulfilling her prescribed obligations as a woman. She was a devoted wife, the loving mother of fifteen children, and a beloved midwife and nurse.

Despite Hutchinson's stature and the wide respect accorded her, church authorities were upset by her ideas and the growing factionalism in the community that such ideas encouraged. Charging her with both religious heresy and behavior unfitting a female, they repeatedly called her to trial in 1637 and 1638. Here she was told: "You have rather been a husband than a wife, and a preacher than a hearer, and a Magistrate than a subject." Clearly, Hutchinson had stepped out of her "place" and had challenged home, church, and state. Consequently, Hutchinson was banished from the colony and excommunicated from the church. Along with many of her followers, she left Massachusetts Bay, settled in Rhode Island, where she continued her resistance, and then moved to New York. In 1643, Hutchinson, two of her sons, and three of her daughters were killed by American Indians because of a tragic misunderstanding over payment for the land Hutchinson occupied.

Neither Hutchinson's punishment nor her death marked the end of the antinomian controversy or of women's resistance to restrictions on their lives. In 1638, the Massachusetts court ordered a number of other women dissenters to be whipped or cast out of the church. In 1641, Ann Hibbens was excommunicated for slander and was denounced for resisting the authority of her husband, "whom she should have obeyed and unto whom God put her in subjection." In 1644, Ann Eaton, an opponent of infant baptism, was excommunicated for lying and for stubbornness. Twenty-two years after the Hutchinson affair, one of Hutchinson's major supporters, Mary Dyer, was hanged in Boston. As a Quaker proselytizer, Dyer was thought to be "troublesome" and "notoriously infected with error."

A similar problem erupted with the women of Salem, Massachusetts.

Here, women who questioned religious and other authorities were branded witches. Throughout the witchcraft trials of the 1650s and 1660s, Salem tribunals ordered women to be whipped, chained to posts, jailed, excommunicated, and executed. In 1648, for instance, Margaret James was executed for having a "malignant" touch, using suspicious medicines, and acting in an intemperate fashion at her trial.

In a later outbreak of the witchcraft scare during the 1690s, women and a few men were branded witches in some forty other towns, mainly in New England. These women were usually middle-aged, reputed to be contentious, and involved in community affairs. Their accusers were usually young, unmarried women, and children who were perhaps revolting against authority. Indeed, when Massachusetts looked back on the affair in the early 1700s and exonerated all those accused of witchcraft, the legislature contended that "evil spirits" had motivated the accusers, rather than the accused.

Recent work on seventeenth-century witchcraft in New England suggests that women who achieved even a modicum of economic success were more likely to be accused of practicing witchcraft than those who had not. Wives or widows who were active in commerce or participated in business endeavors received an unusually high number of charges and convictions. Whether they were actually religious dissenters or were threats to prevailing conceptions of womanhood is unclear in most cases. But it is evident that their economic activities diverged sharply from Calvinist teachings regarding women.

Women who rebelled against the model of womanhood by becoming business people appeared not only in New England but in the middle and southern colonies as well. In the South, for example, young Eliza Lucas practiced her own brand of noncompliance. Her father served as a governor of Antigua in the West Indies, although her invalid mother was incapable of running the family plantations in South Carolina. In 1739, seventeen-year-old Eliza took over the management of three plantations in the Charleston area. She taught herself bookkeeping, accounting, and other skills needed to run such an extensive business. She also learned all that she could about the cultivation of rice, South Carolina's major crop at the time. She wrote a friend: "I have the business of three plantations to transact, which requires much writing and more business and fatigue of other sorts than you can imagine."

At her father's urging, Lucas began to experiment with other crops. One of these was the indigo plant, which produced a blue dye very much in demand by the British textile industry. Although neighboring planters thought her to be an eccentric young woman, she believed that indigo might pull the economy of South Carolina out of the doldrums.

The path was not easy for Eliza Lucas. She worked in the fields alongside her overseer, studied the involved process of retting the indigo plant into dye-cakes, and finally accepted the aid of a knowledgeable indigo maker sent by her father from the West Indies. This man feared that her success would undermine his own island's sale of indigo. He quarreled with Lucas and sabotaged the retting equipment. Despite these difficulties, Lucas finally produced the plantation's first batch of dye-cakes in 1744. Upon observing her success, neighboring planters sought her aid. She graciously gave them both indigo seeds and advice. Eventually, indigo became the second largest crop for export in South Carolina.

Although she was atypical in many ways, Lucas also embodied the well-bred southern woman. She studied Plutarch, Virgil, French, and shorthand. She was involved in the prescribed female activities of teaching the plantation children, doing needlework, and playing the pianoforte. She kept a letterbook filled with charming phrases and interesting observations that is one of the most significant collections in existence kept by a colonial lady.

In 1744, Lucas married Charles Pinckney, widower of her best friend and twenty years her senior. During their happy marriage, she continued to supervise the family lands while her husband and two of her sons, Charles Cotesworth and Thomas, engaged in politics. She also established the culture of silkworms in Charleston and founded a smallpox hospital. When she died in 1793, George Washington requested the privilege of being one of her pallbearers.

What conclusions can be drawn from the lives of Bradstreet, Hutchinson, Lucas, and the many other women like them? It appears that they personified a resentment and tension that was perhaps experienced by many women when urged to accept roles that did not fit their own talents, interests, and values. Because such women seldom directly articulated or examined their frustrations, it is impossible to assess how clearly they understood their own actions. They did not declare themselves to be supporters of women's rights or feminism. They did not express their ideas in terms of an ideology or a reform crusade for women. Whether they actively chose to resist the model or were simply following their own convictions is thus indiscernible. The fact remains, however, that these women's individual actions did indeed constitute an assault on the accepted image of womanhood.

The contradictions in these women's lives indicate that the history of white women between 1607 and 1776 is complex and does not easily lend itself to generalization. Yet although women's experiences obviously differed from woman to woman, region to region, and decade to decade, an overview can be constructed. There were similarities in the lives of colonial women, whether they lived in the South of the 1660s or in the New England of the 1700s.

Whether she was married or single, the central focus of a white colonial woman's life was her household and family. A typical colonial household might include a married couple, their children, and perhaps an unmarried aunt, uncle, or grandparent. Perhaps as many as one third of these households also included an indentured servant, hired field-workers, or a number of black slaves.

Since the majority of widows chose not to remarry, a large number of households were headed by women. According to a guidebook published in 1750, *A Wedding Ring Fit for the Finger*, this was perfectly acceptable. Its author explained that, "when the great light goes down, the lesser light gets up." In other words, although a wife was subject to her husband when he was present, she could "be sovereign in her husband's absence." The colonial family was based on a patriarchal system in which the husband, if alive, was the recognized head.

In this structure, work was divided according to sex, with women dominating the home and men dominating the fields or other place of business. But the family organization was not to be a dictatorship. Rather, marriage was often referred to as being egalitarian. A wedding sermon in Boston in 1750 stated: "Our ribs [women] were not ordained to be our rulers. They are not made of the head to claim superiority, but out of the side to be content with equality." Particularly in New England, husbands were cautioned by the courts and community opinion to extend honor and respect to their wives. It was also widely assumed that, since men possessed a highly loving nature, their affection for their spouses would soften the hierarchical organization of the family. Thus, Adam's Rib often had a degree of functional equality although her husband directed family affairs.

In spite of the usual image of our foremothers and fathers, sexual intimacy was an important part of their lives. Men, especially among the Puritans, were expected to satisfy the sexual needs of their wives. Failing to do so, whether through impotence or neglect, was cause for divorce. While believing in sensuality within the bounds of marriage, most colonists were strongly opposed to adultery. Such "inconstancy" was punishable by fines, whipping, the pillory, or even death. Legislation in Massachusetts Bay prescribed whipping and the wearing of the "capital letters A.D. cut out in cloth and sewed on their uppermost garments."

Other causes of divorce included desertion, neglect, cruelty, and bigamy. Divorces were easier to obtain in the colonies than in England but were still costly and time-consuming. Since only those with the necessary resources could pursue a divorce, it is assumed that a large amount of informal separation and desertion took place. Unfortunately, people seldom leave written evidence of such actions.

Solid evidence that sexual crimes occurred between women and men exists. A considerable number of children were born as a result of seduction or rape. These occurrences were not always unpleasant or violent. A Virginia woman of the seventeenth century was so pleased with the outcome of her seduction of a man in an open field that she swore to give him "as much cloth as would make him a sheet." But in many cases, women were victims of physically aggressive males. One Massachusetts woman of the same era reported that a man flung her down in the street; another, that her master caught her by the wrist and "pulled her against the side of the bed."

Because sexuality and childbearing played a prominent role in the lives of colonists, women by necessity devoted a large amount of time to pregnancy and childbirth. As has been said, colonial women bore an average of eight children. Wed in 1685, Sarah Steins Place, a typical New England woman, bore her first child in 1686 and her eighth in 1706. These frequent pregnancies were likely to take a mother's life in one out of every thirty cases. Those women who survived would spend almost twenty years with an infant at her side and almost forty rearing her children to adulthood.

Until the mid-1700s, virtually all babies were delivered by female midwives. The term midwife came from the English "mid-wif," or with-women, thus indicating that birthing was exclusively a female affair during these years. Midwives usually held a respected position in the community and were revered as friends as well as medical practitioners. The midwife's primary function consisted of assisting the mother to deliver naturally. She might use herbal teas, wine, or liquor to lessen the pain, but she avoided mechanical devices and drugs. This situation would change drastically with the introduction of formal medical training, licensing, and obstetrical forceps, all of which led to the introduction of male physicians into the delivery room.

Throughout the colonial period, women prepared for childbirth by abandoning corset stays, wearing flat shoes, and refraining from carriage rides. A pregnant woman also avoided "sudden frights, strong passions, or ungratified longings" to protect her unborn child. Guidebooks advised expectant mothers to pray and to contemplate the possibility of death. Anne Bradstreet expressed her own fears of yet another birth in a poem written for her husband in the mid-1600s. "How soon, my Dear, death may my steps attend/ How soon it may be thy lot to lose thy friend."

As the day of the birth approached, the mother-to-be was joined by her mother, aunts, sisters, friends, and the midwife. They laid out linen, readied basins and towels, told bawdy jokes to lighten the tension, walked the expectant mother about to relieve the pain, and held her by the arms as she delivered her baby through a low stool with an open seat. They then helped care for the mother and newborn babe while celebrating its birth with a feast. The father was admitted only briefly, and other men were barred from the chamber for several weeks. The overwhelming tone of the event was one of encouragement, support, and warmth.

Friends and family soon dispersed. The new mother was free to return to her regular round of duties and chores. Her household, now somewhat expanded, received her attention once more. She also resumed the numerous other undertakings that engaged women's minds, energies, and talents during these years.

One of these activities was the production of handiwork and craft work. Women's needlework skills resulted in finely stitched samples, bed rugs, coverlets, pillow shams, and other textiles. Women also hooked, embroidered, and appliqued rugs. They watercolored and embroidered pictures, portraits, and mourning pictures, which recorded family deaths. They painted stoneware crocks, worktables, sewing boxes, and dishes. And they stitched a large variety of quilts, many of which chronicled births, deaths, marriages, and other significant family events. Extant examples of women's craftwork include a bed rug created by Phoebe Billings of Massachusetts during the early decades of the 1700s, a crewelworked bed ensemble designed by Mary Bulman of Maine during the 1740s, and a firboard or overmantel painting by Sibyl May of Connecticut during the 1750s. Such artifacts, combined with written descriptions of early American women's creations, indicate that colonial women adorned their homes with exquisite folk art demonstrating both originality and talent.

But all of colonial women's activities were not geared toward their homes. Early American women also engaged in welfare by caring for widows, orphans, criminals, the disabled, and the poor in a day when social institutions such as hospitals and prisons were few in number. In addition, women participated in church affairs. Although denied full participation and the right to hold office, most women were expected to attend religious services and ceremonies. Only a minority sect, The Society of Friends, or Quakers, extended to colonial women equality, participation in the ministry, and a reprieve from the doctrine of St. Paul that demanded the silence of women in church. Quaker women also participated in Quaker government through "women's meetings" instituted in 1681. In all other religious organizations of the 1600s and most of the 1700s, however, women's roles were strictly circumscribed.

When the religious revival movement known as the Great Awakening erupted in the colonies in the 1730s and 1740s, women flocked to revival meetings in numbers equal to men. Revivalism offered women more opportunity for social interaction and freedom for self-expression than the more traditional and formal religious services had. A proliferation of meetings, ministers, and sects diffused authority and created an opportunity for women to assert themselves. Women helped to judge members for admission, to select ministers, and to organize religious services. During the 1760s, Sarah Osborn of Newport, Rhode Island, spoke to hundreds of people in her home each week on religious matters.

Perhaps women favored revivalism because most other public spheres were essentially closed to them. Education for women was limited to the basics and to female "accomplishments" such as needlework, singing, and playing the pianoforte. In the South, planters' daughters sometimes acquired some education due to the common practice of allowing young women to sit in on sessions given by tutors hired to instruct young men. Political involvement was also limited. Although women had occasionally voted in early town meetings or spoken out in local gatherings, increased settlement brought with it consolidation of political power in male hands. Not only the vote but also officeholding, judgeships, jury service, and public debate were restricted to men. It is little wonder that scores of energetic and talented women found their outlet through folk art, social service, or religion. Even on the edges of society, along the colonial frontier that slowly pushed westward toward the Appalachian Mountains by the mid-1700s, women found that their labor, childbearing abilities, and other important contributions were valued but not rewarded by inclusion in public life.

Historian Julia Spruill pointed out that, on the North Carolina frontier, women worked alongside their men doing the heavy labor involved in clearing forested land for farms, planting crops, constructing homes and barns, and raising stock. Frontierswomen were esteemed for their domestic skills as well as their abilities outside of the home; yet as settlement progressed traditional ideas of women's work and roles soon appeared. Although women on the colonial frontier might wield a certain degree of influence within their families, they were usually expected to play customary, docile roles publicly.

Of course, all of these generalizations regarding colonial women speak only of the historical experiences of the white women who helped to develop the British colonies in North America. They have little relevance to either the native women who inhabited the land long before their white counterparts arrived or to the black women forced to immigrate to America against their wills.

Anthropologists and historians interested in American Indians are actively engaged in remedying this situation by reconstituting the story of America's native women. To do this, they have to overcome centuries of anti-Indian prejudice that has distorted the picture. Source materials often reflect the idea of either a Noble Savage or a barbarous one. In either case, the image is mythical.

The continent of North America had been populated by a large number of native peoples for thousands of years before European explorers and settlers arrived. American Indians had a rich culture, complex economic and religious life, technology, agriculture, social structure, and a fascinating history of their own. In reality, then, American history begins well before 1607. After the English and other settlers began to fan out along the coast of North America, the Indian presence continued to shape and determine many facets of American history. Indians, for example, contributed their energies as laborers, guides, and teachers of farming, hunting, and other skills. Indian women offered their talents as spouses and companions, traders, craftspeople, and agriculturalists. Among many other contributions, maize, or Indian corn, facilitated the survival and expansion of the colonies. Indian culture and arts bestowed beauty and creativity to the infant white civilization. And the Indians' love of liberty and fierce independence helped to shape the colonists' conceptions of freedom.

Yet American history textbooks have customarily emphasized only one Indian woman, Pocahontas. Held up to generations of Americans as a significant historical figure, her story is indeed an interesting one. This native woman, originally named Matoaka, was the daughter of Powhatan, an Indian king in early Virginia. In 1607, she intervened with her father to save the life of Captain John Smith of Jamestown. Evidently, it was Smith who first called her Pocahontas.

During the following years, the young woman performed many acts of kindness for various Jamestown settlers. In 1613, she met John Rolfe, the colonist responsible for introducing the cultivation of tobacco to Jamestown. When she agreed to marry Rolfe, she was instructed in Christianity and baptized Rebecca. After the couple's marriage in 1614, they lived in Jamestown and had one child. In 1616, they went to England, where Rebecca was presented at court and touted as an Indian "princess." In 1617, Rebecca died and was buried in England. She was virtually forgotten until the mid-eighteenth century, when several authors and playwrights seized her romantic story for their work.

Other examples of biased historical reporting are the many accounts of American Indian women written by missionaries, trappers, traders, travelers, and settlers. Since the majority of them regarded native people as primitive savages to be Christianized, exploited, removed, or exterminated, they frequently viewed native society with a jaundiced eye that tended to magnify, and even create, negative aspects of Indian life. Also, these observers were usually European males from a nonnomadic, agricultural background and were not accustomed to a division of labor in which the women did the village work and the men did the hunting, fishing, and fighting. Consequently, they consistently described Indian women in terms of "squaws."

One typical account of native women written by a missionary in the early 1600s characterized Indian women as "poor creatures who endure all the misfortunes and hardships of life." According to him, Indian women were the servants and slaves of Indian men. Such damaging characterizations bequeathed a very unattractive picture of Indian women to generations of Americans. The image of the "squaw" was far removed from that of the Indian princess. As one bit of doggerel put it, the "squaw" was a "beast of burden, slave, chained under female law from puberty to grave." This stereotype of the squaw, just like that of the princess, continues to cloud Americans' views of early American Indian women.

In addition to problems of biased perceptions, difficulties also arise in gathering source materials. American Indian history is usually based on oral tradition and is passed on by word of mouth from person to person within a native group. Furthermore, it is often guarded jealously from outsiders because it is considered to be a personal and valued possession. The many and complex Indian dialects also made accurate communication and understanding difficult. Researchers thus face many hurdles in collecting evidence. Yet without native sources, they cannot fairly reconstruct the rich historical legacy of the hundreds of different native cultures that existed during the colonial period.

Given these obstacles, it is not surprising that an objective view of the lives of American Indian women has not yet emerged. Nor have the biographies of many early native women been written. The few Indian women who are remembered include Mary Brant, a Mohawk woman, who was a consort of Sir William Johnson, Superintendent of Indian Affairs for the Northern Colonies in the late 1700s. There was also Mary Musgrove, a part Creek woman who became an Indian leader in colonial Georgia; Catherine Tekakwitha, a Mohawk convert to Catholicism, whom missionaries idealized to unconverted Indians; and Nancy Ward, a Cherokee leader, who befriended settlers on many occasions. Like Pocahontas, these women are remembered primarily for their usefulness to whites. Their stories give few clues to the lives of most Indian women during these years.

It is known, however, that contact with English settlers changed the lives of native women in the coastal Algonquian language groups that included the Wampanoag and Narragansett in New England and the Powhatan in Chesapeake Bay. By the 1630s, these bands had been ravaged by plague and smallpox epidemics. By the mid-1600s, the 10 percent who survived were dependent upon such English trade goods as weapons and clothing. Food was produced by their women. Among the agricultural Algonquian, women produced about 90 percent of the food supply through farming. In addition, they fished, gathered wild plants, produced domestic household goods, processed and stored food, and aided in hunting.

While many observers felt that native women were overburdened with work, others suggested that their lives were not as demanding as they at first appeared. For instance, Roger Williams, religious leader and founder of Rhode Island, noted that native women and men worked together on such tasks as clearing a field for cultivation or harvesting a crop. Mary Jemison, an Indian captive during the 1700s, reported that women's chores were "not so severe" and "probably not harder" than those performed by white women.

Moreover, native women held power in a number of areas. They routinely acted as businesspeople and entrepreneurs by actively engaging in barter and trade. Among themselves, they exchanged crops and other goods; to the English they offered skins, baskets, and other items in return for needles, textiles, kettles, tea, stockings, and shoes. In addition, women could wield influence by rising to the position of leader, or sachem. Although the office of sachem was inherited, it was retained only by keeping the respect of the group who supported the sachem with contributions of food. Quaiapan served as a Narragansett sachem during the 1660s and 1670s, while Weetamoo led as many as 300 Pocasset Indian men in warfare during those years. Native women also served as shamans, or priests. In this role, they acted as religious leaders and medical practitioners. Among some bands, women even served as both shamans and warleaders, a position that involved much power and respect. Finally, many native groups were matrilineal and matrilocal, patterns that underwrote the influence of women in both their families and bands.

Colonial observers were perhaps misled about the supposedly "degraded" position of native women by the system of sexual segregation observed among most coastal Algonquian groups. Women often ate separately, performed their own dances, and spent their menstrual periods in special huts. At the same time, sexual assault and other vulgar behavior was virtually unknown, with rape being the only capital offense punishable by the entire band. When native women's roles as agriculturalists, domestic laborers, and people of influence were observed by later generations of Euro-Americans among inland and plains Indians, the prism of white culture, values, and belief systems once again distorted the picture.

The history of early black women has fared even worse than that of native women. Since blacks were considered lowly and inferior, their experiences were recorded only incidentally. Records of the London Company show, for instance, that the first load of 20 blacks arrived at Jamestown in 1619. By 1648, Virginia's black slave population had reached 300. Various records indicate that blacks lived and labored not only in the colonial South, but in the middle and New England colonies as well. For example, laws of several northern colonies and of all the plantation colonies demonstrate the strong sentiment that existed against miscegenation, that is, interbreeding of whites and blacks. And diaries and letters of early settlers frequently mention black field hands and women who served as nursemaids, washwomen, and domestic servants.

Blacks, like Indians, were viewed with great prejudice. They, too, were seen as uncivilized barbarians who knew nothing of Christianity. Brought from a far and unknown land in chains, black slaves seemed to most colonists to be sons and daughters of Satan. It is thus understandable that one of the few existing accounts of an early black woman is that of Tituba, a West Indian slave accused of practicing witchcraft in Salem.

As the number of blacks in America increased, so did the fears of the whites. By the close of the colonial period in the 1770s, there were 48,460 black slaves in the North and 411,362 in the South. Whites increasingly viewed blacks as troublemakers who rebelled or ran away. Indeed, both slave men and women often ran away, according to public notices and newspaper advertisements for their return. One such announcement that appeared in the *South Carolina Gazette* in 1834 stated: "Run away about five weeks ago from Hugh Campbell, a Negro wench named Flora, she has a scar on her forehead." Flora's owner offered a thirty shilling reward for her return.

White worries about runaways and rebellions eventually led to the denial of education for and written communication between black people on the theory that such opportunities would only foster conspiracies among slaves. Denied a written outlet for their thoughts and used to the custom of oral history from their African homes, black Americans relied on oral tradition to register their history. Historian Gerda Lerner has pointed out that black women's history faces another predicament. As a group, black women have been the target of double oppression. They have been discriminated against as blacks and as women. This leads to the neglect of their history by both black historians and women's historians. If they appear in history textbooks at all, it is usually often as hapless victims of the slave system.

Actually, the first black women to come to the colonies did so as indentured servants, a temporary status during which the black woman's labor was exploited in both house and field but that was supposed to end after a period of years. As early as the 1640s, however, Virginia court records noted that black people were sold "for life" and that the status of many black children was that of "perpetual servant." In 1652, one Virginia planter purchased a young black woman as well as "her issue and produce during her . . . Life tyme and their successors forever." By 1662, slavery was legalized in all the colonies.

The issue of the legal position of black women was soon resolved. In 1662, Virginia passed legislation decreeing that all black children would automatically inherit their mother's condition, that "all children born in this country shall be held bond or free according to the condition of the mother." It also stated that any "Christian" that was engaged in "fornication with a Negra man or woman, he or she offending shall pay double the fines imposed." Other colonies soon followed suit with laws supporting black slavery and forbidding miscegenation. By the mid-1700s, every colony prohibited cohabitation between the races.

Black women in colonial America were plagued with heavy workloads, broken families, and a short life expectancy created largely by a lack of immunity to unfamiliar diseases. Although black women who produced many children were highly valued, their poor health, early death rates, and depression and alienation under slavery created a low fertility rate. In addition to producing future workers, black women were also expected to provide cheap labor. In the South, the black slave woman was put to work in both plantation house and fields, while in the North she engaged in domestic tasks or was hired out.

Black slave women, much like American Indian women, played a vital role in the colonial economy. Yet their contributions were frequently overlooked and undervalued. Another conclusion that can be drawn regarding native and black women in early America is that their lives, roles, and actions frequently diverged from the Euro-American ideal of womanhood. Rather than being passive and weak, they were often assertive and strong. Although they did cook, sew, and care for their families, they also performed heavy labor, resisted their oppressors, and filled leadership roles. Like many of their white counterparts, the reality of their lives regularly deviated from the myth of what they "should" be.

The process of inventing the model of the American woman had only begun during the years of settlement. The colonial period was not only the childhood of the new nation; it was the infancy of the development of the "true" American woman. Traditional ideas of women's roles came to the American colonies as part of the settlers' cultural baggage. Here they were shaped by the demands of the new and often rugged environment.

Gradually, customary views of women experienced alteration. The reality of many women's lives deviated from the prescribed image. During the years after 1776, however, the invented American woman would tend to grow and codify along with a new nation—the United States of America.

SUGGESTIONS FOR FURTHER READING

Anderson, Marilyn J. "The Best of Two Worlds: The Pocahontas Legend as Treated in Early American Drama." *The Indian Historian* 12 (Summer 1979): 54–59, 64.

Barker-Benfield, G. J. "Anne Hutchinson and the Puritan Attitude Toward Women." *Feminist Studies* 1 (1972): 65–96.

Berkin, Carol Ruth. "Within the Conjurer's Circle: Women in Colonial America." In *The Underside of American History,* 3d ed., edited by Thomas R. Frazier, 79–105. New York: Harcourt, Brace and Jovanavich, 1978.

Berkin, Carol Ruth, and Mary Beth Norton, eds. *Women of America: A History.* Boston: Houghton Mifflin Company, 1979. Parts I and II.

Buel, Joy Day, and Richard Buel, Jr. *The Way of Duty: A Woman and Her Family in Revolutionary America.* New York: W. W. Norton & Co., Inc., 1984.

Demos, John. *A Little Commonwealth: Family Life in Plymouth Colony.* New York: Oxford University Press, 1970.

————. *Entertaining Satan.* New York: Oxford University Press, 1982.

Dewhurst, C. Kurt, Betty MacDowell, and Marshal MacDowell. *Artists in Aprons: Folk Art by American Women.* New York: E. P. Dutton, 1979.

Dye, Nancy Schrom. "History of Childbirth in America." *Signs* 6 (Autumn 1980): 97–108.

Friedman, Jean E., and William G. Shade, eds. *Our America Sisters: Women in American Life and Thought.* Lexington, MA: D. C. Heath and Company, 1982. Part I.

Green, Rayna. "The Pocahontas Perplex: The Image of Indian Women in American Culture." *The Massachusetts Review* 16 (1975): 698–714.

Gregory, Chester W. "Black Women in Pre-Federal America." In *Clio Was a Woman: Studies in the History of American Women,* edited by Mabel E. Deutrich and Virginia C. Purdy, 53–70. Washington, D.C.: Howard University Press, 1980.

Gordon, Michael, ed. *The American Family in Social-Historical Perspective.* New York: St. Martin's Press, 1978.

Hubbell, Jay B. "The Smith-Pocahantas Story in Literature." *The Virginia Magazine of History and Biography* 65 (July 1957): 275–300.

James, Edward T., ed. *Notable American Women, 1607–1950: A Biographical Dictionary.* Cambridge, MA: Belknap Press, 1971.

Jordan, Winthrop D. *White over Black: American Attitudes Toward the Negro, 1550–1812.* Chapel Hill: University of North Carolina Press, 1968.

Kessler-Harris, Alice. *Women Have Always Worked: A Historical Overview.* New York: McGraw-Hill, 1982.

Koehler, Lyle. *The Search for Order: The "Weaker Sex" in 17th Century New England.* Urbana: University of Illinois Press, 1980.

Lindemann, Barbara S. "'To Ravish and Carnally Know': Rape in Eighteenth-Century Massachusetts." *Signs* 10 (Autumn 1984): 63–82.

Medicine, Beatrice. "Bibliography of Native American Women." *The Indian Historian* 8 (1975): 51–53.

Norton, Mary Beth. "The Evolution of White Women's Experience in Early America." *American Historical Review* 89 (June 1984): 593–619.

Ryan, Mary P. *Womanhood in America: From Colonial Times to The Present.* New York: New Viewpoints, 1979. Chapter 1.

Scholten, Catherine M. "On the Importance of the Obstetrick Art: Changing Customs of Childbirth in America, 1760–1825." *William and Mary Quarterly* 34 (July 1977): 426–445.

Smith, Daniel Scott, and Michael S. Hindus. "Premarital Pregnancy in America, 1640–1671: An Overview and Interpretation." *Journal of Interdisciplinary History* 5 (1975): 537–570.

Spruill, Julia Cherry. *Women's Life and Work in the Southern Colonies.* New York: W. W. Norton and Company, 1972.

Ulrich, Laurel Thatcher. *Good Wives: Images and Realities in the Lives of Women in Northern New England, 1650–1750.* New York: Oxford University Press, 1983.

Watson, Alan D. "Women in Colonial North Carolina: Overlooked and Underestimated." *North Carolina Historical Review* 58 (January 1981): 1–22.

Wells, Robert V. "Demographic Change and the Life Cycle of American Families." *The Journal of Interdisciplinary History* 2 (Autumn 1971): 273–282.

Woloch, Nancy. *Women and the American Experience.* New York: Alfred A. Knopf, 1984. Chapters 1–2.

Wertz, Richard W., and Dorothy C. Wertz. *Lying-In: A History of Childbirth in America.* New York: Free Press, 1977.

Young, Philip. "The Mother of Us All: Pocahontas Reconsidered." *Kenyon Review* 24 (Summer 1962): 391–415.

This Charles Willson Peale portrait of Mary Gibson Tilghman and her sons was painted in 1789. Done only a year before her death in 1790 at age twenty-four, it might have been a model for the image of the Republican Mother that developed during the Revolutionary era. Courtesy of the Maryland Historical Society, Baltimore, Maryland.

CHAPTER 2

Republican Motherhood:
The American Revolution and
Early New Nation
1776–1816

ON 2 July 1776, the Continental Congress voted to support independence of the American colonies from their mother country. When Congress released the news of independence on July 4, it was the occasion of celebration for those who were Patriots, or supporters of the new government. These people favored a revolution that would lead to the establishment of an independent nation. For Loyalists, those who backed the English, it was the cause of great consternation. These people preferred to remain within the British Empire. But few colonists, whatever their political sympathies, were surprised. A widespread desire for self-government had been evolving for many years due to the economic, social and political differences between Great Britain and her colonies in North America.

Although historians have generally focused on male activities during the American Revolution and when the new American nation was hammered out, women were also highly involved. Despite the fact that women contributed their skills and energies to the growth and progress of their country, they were not rewarded with widely expanded roles and statuses. Instead, the traditional conception of women as wives and mothers survived the Revolutionary era and was in some ways strengthened during these years. Rather than being destroyed by the national upheaval, this conception was increasingly cast in a conventional mold. The idea of women's "sphere" grew in stature and impact. At the same time, in practice, serious questions were being raised concerning its validity in light of women's participation in resistance, war, and the founding of the new nation.

The resistance phase of the colonies can be traced back to 1763, the year in which the French and Indian War ended. Dissatisfied colonists registered unending complaints concerning the provisions of the treaty that concluded the war and the many pieces of legislation that flowed out of Parliament in an attempt to control its unruly American subjects. The usual historical account of the resistance period is marked by such names as Sam Adams, Thomas Hutchinson, Thomas Jefferson, and Thomas Paine, and such organizations as the Stamp Act Congress, the Sons of Liberty, and the Continental Congress.

A major omission from the history of the resistance years are the many contributions of female Patriots. A large number of colonial women involved themselves in resistance to the British almost immediately. They willingly boycotted the importation of many of their favorite goods, especially tea. They formed themselves into anti-tea leagues, in which they experimented with brewing herb teas from raspberry, sage, and birch leaves. The most popular home grown tea, called Liberty Tea, was derived from loosestrife plants, members of the primrose family that commonly grew in the fields and roadsides of New England.

Colonial women further supported anti-importation by refusing to purchase British textiles. Instead, they produced their own cloth and remade their families' old clothes. In 1768, a New York newspaper described the "glorious example" of two Newport women who "spun fully sixty yards of good fine linen cloth nearly a yard wide, besides taking care of a large family." By the time that the Revolution actually began, women were experts at "making do." In 1777, one woman told a British officer:

> I have retrenched every superfluous expense in my table and family. Tea I have not drunk since last Christmas, nor bought a new cap or gown since your defeat at Lexington: and, what I never did before, have learned to knit, and am now making stockings of wool for my servants: and this way do I throw in my mite for the public good. I know this, that as free I can die but once: but as a slave I shall not be worthy of life.

Besides supporting boycotts and nonimportation, women Patriots assisted in political actions against the British. They joined the Daughters of Liberty, who, along with the Sons of Liberty, held bonfire rallies, distributed anti-English propaganda, and hung tax collectors in effigy. The Boston Tea Party was initiated by Sarah Bradless Fulton, who was later known as the "Mother" of the famous event.

Some women organized active demonstrations on their own. In 1777, a group of Massachusetts women forcibly opened the warehouse of a merchant who was hoarding goods in order to sell them later at inflated wartime prices. It was reported that "a number of females, some say a hundred or more, assembled with a cart and trunks, marched down to the warehouse and demanded the keys, which he refused to deliver." One woman then grabbed him by his neck, pushed him into a cart, and seized the keys. After opening the warehouse, the women hoisted out hogsheads of coffee and drove off with them while a large group of men stood by in amazed silence.

Women pressured men in other ways to defy the British. Some young women refused to dance with or court men who had not declared their anti-English sentiments. Some wives denied their husbands "conjugal rights" until they swore their opposition to Great Britain. And a large number of women encouraged their husbands and sons to volunteer as members of the Continental Army.

Pushing their men toward the front lines meant great sacrifice for women who would now have to run the family farms and businesses by themselves, as well as to sell produce to supplement their husbands' irregular soldier's pay. When Abigail Adams's husband, John, urged her to "rouse your whole attention to the family, the stock, the farm, the dairy" in his absence, she responded by becoming an expert farm manager. It was her hope that, in time, she would have the "reputation of being as good a farmeress as my partner has of being a good statesman."

While single-handedly tending their families and farms, women Patriots organized women's associations that devoted untold hours to sewing clothes, rolling bandages, and preparing foodstuffs. In addition, they spent huge amounts of time and energy organizing charity fairs and other events to collect money for food, clothing, and sanitary supplies such as bandages for the army. In a fund-raising broadside printed in 1780, a Philadelphia woman explained that women were motivated by the "purest patriotism" in aspiring "to render themselves really useful." The campaign raised $30,000, which was used to purchase soldiers' shirts. In 1781, George Washington publicly praised the Ladies Association of Philadelphia for their fundraising efforts. They had "embellished" the American character, he stated, "by proving that the law of country is blended with those softer domestic virtues" of women. He added that these women deserved "an equal place with any who have preceded them in the walk of female patriotism."

Women not only created food and other goods, they also destroyed them rather than permit them to fall into the hands of the British. Rebecca Motte of South Carolina handed flaming arrows to soldiers to shoot at her home so that English soldiers would be forced to evacuate it. She quietly proclaimed, "I am gratified with the opportunity of contributing to the good of the country." She added, "I shall view the approaching scene with delight." Catherine Schuyler of Albany, New York, similarly burned fields of wheat to keep them from the enemy. Implementing a scorched earth policy, these and other women gladly destroyed their own homes and food supplies for the American cause.

None of these activities seem to diverge too far from the usual realm of female activities. But it is not widely recognized that women also collected lead, melted it down, and produced the shot used by the army. They manufactured and assembled arms. And they converted their businesses to wartime production. A Mrs. Proctor of Salem converted her tool factory to a rebel arsenal, while "Handy Betsy the Blacksmith" lent her expertise regarding cannon and other arms.

Other women became involved because of their technical skills. Mary Katherine Goddard, a leading printer and newspaper publisher in Baltimore, printed the official version of the Declaration of Independence in 1777. In 1775, she had been appointed postmaster of Baltimore and was probably the first woman to fill such a post. By the time of the Revolution, she was a successful and respected businessperson, an achievement recognized by the Continental Congress when it contracted with her for the Declaration.

Other women aided the Revolution by acting as saboteurs and spies. Lydia Darrah, a Quaker woman in Philadelphia, listened at the door of a room in her home, which British officers had taken over for meetings. When she heard attack orders read, she went through the British lines on the pretense of getting flour milled. She located an American officer to whom she entrusted her secret. A few days later, she placidly observed a British officer's despair at finding the American cannon mounted and prepared to receive his attack. "We have marched back here like a parcel of fools," he fumed.

Other attacks were thwarted by courageous women disguised as men. In Massachusetts, a group of women dressed themselves in their husbands' clothes and carried pitchforks in order to guard a nearby bridge. Here they unhorsed and searched a British courier. When they discovered dispatches concealed in his boot, they conducted him to the local jail for detention. In South Carolina, Elizabeth Marshall and her daughters-in-law also dressed as men. They, too, accosted a courier and seized his dispatches, thus blocking the passage of essential military intelligence.

Other women went directly to the front to offer their services. Mary Ludwig Hay McCauley was a camp cook, washwoman, and nurse. She was known as Molly Pitcher because she carried so many pails and pitchers of water to the men. When she saw her husband fall, she took over his cannon, keeping it in operation for the rest of the Battle of Monmouth. Soldiers remembered her as a warmhearted, energetic woman who swore volubly and chewed tobacco. In 1822, the Pennsylvania legislature rewarded her war service with a small pension.

Less well known is Margaret Corbin who fought and was wounded in the Battle of Fort Washington. Like Molly Pitcher, she followed her husband to the front, where she served as a nurse, cook, and washwoman. When he died at her side, Corbin filled his battle post until she was disabled by three grape shot that permanently cost her the use of one arm.

In 1779, she too received a small pension for her heroism. Known as "Captain Molly," Corbin was the first woman pensioner in the United States.

Deborah Sampson was a different type of revolutionary soldier. In 1782, she enlisted in the Continental forces under the name of Robert Shurtleff. Her unusual height, strong features, and great stamina protected her from discovery until she was hospitalized with a fever. After being exposed as an imposter, she was quickly discharged in 1783. She later wrote that she had "burst the tyrant bonds which held my sex in awe and clandestinely, or by stealth, grasped an opportunity, which custom and the world seemed to deny, as a natural privilege." She was granted a pension as a war veteran in 1792.

Scores of other women invaded the camps of the Continental Army, pledging to help in any way possible. Martha Washington, for example, wintered with her husband at Valley Forge. Here, she went from hut to hut carrying food to the sick and consoling the dying. Emily Greiger performed another type of service by volunteering to carry a message after the male soldiers in camp declined to do so. When she was detained by a British scout, Geiger ripped up the document and swallowed it. The next day she promptly delivered the message that she had quickly committed to memory. Yet another task that women often performed was combing the battlefields for the dead, whom they identified and gave proper burial.

This impressive description of women's war efforts actually only touches on their enormous involvement. Although a good deal of scholarly work has been done on revolutionary women, there is still much to be discovered about women who acted both as individuals and as organized groups to aid the cause of American liberty. Future research will be devoted not only to learning more about the women who worked at home and on the front but also to those who pledged their literary and intellectual talents to the war effort.

Phillis Wheatley, a black slave, was one such woman. She was purchased by a wealthy Boston merchant, John Wheatley, in 1761 as a personal servant. The Wheatleys soon recognized the young girl's nimble mind and gave her opportunities not usually given a slave. Phillis Wheatley became a Latin scholar, a poet, and a witty conversationalist. One of her most celebrated poems was "Ode to General Washington," published in the *Pennsylvania Magazine* in 1776. It identified her as a Patriot and gained her a personal invitation to visit General Washington's headquarters in Cambridge, Massachusetts.

Mercy Otis Warren was another patriotic poet. In addition, Warren was a historian, playwright, and propagandist of the Revolution. She turned her talents to political activism by writing three anti-British satirical plays during the war years. In the late 1770s, Warren began her major literary work, the three-volume *History of the Rise, Progress and Termination of the American Revolution,* which appeared in 1805. In 1790, Warren published a collection of verse entitled *Poems, Dramatic and Miscellaneous.* This volume included two pieces advocating human freedom. Warren's work indicated that she was not only a supporter of the principle of American liberty but was also an early enthusiast for the cause of female independence as well. She once commented to a friend that women should accept their "appointed subordination" only for the sake of "Order in Families," not due to any inferiority on their part.

During much of her lifetime, Warren was a close friend and frequent correspondent of Abigail Adams. According to historian Mary R. Beard, the voluminous correspondence of the two women is believed to have been the basis for the Committees of Correspondence, agencies for communicating insurrectionist ideas and actions from colony to colony. Beard pointed out that these two women discussed political events not only with each other but also with a number of men involved in the protest movement. Warren's and Adams's questions and comments elicited serious and often lengthy replies, which they then read to a group of people interested in discussing the issues involved.

Adams is today perhaps the best known woman of the Revolutionary era. Her letters to her husband, John, while he served in the Continental Congress have been quoted repeatedly by contemporary feminists. She is especially recognized for her attempts to extend the concepts of liberty and independence to other groups of people besides propertied white males.

In 1776, recognizing that a new form of government would have to be devised for the United States, Adams wrote to her husband: "In the new Code of Laws which I suppose it will be necessary for you to make I desire you would Remember the Ladies, and be more generous and favourable to them than your ancestors." She asked that he not "put such unlimited power in the hands of the Husbands" because "all Men would be tyrants if they could." She concluded by stating: "If perticular care and attention is not paid to the Ladies we are determined to foment a Rebelion, and will not ourselves bound by any Laws in which we have no voice, or Representation."

Adams was not asking for a social revolution in sex roles. She did not argue that women should vote or hold public office. She did not espouse equality for women or an abandonment of their domestic roles. Rather, Adams envisioned a legal system that would protect women from unlimited power in the hands of men.

John Adams responded to his wife's request in a joking manner. He wrote to her that he had heard that the Revolution had "loosened the bands of Government everywhere," even to the point of stirring up American Indians and black Americans. But, he added, her letter was "the first Intimation that another Tribe more numerous and powerfull than all the rest were grown discontented." Adams suggested to her friend Mercy Otis Warren that they petition the new Congress regarding the situation of women. She soon dropped her case with the statement to John: "I can not say that I think you very generous to the Ladies, for whilst you are proclaiming peace and good will to Men, Emancipating all Nations, you insist upon retaining an absolute power over Wives." Her last retort warned him that "we have it in our power not only to free ourselves but to subdue our Masters, and without violence throw both your natural and legal authority at our feet."

Adams's words were courageous yet in a sense empty in a day when women's rights and feminism were not major issues. She had few allies to back up her ideas and help her to mount the revolution of which she spoke. Yet she was still an effective reformer in certain ways. As her son, John Quincy Adams, wrote after her death, "her life gave the lie to every libel on her sex that was ever written." She was an accomplished business manager and self-proclaimed "farmeress" when John was away, which was a good deal of the time. Her wise investments and sound management provided the money to send her sons to Harvard, underwrite John's political career, finance the furnishing of several foreign legations and the newly constructed White House, and support the Adamses after John's retirement from the presidency.

Abigail Adams was also concerned with the anomaly of slavery. She was firmly convinced that the slave system destroyed the character of both individuals and society as a whole. In 1797, Adams sent a black servant boy to evening school. When her neighbors visited her to make known their objections, she strongly advocated the principle of "equality of Rights." Arguing that the young man was a freeman, Adams maintained that he had a right to an education. "Merely because his Face is Black, is he to be denied instruction? How is he to be qualified to procure a livelihood?" she asked. As a result of her impassioned defense of the young man's right to an education, the case was dropped.

Adams was the most visible, and probably the most vocal, woman of the Revolutionary era. But she clearly did not stand alone. There were many women who violated the dictates of the female role in order to follow their own interests and convictions. Whether they engaged in political activities, fought alongside men, wrote letters and tracts, or pursued other "unfeminine" activities, their actions challenged the model of American womanhood. Like the many assertive and irrepressible colonial women who preceded them, women of the war years displayed a high degree of independence of thought and spirit. Not content with the passivity and submissiveness that was widely believed to be their inherent nature, these women defied convention to follow their own desires, talents, and convictions.

In many cases, women were able to undertake "male" activities without much public or private censure. It was, after all, a time of national crisis that demanded the relaxation of the usual rules. Women who worked, fought, or wrote to help the cause of freedom were seen as patriotic and loyal to their country, if not to the dictates of their gender roles. Women who neglected the female sphere in order to participate in the larger public realm were indeed Patriots of the first order in many people's eyes.

It would seem logical to expect that these energetic and courageous women might be rewarded with some of the fruits of the Revolution. Perhaps they too would be granted a modicum of liberty and freedom. It also seems reasonable to expect that traditional beliefs regarding the weakness and inferiority of females would fall by the wayside as a consequence of these brave women's deeds. Surely, the post-Revolutionary years would be golden ones for American women. They would certainly expect to partake of the democracy that was so widely discussed throughout the new nation, especially since they had helped to secure it.

In recent years, historians of women have devoted a good deal of time to exploring whether the American Revolution did in fact produce any marked improvements in women's lives. They have collected and examined a wide variety of source materials in an attempt to assess the impact of the wartime period on women's roles. In fact, this research has resulted in a fascinating dialogue among historians who are unearthing contradictory findings. The issue of whether the Revolution helped or hindered the progress of American women is a provocative and stimulating debate.

In an essay in 1976, historian Joan Hoff-Wilson argued that the American Revolution brought about only an illusion of change for women. According to her, the war pushed America toward industrialism, a system that would move many women into factory jobs that were poorly paid and low in status. Women would thus lose whatever respect and autonomy they had as commanders of their households. Furthermore, the ideology of the new nation demanded "Republican Mothers," whose primary task was to train their sons for future citizenship and their daughters for future domesticity. In Hoff-Wilson's view, neither of women's new roles—that of factory worker or of Republican Mother—offered women any improvement in their positions. On the contrary, the female descendants of colonial women lost the economic authority and professional opportunities that their mothers and grandmothers had enjoyed.

In 1980, an important study by Mary Beth Norton challenged Hoff-Wilson's perception of the impact of the war on American women. In Norton's view, the Revolution had a positive effect on women's lives. The economic and social disruption that it created gave women the chance to take over farms, plantations, businesses, trades, and professions while men were involved in war-related duties. Norton's thorough examination of various types of evidence led her to the belief that the Revolution had an "indelible effect upon American women."

According to Norton, the changes were not to be found in the area of law and politics, but in women's private lives. Reform did not consist of the rewriting of legal codes, the granting of the vote to women, and the emergence of a strong feminist movement. Rather, it appeared in the reorganization of family structure and in women's aspirations. Norton maintained that the Revolution's effect on women could be determined only by an "analysis of women's private writings" rather than by an "examination of formal actions implemented by men."

Unlike Hoff-Wilson, Norton identified certain social and philosophical factors in the Revolution that encouraged the emergence of a generation of women with a strong sense of self. Moreover, women now lived in a world that offered them increased opportunities in education and other public activities. Norton observed that, while women of the Revolutionary era could not escape certain feminine standards, their domestic roles as wives and mothers were seen as having an impact upon the larger society. All Americans finally recognized the importance of motherhood. But, Norton added, the "republican definition of motherhood" would in itself eventually become a tremendous restriction on the development of American women. Norton concluded that, in the final analysis, "the legacy of the American Revolution for women was thus ambiguous."

Historian Linda K. Kerber presented similar findings in her investigation of how the Revolution affected women. "This is a difficult question to answer," Kerber wrote. "The war raised once again the old question of whether a woman could be a patriot—that is, an essentially political person—and it also raised the question of what form female patriotism might take." Basic assumptions about women were challenged. For example, coverture, the control of a married woman's property by her husband, suggested that she had little political identity of her own. If he fought for the Loyalist side, was she automatically a Loyalist as well? Was she responsible for her own crimes of treason and espionage? Could she, like the new nation, free herself of a burdensome master through divorce?

Kerber's study points out just how complex the situation of women actually was during the era of the Revolution and early nationhood. She emphasizes that, while many women experienced political involvement during the war itself, they soon learned that the new republic granted them few opportunities as political beings. Instead, women soon discovered that their value to the nation lay in Republican Motherhood, a concept that entrusted women with the morality of the nation's future citizens. According to Kerber, the conservative nature of the Revolution revealed itself in its failure to integrate women as true participants in the political community. Kerber noted: "It is possible to read the subsequent political history of women in America as the story of women's efforts to accomplish for themselves what the Revolution had failed to do."

This spirited discussion among historians of women is at once both intriguing and confusing. It offers few definitive answers to the question of how the Revolution changed women's status. It is unclear whether the war's ideology and economic impact caused improvement or decline in the condition of American women. Perhaps it is enough to acknowledge the incredibly complicated dimensions of the debate and to realize that there is no one answer to the many questions involved in it. Instead, a reasonable way to proceed in assessing the effect of the Revolution on women may be to recognize that the Revolution did cause change. Whether for better or for worse, women's lives were affected in many diverse areas by the war and the necessary aftermath of establishing a new nation.

Undoubtedly, the development of the concept of Republican, or Moral, Motherhood precipitated numerous alterations in women's roles during the late 1700s and early 1800s. During the colonial period, women had been viewed primarily as wives, helpmeets, and ornaments. Seventeenth- and eighteenth-century Americans did not idealize motherhood and often seemed unconcerned about it. Neither the helpmeet nor the ornament image of women placed any emphasis on mothering.

Maternal love was apparently taken for granted and was not considered to be a matter that needed direction or guidance. If anything, there was more discussion of fatherhood, since the father was the dominant member of the family. Because men worked in or near the home during the years of settlement, they were able to help rear their children. Mothers, on the other hand, were so busy with their many chores that they often relied on their husbands or other adult members of the household to care for their children.

By the end of the eighteenth century, however, these casual attitudes toward motherhood had changed dramatically. Topics such as breast-feeding, discipline, and the instilling of morality in young children now elicited the attention of ministers, authors of guidebooks, and physicians, among others. The Moral Mother was increasingly charged with nurturing loyal and effective citizens for the newly founded nation. She was responsible for protecting virtue and morality in the United States.

A number of social changes produced this modified perception of women's roles. Many men now worked away from the home, regularly leaving the care of children in the hands of women. The increasing availability of certain factory-produced goods began to alleviate the burden of incessant domestic labor, thus giving women more time for child care. And women read more than ever before, thus opening themselves to the rapidly growing literature on motherhood.

Perhaps many women also recognized that Republican Motherhood was in a way an upgrading of their inferior status. If so, such a realization would make it possible for them to accept its tenets willingly. The potential gain in prestige would also make it palatable to immigrant women who had little in their backgrounds to prepare them for notions of democracy and republicanism, especially in relation to mothering. Representing a growing diversity of cultural experiences, including eastern European, Jewish, and Catholic, immigrant women could identify with a role that granted them increased respect even if they did not yet understand its importance to their new country.

Not only women but men as well gradually accepted the idea that females were innately more loving and nurturing than males. During these years, mother's love was recognized as an inborn instinct. Maternal fondness and tenderness toward children were highly acclaimed. In summary, motherhood was idealized, romanticized, and sentimentalized by Americans who believed that the future of their new nation somehow depended on it.

Naturally, such drastic revisions in the image of women affected many elements of family life. Birthing itself was rapidly becoming a more complicated affair. By the time of the Revolution, an expectant mother's personal support network of family, friends, and midwife had largely been replaced by male physicians. The change was primarily due to the introduction of obstetrical forceps, as well as a growing concern about the welfare of the mother. Men moved into the field of midwifery by promising women help with difficult deliveries through the use of forceps, but eventually they took over almost all deliveries.

Dr. William Shippen of Philadelphia led the revolution in birthing techniques. After studying medicine, including midwifery, in London, Shippen returned to Philadelphia in 1762. He brought with him British standards concerning hospitals, medical training, and professionalism. At his urging, the only hospital in America, the Pennsylvania Hospital, initiated formal medical training and lectures in midwifery. Shippen became Professor of Anatomy, Surgery, and Midwifery. Since women were not admitted to formal medical training, they were denied knowledge of the forceps and were effectively limited in their practice as midwives. In 1763, Shippen's entry into the practice of midwifery in Philadelphia marked the beginning of male control of the delivery room.

By 1807, five medical schools in America offered courses in midwifery to male students. The increasing presence of trained male doctors in the delivery room transformed the birth process. Instruments and anesthesia came into regular use and the Caesarean section became a common emergency procedure. Because both wives and husbands often felt uncomfortable with the presence of a male, the doctor communicated with the pregnant woman through a nurse and avoided performing a vaginal examination. Standards of modesty and of delivery-room etiquette often caused improper medical care. Since the doctor usually worked under a sheet to avoid seeing the woman's body, accidents were common. A Dr. Dewees warned his students to be careful so that "no part of the mother is included in the locking of the blades" of the forceps. Apparently, this accident was common. Because the infant's umbilical cord also had to be cut under covers, newborn babies were sometimes mutilated as well. One story passed on to medical students told of a doctor who caught a newborn infant's penis in the blade of his scissors.

The whole aura of the birthing ceremony also changed. Rather than being an open event involving many supportive people, it was now conducted in a darkened room by a professional, aloof male physician. It was no longer a matter of nature but a disease that demanded scientific management. Oddly enough, the new strictures surrounding childbirth actually indicated more sympathy for the expectant mother, rather than less as it may appear. Changing attitudes toward the importance of motherhood called for more mothers to survive childbirth. In this sense, the entry of male physicians and instruments into the delivery room was a sign of the enhanced value of women.

Another consequence of the growing emphasis on motherhood was an interest in child-care practices. Manuals such as *Mother's Cathechism and Maternal Instruction* appeared in large numbers. The prevailing view of children became less one of a miniature adult to be rescued from original sin and more one of a pliable and innocent being whose upbringing demanded specialized equipment, toys, and books. Children were increasingly seen as individuals. Thus, from the concept of motherhood came the concept of childhood.

A recent study of one Connecticut town during the end of the eighteenth and the beginning of the nineteenth century demonstrates that other significant modifications occurred in family structure and interaction during this period. The proportion of single women increased while family size slowly decreased. By 1796, for example, 8 percent of Baltimore's households were headed by women, two thirds of whom were widows and one third single women. An increase in the number of women in the general population created a more competitive marriage market in the closing decade of the eighteenth century. Widowed and single women supported themselves by working as seamstresses, laundresses, dyers, starchers, lace makers, and mantua makers. They also ran small businesses supplying groceries, dry goods, millinery, hardware, and other small goods.

Other changes were also evident. Women now controlled more personal and real property. They also applied for and were granted a large number of divorces, many more than men. This statistic might be interpreted as a consequence of an enhanced spirit of independence among women, along with a willingness on the part of society to take women's needs more seriously. Certainly, a new ideal of companionate marriage was developing. An anonymous article of the 1790s declared that an ideal marriage was one based on "mutual esteem, mutual friendship, mutual confidence, begirt about by mutual forbearance." Possibly the heightened worth of motherhood raised expectations regarding the contributions of men to marriage and family relationships. To protect their vulnerable children, women were perhaps no longer willing to endure their husband's adultery and alcoholism.

Another area of change that defies concrete explanation is the emergence of women artists. Although women continued to be heavily involved in the production of folk art and craft work within their homes, a number of them moved into the creation of more conventional works of art. They achieved this without the benefit of formal training or study abroad because these activities were believed to be unseemly for women.

Despite these limitations, several women gained public recognition for their pastel drawing during the late eighteenth century. Ruth Henshaw Bascom of Massachusetts was known for her pastel crayon portraits. Also proficient at needlework, Bascom reportedly never accepted money for any of her works. Sarah Perkins was a Connecticut pastelist who also produced portraits during the 1790s. Her work was cut short after she took charge of her seven brothers and sisters at the age of twenty, married a widower with five children, and then had four children of her own.

Other women artists worked in the medium of watercolor. Sophia Burpee sometimes combined her watercolors with embroidery. Ruby Devol Finch executed watercolor paintings, especially of the Parable of the Prodigal Son, as well as miniatures and family records. Like Finch, Mary Parke painted Biblical scenes in watercolors. Susanna Heebner of Pennsylvania also focused on religious themes. Her manuscript illuminations combined religious poetry, moral teachings, and brightly colored decorations.

Probably the best known female artist of this era was Sarah Miriam Peale. As the youngest daughter of James Peale, a renowned miniaturist and portrait painter, Peale had artistic advantages not available to other women. Trained by her father and her uncle—acclaimed natural history painter and portraitist, Charles Willson Peale—Sarah Peale became an accomplished portrait and still-life artist. Her clients included heads of state and generals. She was the first woman to have her work exhibited at the prestigious Pennsylvania Academy of the Fine Arts.

The public acceptance of these women as artists certainly indicates an important change in perceptions of women. Now accepting themselves as individuals who possessed at least a modicum of talent and ingenuity, women were expanding their horizons. Women began to blossom in other areas, particularly in education. The rhetoric of the 1780s and 1790s declared that reason and rationality were masculine qualities and not common among women. Yet, at the same time, many Americans believed that women must be educated for their roles as Republican Mothers. Several women took advantage of this ambivalence in order to argue for the improved education of women.

Judith Sargent Murray, an author and early feminist, was one of the first Americans to argue publicly for increased educational opportunities for women. In 1779, writing under the pen name of Constantia, Murray declared that men and women had equal minds that deserved equivalent educations. "Are women deficient in reason?" she asked. "We can only reason from what we know, and if an opportunity of acquiring knowledge hath been denied us, the inferiority of our sex cannot fairly be deduced from thence." If women were "allowed an equality of acquirements" in the realm of education, they would "meet on even ground" in their achievements.

At the same time, Abigail Adams, in her letters to her husband, was exploring the meaning of the Revolution for women's education. After reading the Declaration of Independence, Adams understood that women's primary duty was to cultivate wisdom and loyalty in their children, thus preserving virtues necessary to a free republic. But how would women train "Heroes, Statesmen and Philosophers," she wondered, if they themselves were not "learned." In 1778, she reminded John of the "trifling narrow contracted Education" of women in the new United States. "You need not be told," she wrote, "how much female Education is neglected, nor how fashionable it has been to ridicule Female learning." Adams continued to worry about the matter and, by 1787, concluded that women were "rational Beings," whose minds "might with propriety receive the highest possible cultivation." Adams recognized that an educated woman would "draw upon herself the jealousy of the Men and the envy of the Women," but she believed that the only "way to remedy this evil" was "by increasing the number of accomplished women," thus forcing their acceptance by society.

As women's education became an ongoing debate, it was obvious that most Americans believed that the new republican woman should be rational, competent, and self-reliant. As Linda Kerber has pointed out, women were now to be educated for the good of the republic. This view did not support "intellectual" women or the departure of women from the home as their primary sphere. Rather, it emphasized the idea that women's duties in the home had achieved a new significance. The celebrated Dr. Benjamin Rush of Philadelphia explained it this way: "Let the ladies of a country be educated properly and they will not only make and administer its laws, but form its manners and character."

In 1787, Rush presented a model curriculum for republican women to the board of visitors of the Young Ladies Academy of Philadelphia. He maintained that "female education should be accommodated to the state of society, manners, and government of the country in which it is conducted." The course of study of this academy, which claimed to be the first of its kind chartered in the United States when it opened in 1787, included reading, writing, arithmetic, English grammar, composition, rhetoric, and geography. The curriculum represented an alteration in ideas regarding women. Prominent men had, for the first time, devoted their time and energy to advocate the concept of a sound education for women.

Yet addresses by the academy's graduates reflected these young women's acceptance of the *status quo*. "I believe I must give up all pretensions to profundity," one stated, "for I am more at home in my female character." Only a few of these women made any mention of equal education and widening the accepted female sphere. But the academy's founders did not intend it "as constituting an Era altogether new." Instead, there is strong evidence that the school's founders wanted to lessen women's discontent while improving the education of the mothers of the new country's future citizens.

In the South, too, women were taking advantage of increased educational opportunities. Women's academies were at the center of the movement away from superficial education in "female accomplishments" to more solid training in subjects that would contribute to women becoming more effective mothers and more informed citizens. In 1805, a Virginia planter requested that his daughter send him a complete account of her academy education: "It is not enough for me to know that you make as much progress in your French and Geography as you possibly can! I wish to know precisely what that progress is—I wish to know how each day is employed—what proportion is devoted to study, to writing, to cyphering, to reading, to sewing, to amusement, to idleness." Southern women flocked to academies in order to gain, if not equality, at least an improved quality of life as wives, mothers, and plantation mistresses.

During the closing decades of the 1700s and the opening years of the 1800s, women asserted themselves not only in educational institutions but in religious ones as well. Although a woman's ability to reason was often questioned, her sense of piety was not. During the early 1700s, male church membership had begun to decline. By the Revolutionary era, the number of women church members far outnumbered men. Soon most congregations had a majority of female members. Religious activity offered women a voice and a role, however limited it might be. Women, subordinate in other areas of life, discovered an opportunity to express themselves in the churches. During the 1770s, Mother Ann Lee even promoted a new sect, Shakerism. And during the 1780s, revivalist Jemima Wilkinson attracted numerous followers.

As church audiences became largely female, ministers found it necessary to "feminize" their message to meet the needs of their listeners. Clergymen turned their attention to topics of concern to women, such as the family, public and private morality, the refinement of society, and missionary endeavors. They also stressed the crucial role of godly mothers and the importance of women's morality, thus adding the church's voice to the growing emphasis on motherhood.

When the Second Great Awakening occurred in the late 1790s, women were in its forefront. As religious, emotional, and highly moral beings, they saw themselves as the inculcators of virtue not only in children but in men as well. They actively recruited men for conversion, an act that implied the superiority of their female religious nature. Women also openly expressed anger against authority, particularly that of ungodly men and controlling ministers. Through religion, women vented the tensions caused by other limitations on their lives.

The political realm was one such source of frustration for women. They soon learned that the brave statements regarding freedom and liberty for all contained in the Declaration of Independence did not include them. John Adams argued that, while women were theoretically part of the new government of the United States, their influence was exercised in the home rather than in any public political capacity. Thomas Jefferson, the author of the Declaration, believed that "the tender breasts of ladies were not formed for political convulsion." Consequently, republican women found that the United States Constitution included no rights or protections for them. Women received no new legal codes nor were they freed from coverture and the limitations of marital unity. They had no representatives in governing bodies nor any emissaries or planks in the platforms of the first political parties. Their occasional right to vote in some local and state elections was exercised for the last time in 1807 in New Jersey.

Clearly, the many political ramifications of the Revolution and the new nation's government did not extend to women. Even in such egalitarian frontier regions as those along the Cumberland River, women were not granted political privileges during the 1780s and 1790s. They were not rewarded with increased opportunities, although their effort and energy was crucial in expanding the new country toward the west and south.

These women aided the formation of the new states entering the union after the Revolution—Kentucky in 1792, Tennessee in 1796, and Ohio in 1803.

Frontierswomen fought alongside their men in wresting the land from its native owners, worked to clear the land with oxen, mules, horses, and primitive machinery, and struggled to raise their children as educated "proper" people. When they lost their men, many frontierswomen continued to work on their own. It has been estimated that almost two thirds of early women settlers in Tennessee alone were widowed by Indian wars by the 1790s. Yet few left the frontier to live with families in the more settled eastern regions. Widowed in 1781, Leah Lucas stayed on the Cumberland frontier, farming the family land and raising five children.

Other women who did have husbands also learned to manage farms, children, and crises on their own while their men were absent on long trips. Married to hunters, traders, trappers, surveyors, and politicians, Cumberland women stayed home and minded the family enterprise. Daniel Smith, for example, was gone from his family more than a year when he helped to survey the North Carolina-Virginia line in 1779–1780. Thus, women often tilled the fields, built houses and out-buildings, bred animals, cared for their children, and did a multitude of heavy tasks.

Even when men were on the scene to care for the fields and stock, frontierswomen's work was extensive and exhausting. A woman managed the house, children, and dairy—all complex tasks requiring training and skill. Women's labor and management abilities were often recognized by their menfolk in their wills, which commonly left property to a spouse and assigned a wife as executrix. There was also a good deal of respect given to women, but they were not widely encouraged to explore new roles in the public arena.

American Indian women fared even worse in the new nation of the Revolutionary period than did Euro-American women. Along with Indian men, native women suffered because of white expansionism. As the white population moved westward, it became increasingly impatient with native concepts of communal landholding. Puzzled by the Indian belief that land belonged to everyone and thus could not be transferred to an individual through a piece of paper, whites resorted to threats and trickery to get Indians to agree to land sales. Convinced of the validity of "private property"—and of their God-given right to the land—whites pushed Indians farther and farther west.

Most whites seemed to overlook or ignore the fact that the brisk trade conducted with Indians significantly aided the economic development of the American frontier. They minimized Indians' contributions to western development as porters, laborers, traders in furs and other goods, guides, bridge builders, explorers of routes, and suppliers of food and other necessary commodities to white migrants. Because most Indians preferred their own cultures and refused to assimilate to white ways, whites destroyed them or pushed them farther westward.

This displacement of American Indians was accompanied by white exploitation of native women. As a case in point, the American fur trade weakened the status and power of Indian women by utilizing them as poorly paid and low-status interpreters, workers, and liaisons. The "civilization" that the fur traders carried to native women included venereal disease, prostitution, and abandonment by white husbands. At the same time, factory-produced goods began to undermine the use of items such as textiles and pottery produced by native women. And white attitudes regarding the inferiority of women denied Indian women any recognition or reward for the significant role that they played in the development of the fur trade itself.

Thus, the importance of Indian women to their particular societies gradually diminished. Like white women, they were increasingly relegated to the domestic sphere. Opportunities for women to become political leaders of their communities, serve as shamans or warriors, and actively engage in trade began to decrease. In Iroquois society, for instance, a group of female elders had long served as sachems on tribal councils, the most powerful ruling body. White leaders, however, disapproved of such power in the hands of women and now effectively denied it to Iroquois women by refusing to deal with them. Under the matrilineal system of the Cherokee, women held property, kept their children in case of a divorce, and decided whether captives would be adopted or punished. As a result of intermarriage with whites and the United States government's "civilization" policy, the Cherokee were encouraged to abandon this arrangement in favor of a patrilineal pattern of inheritance. Cherokee women had lost further power by 1800, when a depleted game supply caused Cherokee men and African slaves to take over the agricultural tasks that belonged to women.

Unlike their white counterparts, Indian women did not have a "republic" for which to labor within the home. In addition, they were neither "virtuous" nor moral in white eyes and were becoming less so in the Indian view as well. Their possibilities for achievement were diminishing and were not being replaced by prominence as mothers. By the early years of the 1800s, the situation of Indian women bore less resemblance to that of white women than ever.

Of course, white society was largely unconcerned about the position of American Indian women. The native women who commanded the attention of whites continued to be those that helped them to achieve their ends. Thus, Sacajawea, an Idaho Shoshoni, gained historical fame among whites when she aided the Lewis and Clark expedition as an interpreter and guide between 1804 and 1806. In another case, Marie Dorion, an Iowa Indian, was remembered as the only woman on the famed expedition to Astoria (1811–1812) on the Columbia River and as an Indian who warned whites of a native attack. It is from the shackles of such stereotypes that Indian women's history is currently struggling to emerge.

Like American Indian women, black women were also objects of exploitation by whites. With the growth of industrialization in the North and the cotton culture in the South after the Revolution, black slavery gradually declined in the northern states while it became dominant in the southern ones. As profits from cotton began to rise, white slaveowners intensified their efforts to extract the most labor possible from black slave women. After Congress abolished the slave trade in 1808, black women were also expected to become "breeders," that is, to produce as many slave children as possible. Prizes, promises of freedom, and other rewards were frequently offered to slave women who bore ten or more children.

Black slave women also labored as nursemaids, midwives, domestic servants, and field hands. On the larger plantations, they served as seamstresses, nurses, poultrymaids, and dairymaids. Since the number of trades and crafts that black women were allowed to pursue were limited, compared to those open to black slave men who worked as blacksmiths, coopers, overseers, and in other similar capacities, more women worked in the fields than did men. The black female field hand was routinely expected to perform domestic tasks as well. One Virginia planter of the late 1700s described a favored slave as "a stout able field wench and an exceedingly good washer and ironer."

These black women were regarded as chattels rather than human beings. They were listed in property inventories of plantations by first name, age, and monetary value. On the auction block, they were scrutinized much like livestock. At one slave sale, a small buyer "took one of the prettiest women by the chin and opened her mouth to see the state of her gums and teeth, with no more ceremony than if she had been a horse."

In spite of the indignities and degradation of the slave system, black women provided the glue that held slave families together. Familial ties were extremely important to black slaves; yet they lived with the constant threat of separation from their kin. Slaves continually protested against their inability to establish families and preserve family units. In 1774, a group of Massachusetts slaves petitioned the state legislature for their freedom, stressing the destructive nature of slavery on family life: "How can a slave perform the duties of husband to wife or a parent to a child? How can a husband leave his master to work and cleave to his wife? How can the wife submit to her husband in all things?" Although

Massachusetts and other northern states manumitted their slaves, the southern slave system continued to exploit black women while often wrenching their families from them.

One change that the Revolution did bring about for black Americans was the hope of eventual abolition from their slave status. During the war itself, the presence of British armies encouraged slaves to escape their owners. Moreover, the British often harbored runaway slaves and granted them freedom as a means of weakening the efforts of southern Patriots. After the war, the British transported many slaves who had joined them to Nova Scotia in Canada. These former slaves frequently escaped in family groups that included women and children. Over half of the twenty-three slaves who fled Thomas Jefferson's Virginia plantation during the war were women and girls.

At the war's conclusion, many Americans supported the abolition of slavery. A number of slaveowners in the upper South chose to free their slaves in a burst of abolitionist enthusiasm. This move created a free black population that included many women. Other Americans began to form abolitionist societies. As long-time opponents of slavery, the Quakers were in the forefront of this activity. Abolitionist societies, organized in Philadelphia and elsewhere in the middle states, sought to convince Americans that their freedom should extend to blacks. Using the Declaration of Independence as a basis, they claimed that liberty for one and all should transcend distinctions of color. And several states passed abolition provisions. The Massachusetts Constitution of 1780, for instance, included a Declaration of Rights stating that "all men are born free and equal." Under this provision such slaves as Elizabeth Freeman (also known as Mum Bett) finally received liberation from their slave status.

Other Americans argued that black slaves who participated in the Revolution should be rewarded with their freedom. Yet, in practice, this policy was seldom implemented. A black woman who served as a bullet runner for American troops remained a slave until she was nearly 80, at which time she escaped to Canada. Another black woman who served a colonel for forty years was denied her impassioned plea for freedom in 1782.

Pennsylvania was a leader in attempting to erase the contradictions between the nation's freedom and the servitude of some of its citizens. During the Revolution, Pennsylvania passed the Gradual Abolition Law which in turn led to an increase in the state's black population. The Census of 1790 recorded 10,301 blacks in Pennsylvania—6,540 free and 3,761 slaves. But the state's abolition provisions attracted such an influx of blacks, many via the early Underground Railroad, that the total had jumped 176 percent by 1800. By 1800, Pennsylvania's black population numbered 16,270—14,564 free and 1,706 slaves.

The situation of free black women in Pennsylvania did not markedly improve as a result of the experiment in gradual abolition. They were often denied employment. When employed, they worked on farms or as domestic servants for impossibly low wages. And they lived with the ever-present fear of being captured and sold into slavery.

Evidently, the Revolution had not dramatically altered the lives of women—white, Indian, or black—in any major way. They were still viewed and treated largely in prejudicial and discriminatory terms. The writings in the 1780s of two male commentators illustrate the ways which most Americans viewed native, black, and white women during the late eighteenth century. The perceptions that they recorded were common and are extremely useful in gaining insight into women's historical experiences. The ideas of these two educated, sophisticated men distinctly reveal the stronghold that images and stereotypes of women and womanhood had over people's minds in this era.

One of these writers was Thomas Jefferson. Regarding Indian women, Jefferson noted that they were forced to submit to "unjust drudgery," as was the "case with every barbarous people." They bore fewer children than white women, for, as "with all animals, if the female be badly fed, or not fed at all, her young perish." To Jefferson, such "obstacles of want" were simply nature's way of limiting "the multiplication of wild animals." He concluded that, when married to a white man, an Indian woman who was fed properly, exempted from "excessive drudgery," and protected from danger could bear as many children as white women. His view, like that of most white Americans at the time, was based more on prejudice and ignorance than knowledge.

Jefferson displayed a similar bias when he turned his attention to black women. He lamented the absence of "flowing hair" and "symmetry of form" in black women as compared with whites. Moreover, "the veil of black" gave their faces an "eternal monotony" that contrasted unfavorably with the "fine mixtures of red and white, the expressions of every passion by greater or less suffusions of color" that appeared in white women's faces. Observing that blacks slept frequently, he explained that an "animal whose body is at rest, and who does not reflect, must be disposed to sleep of course." Jefferson could not identify an occasion when a black "had uttered a thought above the level of plain narration," nor displayed "even an elementary trait of painting or sculpture." He dismissed Phillis Wheatley as an example of religious zeal, rather than of talent. "The compositions published under her name are below the dignity of criticism," he concluded.

Given the fact that Jefferson was considered a democratic, liberal thinker, his attitudes seem rather prejudiced, even for his time. If these were the ideas of a sophisticated, well-educated liberal, then the chances are that the mass of Americans were even more unenlightened. Jefferson's descriptions of American Indian and black American women certainly do not indicate the existence of a crucible of liberty for them.

The second writer was Hector St. John de Crèvecoeur, a New York farmer of French background, who demonstrated a very different set of prejudices in his discussion of white women in America. The images of his own wife that inspired his love focus upon her spinning, knitting, or nursing a child. He claimed that, like him, American men did not expect a dowry with a wife, for they realized that a "wife's fortune consists principally in her future economy, modesty, and skillful management." According to Crèvecoeur, if a farmer were "blessed with a good wife," he had the opportunity to live better than "any people of the same rank on the globe."

Several significant points emerge from the writings of these two influential men. Their essays discuss white women largely in terms of their domestic roles and native and black women primarily in terms of their race. They extol white women's contributions to the nation and denigrate those of native and black women. And they show that even educated, liberal observers were deeply affected by prevailing stereotypes of women.

Clearly, women's image and "sphere" had been tested by the confusions created by the American Revolution and the forming of the new nation. Changes in thinking regarding women included the ideal of companionate marriage, legitimacy of women's education, an increased respect for motherhood, and talk of enhanced self-esteem for women. Yet the traditional conception of women solely as wives and mothers had not only survived, but had expanded its dimensions and increased its influence. At the same time, however, many women had grown restive with the restrictions on their lives and had begun to question their validity.

This ambivalent situation would soon be disrupted by two major occurrences—the Industrial Revolution and the westward movement—which would alter both the stereotypes and the actuality of American women's lives. The Industrial Revolution, already well on its way by 1800, along with growing westward migration marked by the flow of people toward the Mississippi River after the Revolution, would soon revise the parameters of the model. How these two movements affected both the image and the reality of women's lives is the next chapter in the story of the experiences of American women.

SUGGESTIONS FOR FURTHER READING

Akers, Charles W. *Abigail Adams: An American Woman.* Boston: Little, Brown and Company, 1980.

Berkin, Carol Ruth, and Mary Beth Norton, eds. *Women of America: A History.* Boston: Houghton Mifflin, 1979. Part II, 3.

Bloch, Ruth H. "American Feminine Ideals in Transition: The Rise of the Moral Mother, 1785–1815." *Feminist Studies* 4 (June 1978): 101–126.

Bogdan, Janet. "Care or Cure: Childbirth Practices in Nineteenth Century America." *Feminist Studies* 3 (June 1978): 92–99.

Chambers - Schiller, Lee Virginia. *Liberty, A Better Husband: Single Women in America, The Generations of 1780–1840.* New Haven: Yale University Press, 1984.

Clark, Ella E., and Margot Edmonds. *Sacagawea of the Lewis and Clark Expedition.* Berkeley and Los Angeles: University of California Press, 1979.

Clinton, Catharine. *The Other Civil War: Women in the Nineteenth Century.* New York: Hill and Wang, 1984. Chapter 1.

———. "Equally Their Due: The Education of the Planter Daughter in the Early Republic." *Journal of the Early Republic* 2 (Spring 1982): 39–60.

Cody, Cheryll Ann. "Naming, Kinship and Estate Disposal: Notes on Slave Family Life on a South Carolina Plantation, 1786–1833." *William and Mary Quarterly* 39 (January 1982): 192–211.

Dewhurst, C. Kurt, Betty MacDowell, and Marsha MacDowell. *Artists in Aprons: Folk Art by American Women.* New York: E. P. Dutton, 1979.

Dye, Nancy Schrom. "History of Childbirth in America." *Signs* 6 (Autumn 1980): 97–108.

Friedman, Jean E., and William G. Shade, eds. *Our American Sisters: Women in American Life and Thought.* Lexington, MA: D. C. Heath and Company, 1982). Part I, Nos. 5 and 6.

James, Edward T., ed. *Notable American Women, 1607–1905: A Biographical Dictionary.* Cambridge, MA: Belknap Press, 1971.

Kerber, Linda K. *Women of the Republic: Intellect and Ideology in Revolutionary America.* Chapel Hill: University of North Carolina Press, 1980.

Newman, Debra L. "Black Women in the Era of the American Revolution in Pennsylvania." *Journal of Negro History* 61 (July 1976): 276–289.

Niethammer, Carolyn. *Daughters of the Earth: The Lives and Legends of American Indian Women.* New York: Macmillan Publishing Company, 1977.

Norton, Mary Beth. *Liberty's Daughters: The Revolutionary Experience of American Women, 1750–1800.* Boston: Little, Brown and Company, 1980.

Perdue, Theda. *Slavery and the Evolution of Cherokee Society, 1540–1866.* Knoxville: University of Tennessee Press, 1979.

Sheils, Richard D. "The Feminization of American Congregationalism, 1730–1835." *American Quarterly* 33 (Spring 1981): 46–62.

Smith, Daniel Blake. "The Study of the Family in Early America: Trends, Problems, and Prospects." *William and Mary Quarterly* 39 (January 1982): 3–28.

Utley, Beverly. "Brave Women." *American History Illustrated* 3 (1968): 10–18.

Van Kirk, Sylvia. *Many Tender Ties: Women in Fur-Trade Society, 1670–1870.* Norman: University of Oklahoma Press, 1983.

Woloch, Nancy. *Women and the American Experience.* New York: Alfred A. Knopf, 1984. Chapters 3–4.

Wertz, Richard W., and Dorothy C. Wertz. *Lying-In*. New York: Free Press, 1977.

Wright, Mary C. "Economic Development and Native American Women in the Early Nineteenth Century." *American Quarterly* 33 (Winter 1981): 525–536.

Western artist W. H. D. Koerner created this painting of a westering woman in 1921.
Madonna of the Prairie *captures one popular and enduring image of frontierswomen.*
Courtesy of the Buffalo Bill Historical Center, Cody, Wyoming.

CHAPTER 3

The Cult of True Womanhood: Industrial and Westward Expansion 1816–1837

B Y the second decade of the nineteenth century, the United States was caught up in a fever of growth and expansion. A "boom psychology" encouraged capitalists to invest in new industries, people to flock to American cities from the countryside and from other countries in search of jobs, and thousands of others to stream across the Appalachian Mountains toward the beckoning frontier. Industrialization and the westward migration wrought dramatic changes in the face of the new nation between 1816 and 1837.

Prevailing images and realities of women's lives experienced widespread alterations as well. The customary image of women as primarily wives and mothers not only persisted, but was enhanced by a highly developed doctrine of woman's sphere. Yet, at the same time, the actual activities and employment of women were challenging the traditional concept of separate spheres. By the time of the Panic of 1837—a turning point in the nation's history—the invented American woman appeared to be solid on the surface but, upon closer examination, was actually in a state of flux. All that was certain was that industrial and westward expansion had called the model of American womanhood into serious question.

American women felt the impact of the era's growth in many ways, not all of them positive. In 1816, the appointment of the first congressional committee to study women laborers recognized the widereaching effects of industrialization. Among other things, industrialization transformed household production, created social classes of women, and drew huge numbers of women from their homes into paid employment. These changes, along with their attendant problems, would eventually cause dissatisfied American women to challenge the image of women that restricted their lives.

The story begins in 1789, when the first factory for carding and spinning yarn in America was established in Rhode Island. Because most men were engaged in agriculture, proponents of the American factory system suggested hiring women. They did not want to destroy agriculture in order to develop industry. Besides, it seemed natural for women, who had spun and woven in their own homes, to move their customary work into a factory setting. In his Report on Manufacturers of 1791, Secretary of the Treasury Alexander Hamilton advocated factory employment for women because it made development of the new system possible "without taking men from the fields." He added that this would also render women "more useful than they otherwise would be," while farms would prosper as a result of the income brought in by the "increased industry" of farm wives and daughters.

These arguments multiplied many times over during the following years. Tench Coxe, an avid supporter of manufacturing, argued that "the portions of time of housewives and young women which were not occupied with family affairs could be profitably filled up" by factory work. This view soon expanded to include the claim that a new factory was actually a blessing to a community because it furnished employment for its women. A few years later, it was added that women were "kept out of vice simply by being employed and instead of being destitute provided with an abundance for a comfortable subsistence." In 1822, Philadelphia philanthropist Mathew Carey stated that, without the factory, young women would lack "employment and spend their time perniciously—a burden to their parents and society—trained up to vicious courses." But with factory employment, they were "happily preserved from idleness and its attendant vices and crimes."

It is unclear how instrumental these arguments were in propelling women into factories. Women did enter such employment in large numbers, but it was probably because of the increasing need that farm families had for cash income during the early 1800s. The congressional committee of 1816 identified 100,000 industrial workers in the United States, two out of three of whom were female. By 1828, 9 out of 10 textile workers in New England were female.

Thousands of young farm women in New England left their families to relocate in the new mill towns. The best known of these factory villages was Lowell, Massachusetts. Here, women workers lived together in company-owned boardinghouses. Often, these women sent part of their meager wages home to their families, while their brothers remained on the farm to provide agricultural labor or attended college, often on their sister's earnings. As a result of their paid employment, daughters were now seen as a "blessing to the farmer," rather than a liability.

The Lowell women commonly worked twelve to fourteen hours a day, tending two or more machines for about $2.00 a week. They were offered various cultural benefits such as libraries and participation in the company-sponsored literary journal, *The Lowell Offering*. Although the boardinghouses were supervised by matrons, the factory women enjoyed a certain amount of independence. Lowell was frequently held up as a model factory village with ideal working and living conditions.

As early as the mid-1820s, however, it was becoming clear that all was not well among textile operatives. Although wages had not increased, the work pace had. Hours were still long, and working conditions were worsening. Boardinghouses were overcrowded, and goods in the company-owned stores were expensive. In 1824, a group of women protested against low wages and bad conditions by walking out of a mill in Pawtucket, Rhode Island. Many other strikes, or "turnouts," followed in other areas. These culminated at Lowell itself in the 1840s when the first women's labor organization, the Lowell Female Reform Association, under the leadership of Sarah Bagley, began a crusade for a ten-hour workday. The journal of this reform organization, *Voice of Industry*, complained about an increased work pace and other problems while asking the Massachusetts legislature to investigate conditions in the mills.

Women workers did not make much progress with these protests. After all, they were expendable because there were always more young women or, by the 1840s, Irish immigrants willing to fill their places. Women had difficulty supporting labor organizations on their low wages. And, as women, they were denied knowledge of and access to avenues of power such as public officeholding.

Despite the continued problems associated with factory employment, women who found it necessary to help support their families moved to industrial occupations in large numbers. By the 1820s and 1830s, many of these women workers were foreign born. Young, unmarried immigrant women were routinely expected to help support their families. Almost 60 percent of young, single Irish women worked with German and other groups following similar employment patterns to a lesser extent. Even in conservative Italian families, daughters were often expected to work as a temporary relief for an overburdened family budget. And in many Jewish families, both single and married women worked so that their men could continue the much revered religious study of the Torah, especially if they aspired to the respected position of Rabbi.

Women worked primarily in textile factories, cotton mills, shoe factories, and the needle trades. They were typed as "lady operatives" who worked cheaply and could be hired and fired as needed. Yet many women preferred the factory over teaching, sewing, and domestic service, all of which paid less. In 1839, mill worker Malenda Edwards claimed that, "There are very many young ladies at work in the factories that have given up millinery dressmaking and school-keeping for to work in the mill."

Poor pay, bad working conditions, long hours, low status, and inability to organize plagued women factory workers and was even worse for the numerous women who worked in their homes producing parts to be assembled in factories. They were paid "piecework" wages, a minimal fee per part. As a case in point, the country's largest women's shoe factory, located in Lynn, Massachusetts, depended on the needle skills of women pieceworkers to bind or to stitch shoe uppers in their homes. Women also worked at home as seamstresses. After observing Philadelphia seamstresses in 1829, one commentator noted: "It takes great expertness and increasing industry from sunrise to 10 and 11 at night, constant employment which few of them have, to earn a dollar and a half per week."

Perhaps the most underpaid of all women workers were domestic servants. Many early American homes had included "hired help," who were often regarded as members of the family and assisted with all of the ongoing domestic tasks. In the eighteenth century, help was largely replaced by domestics who were seen as servants and assigned specific menial chores performed apart from family members. The large influx of immigrants, especially Irish, provided a source of needy, untrained women for the domestic service market at extremely low wages. In 1837, one observer commented that "a woman who goes out to wash works as hard in proportion as a wood sawyer or a coal heaver, but she is not generally able to make more than half as much for a day's work."

Given the difficulties of women's labor, it is probably not surprising that many women became prostitutes. Many destitute seamstresses and servants turned to this relatively lucrative pursuit in New York and other cities. Immigrant and farm girls were often lured into "white slavery" by operators of brothels. Despite its growth, neither prostitution nor the resulting spread of venereal disease was publicly discussed, acknowledged or even known during these years.

The various types of women workers constituted a new female working class. Gerda Lerner has pointed out, however, that these working women were both isolated and disenfranchised. The issues in which they were interested related to their own immediate situations and included better pay and improved working conditions. Because questions concerning equality, education, and property ownership were not relevant to their lives, they seldom identified with early feminists who advocated reform in these areas. Because of the fluidity of the women's labor market and the scattered nature of their workplaces, mill girls probably even lacked a collective identity.

Although many women became paid workers by the 1830s, more women remained in their homes than not. Here they worked at such customary chores as cooking, food processing, and child care. Frequently, women now exchanged money for many of the goods that they needed instead of producing them. Some women were relieved of certain tasks by the presence of domestic servants. But in many other cases, especially on farms, women continued to labor as domestic artisans and occasionally as field helpers.

Women who remained in their homes did so for a variety of reasons. Many could afford to stay home and devote themselves to the care of their families. The emphasis that the concept of Republican Motherhood placed on child rearing convinced such women that child care should be their first duty. They believed that this involved providing such services as establishing a moral climate for their children or offering moral support for employed members of the family. Frequently, professional and entrepreneurial men preferred to have their wives and daughters remain at home as symbols of their own ability to support a family. When possible, these men enhanced their images of success by hiring domestic servants and nursemaids to aid their wives.

In the South, planters similarly desired their wives to remain within the home and provided black slaves as servants and nurses. The southern woman was restricted by the Cult of White Womanhood, which characterized women as fragile, delicate creatures in need of protection and guidance. In 1854, social theorist George Fitzhugh claimed that, "Women, like children, have but one right, and that is the right to protection." He added that "the right to protection involved the right to obey," and, "if she be obedient, she stands little danger of maltreatment."

Thus middle- and upper-class American women were given a modicum of leisure. This woman was regarded as a "lady," who labored neither at a job nor at home. Her many responsibilities in managing home, children, and servants were overlooked. It was generally assumed that the availability of servants and slaves, combined with factory-produced goods, made the lady of leisure a reality.

In order to help ladies understand and to shape their roles, lifestyles, and behavior, prescriptive literature, such as guidebooks and etiquette manuals, began to flow from the presses. One popular guide cautioned ladies to keep any learning that they might have a secret, "especially from the men, who generally look with a jealous and malignant eye on a woman of great parts and cultivated understanding." Another advised them to turn their talents to instilling virtue in children, men, and servants. Others urged the need for a woman to marry, both for happiness and economic survival. "Her family is the source of all her joy," one proclaimed.

Extensive discussion ensued regarding the "proper spheres of the sexes." It was generally agreed that men were to provide income and take care of public affairs. Women were to establish homes that would "dispel the gloom and restore the ease and comfort" of men after long days spent coping with weighty matters. The world was to be men's undisputed realm, while the home belonged to women. In this system, such fashionable "accomplishments" as playing the piano and speaking French became more important than ever in attracting a "suitable" husband. One young lady duly learned all the appropriate graces, including how to curtsy and dance. When she was about to wed, her mother reminded her that now it would be her "first care to please and make your husband happy."

Raising children also required the lady's attention. The importance of the American mother was celebrated by the expanding publishing industry. Mothers were now seen as the sole shapers of values and character. They were exhorted to mold and train their children into virtuous and responsible people. Women were further cautioned to "let thy children be the darlings of thy tenderness." It was widely assumed that women's maternal love, now believed to be innate, would guide them in the proper disposal of their motherly duties.

Although only a small proportion of women in industrial America actually were leisure ladies, the concept was soon elevated to the status of ideology. It went hand in hand with what historian Barbara Welter has termed the Cult of True Womanhood. This ideology preached four cardinal virtues—piety, purity, submissiveness, and domesticity—as the goals of all true women. In a sense, the ideals of true womanhood offered women a vehicle through which they might become, or at least emulate, ladies.

The image of the "leisure lady" quickly became the ideal of femininity. It decreed that the home was the woman's domain and that she ruled it totally. Her only proper sphere was the care of that home and its inhabitants. Unrelated vocations or activities would only lead her away from the path of true womanhood.

Although ladies were on the other end of the social scale from mill girls and other women workers, they, too, were isolated and disenfranchised. But, unlike their counterparts in the factories, many ladies did care about such topics as education and property ownership because they were extremely important to their own lives. Although women generally found the endeavor of being ladies amusing for a few years, many of them gradually turned to an examination of these serious issues. In practical terms, ladies had more time than female laborers to reflect upon their ills. They also came together through social activities and so could discuss their problems in small groups. And they had the education, money, and time to procure and read feminist literature, such as Mary Wollstonecraft's *Vindication of the Rights of Women*.

The concept of separate spheres increased the discontent of ladies in two ways. First, many railed against the limitations imposed on them by the idea of women's proper roles. Second, as historian Nancy F. Cott has observed, woman's separate sphere caused a group consciousness to grow among women, which in turn led them to identify common problems and manifestations of oppression. The desire of some ladies to find ways to relieve their frustrations would eventually put them in the forefront of the feminist movement. In the meantime, however, most American women seemed to accept the equating of home, morality, and motherhood with women. Ladies, and even many mill girls and farm women, aspired to achieve some degree of "ladyhood" through the development of domestic and feminine virtues.

It may seem strange that the maxim "woman's place is in the home" received so much attention at a time when many women were actually leaving their homes for paid employment. Several scholars have argued that it was precisely because the traditional role of wife and mother was being challenged by industrial developments that Americans felt a pressing need to promote and protect it. One historian has suggested that women were given the home as their undisputed province in the hope that they would stay in it. Another has claimed that, by making women the protectors of virtue, men were free to engage in compromising business practices without fear of polluting their homes and families. But sociologist Carolyn E. Sachs believes that domestic ideology was related to industrialization because it encouraged increased consumption of factory goods by full-time homemakers while maintaining home-bound women as a reserve labor supply. She adds that the concept of women's domesticity also justified low wages and restricted opportunities for female workers whose "real" jobs were in their own homes.

Although the causes for the development of separate spheres for men and women are difficult to pinpoint, their effects are not hard to identify. Extensive changes resulted when large numbers of men moved their work away from the home to cities and factories, while large numbers of women were expected to remain within those homes. For instance, women were effectively cut out of family businesses, which were now formally organized and located some distance from the home. No longer could women learn trades and professions from fathers, brothers, and husbands. As a result, the number of women operating businesses declined compared to the colonial period. Those women who were involved in business usually served other women by supplying millinery, yard goods, or notions.

One exception was Sarah Todd Astor, a businesswoman of the day who did not engage in "feminine" business pursuits. She helped her husband Jacob parlay her dowry of $300 into a lucrative fur business, the American Fur Company. While he traveled to locate and trade furs, she managed the business, processed and graded furs, and gave birth to eight children in their home above the shop. Due to the investment of the profits of the American Fur Company in New York real estate, the Astor fortune was reputed to be the largest in the country at the time of Sarah's death in 1832.

Rebecca Pennock Lukens was another woman of the era who was involved in a male-dominated industry. On his deathbed, Lukens's husband asked her to take over the family iron mill in Pennsylvania. As a Quaker, she was well educated and had always been encouraged to take an interest in the family metalworking enterprise. After her husband's death, Lukens not only saved the mill from bankruptcy but added iron plate rolling to the business, supplying boilers for steamboats and locomotives. She was so successful that she was worth $100,000 at the time of her death in 1854. But, because her daughters were proper ladies who believed in domesticity, control of the Lukens Steel Company went to her sons-in-law instead of to them.

Astor and Lukens were unusual in that they refused to be segregated into feminine businesses. Most women were powerless to resist exclusion, especially from the professions of medicine and law. Because women were generally barred from medical and law schools and from serving internships with practicing physicians and attorneys, they could not hope to pass the licensing examinations that most states now required. By the 1820s, all but three states mandated licenses for medical practitioners. The examinations were based on techniques (such as the use of forceps) learned only in medical schools, so women were incapable of succeeding even if they had been permitted to take the tests.

On the other hand, women were increasingly granted access to the profession of teaching and nursing, which was just beginning to develop as an organized profession. Men were leaving these fields for jobs that paid more and offered continuous employment. Both teaching and nursing offered low pay, little status, and no security, but women rushed in to fill the void. These occupations seemed to be simply an extension of their home duties of teaching and caring for family members. In addition, most women could live with the drawbacks because they planned to marry and fulfill their domestic destinies rather than to fill these jobs for life. Consequently, teaching and nursing became classified as "women's work," with all the attendant disadvantages, such as low pay, because of women's willingness to accept the existing situation.

The development of separate spheres also affected family relationships. Among the lower classes, men, women, and children frequently went to the factory together each day. Yet, at night, women were expected to cook, wash, and care for the children. Such families often lived in the shantytowns, tenements, and slum districts of industrial cities. Disease and epidemics were rife, fire was a constant threat, and the crime rate was reputed to be the highest in the world. Given these dangerous conditions, how was a working woman to practice domesticity and establish an aura of morality in her overcrowded and shabby home? And how could she train and rear children who were already engaged in full-time factory labor by the age of seven or eight?

The life of ladies, of course, was very different. Their social class could not protect them entirely from disease, fire, or crime, but it could provide some amenities such as theaters, restaurants, and country clubs. Like their employed counterparts, ladies' husbands also left the home each day. But these women had many hours in which to complete their domestic tasks, and some had the help of servants as well.

Because household chores and overseeing servants consumed only a portion of their days, ladies sought out a variety of other activities. One of these focused on the need for ladies to dress lavishly in order to enhance their husbands' status. Ladies often became very concerned with their clothing, which was usually ornate and overdone. Ribbons, flowers, flounces, and ruffles bedecked almost every outfit. Intricate hats and bonnets were absolute necessities, as were gloves, a parasol, reticule (purse), and high-buttoned shoes. The outfits themselves contained as much as 100 yards of material and, in combination with whalebone stays and hoops, weighed fifteen to twenty pounds. When chemise, pantaloons, corset, corset cover, petticoats, and hoops were added, getting dressed was a one- to two-hour project in itself. Once dressed, poring over yards-goods samples, ribbons, or bonnet makings in a favorite shop could consume many more hours.

Ladies also paid considerable attention to their complexions, which they believed should be delicate and pale. They protected their hands and face from the sun and avoided the use of "paints" on their faces. Presumably, the lady demonstrated her leisure through a pallor that indicated little activity. Certainly she avoided exercise other than manuevering her hoopskirts into carriages and through doorways. Inactivity combined with tight corseting made the fainting couch a necessary piece of furniture for women who often felt weak and dizzy.

Ladies took great care with their decorum as well as their appearance. They avoided discussing politics and current events, speaking only of approved ladylike topics instead. They used proper language that indicated their modesty: "limb" for "leg" and "female" or "lady" for "woman." European visitors reported that some ladies were so modest that they even covered piano "limbs" with frilled trousers and draped nude statuary.

Filling their spare time could be a problem for these ladies. Most of them busied themselves with fancy needlework such as embroidery and craft work such as the making of hyacinth stands and glove boxes. Almost all of them played the piano, sang, studied French, and pursued other female "accomplishments." They read, but they were supposed to limit themselves to "morally improving" works of literature and poetry.

They also spent a good deal of time visiting with other women during the morning call or afternoon tea. In fact, many women formed close ties with other women. In 1834, author Catharine Sedgwick wrote that these strong, affectionate relationships between women were "nearest to the love of angels."

Wealthy women commonly spent few hours with their children, who were with nannies and tutors. When in their mother's company, boys were allowed to run and play certain games, but girls were expected to sit quietly sewing or reading. They saw their fathers briefly at dinner or bedtime, often in their role as major disciplinarians of the family. The closeness of the colonial American family was clearly unknown to these middle- and upperclass children.

The process of birthing continued to change as well. Male doctors increasingly dominated the delivery room. It became more common for the expectant mother's husband to be included, but whether he was there for emotional support or to police the behavior of the attending physician remains unclear. Perhaps the greatest related change during these years was women's growing demand for birth control information. Many forms of birth control such as abortions, douches, withdrawal, condoms, and devices to cover the cervix date back to ancient times. By the 1820s, women were not only asking about them but were apparently utilizing them; the birthrate dropped, particularly in urban areas.

At the same time, women were being told that their reproductive organs determined their physical health as well as their social roles. A malfunction of the uterus, thought to be linked to the entire nervous system, could cause backaches, headaches, insomnia, irritability, and a whole gamut of "nervous" disorders. Female ailments, as they were termed, supposedly determined a woman's emotions and achievements. Women's disorders were commonly treated through cauterizing the uterus, saline injections, and inserting leeches into the vagina. Not surprisingly, women rejected these practices in favor of such cures as diet reform, animal magnetism, and phrenology. They followed the preachings of health reformers who stressed exercise, fresh air, and the consumption of grains. And they sought out such unlicensed practitioners as Dr. Harriot Hunt, who, in Boston during the 1830s, pursued homeopathic, preventive medicine and studied the psychological bases of women's medical problems.

It seems evident that some serious contradictions existed between the dictates of the image of womanhood and its actual implementation. In reality: many women worked outside of the home; many ladies thought in terms of oppression and property rights rather than submissiveness; and many women attempted to exercise control over their bodies and reproduction instead of accepting "God's will" in such matters.

This discrepancy can be seen in other areas as well. In the arts, for example, women did continue to produce quilts, rugs, bed coverings, wall hangings, and other domestic artwork. The teachings of domesticity encouraged women to enhance their homes with their own artistic creations. One bit of advice assured women that "it is the province of woman to make the home. . . . " and that "If she makes that delightful and salutary—the abode of order and purity, though she may never herself step beyond the threshold—she may yet send forth from her humble dwelling, a power that will be felt round the globe." Consequently, many talented women used needle and thread instead of brush and paint and pieces of cloth instead of canvas.

But many women refused to accept the dogma by practicing the fine arts. They were always self-taught and were usually wives and mothers. One of the most notable of these was Eunice Pinney, who reared five children while becoming a prolific watercolor artist. Her vigorous and forthright work included landscapes, mourning pictures, and religious, historical, and literary scenes. Ruth Henshaw Bascom also combined domestic duties and art by "taking profiles" with pastel crayons.

Other women artists defied other domestic conventions. Mary Ann Willson lived openly with a Miss Brundage, whom she described as her "romantic attachment," and augmented their income by selling her paintings. Highly original and lively, these were done with paints made from berries, brick dust, and vegetable dyes. Deborah Goldsmith traveled alone from town to town plying her trade of limner, or portrait painter. Other itinerant portraitists were Susan Waters and S. A. Shute, who were much in demand by middle- and upperclass Americans who desired their likenesses preserved for posterity.

Such women artists challenged the words of commentators who warned them that "art is the most difficult—perhaps, in its highest form—almost impossible to women." Barred from enrolling in art schools and displaying in galleries, women did indeed have a difficult time learning to be artists. They were believed to have a "natural repugnance" to drawing from "life," or in other words, from nude models. Thus, according to one clergyman, "no virtuous and delicate female, who rightly appreciates the design of her being, and desires to sustain her own influence and that of her sex, and fulfill the high destiny for which she is formed, would desire to abate one jot or tittle from the seeming restrictions imposed upon her conduct."

Despite these stern words, many women did struggle against these limitations. A widespread desire to expand the female sphere erupted not only in art but in education as well. During these years, supporters of "improved female education" began to dispute the widely accepted idea that women's minds were smaller and weaker than men's, thus making women uneducable. In 1818, Hannah Mather Crocker, granddaughter of Cotton Mather, stated in *Observations on the Real Rights of Women:* "There can be no doubt but there is as much difference in the powers of each individual of the male sex as there is of the female: and if they receive the same mode of education, their improvement would be fully equal." Other proponents of women's education also argued that, if women were given "equal advantages" with men, they would soon prove that they were capable of being educated.

Critics responded that there was no reason for women to be educated since they were confined to a domestic vocation. What difference would it make if women's minds were equal to men's since they did not need to use them in the same ways? Reformers turned the principles of domesticity to their own ends when they answered that motherhood demanded education if its practice was to produce salutary adults. While they did not wish to see a woman "emulate the schoolmen's fame," they did believe that a woman's "mental and moral improvement" was necessary for her success as a mother and the happiness of her family. Their assertion that "men will never be wise while women are ignorant" was difficult to dispute.

In 1837, French commentator Auguste Carlier noted: "Ideas in America do not yet seem to be sufficiently settled in reference to the range of women's education. This is often superficial: at other times it embraces the Latin language, mathematics, trigonometry, algebra, etc." Reformers argued for academic subjects while traditionalists supported fashionable accomplishments. Those who emphasized the accomplishments realized that women were expected to attract husbands and then please them. Even the reformers recognized the economic and social importance of marriage to women. They cautioned young women to acquire knowledge with great modesty while "looking up" to the men on whom they depended.

Several women tried to resolve this ongoing debate by educating women in "serious" subjects. Emma Hart Willard upgraded her own Middlebury Seminary to show what women could do with such topics as algebra, trigonometry, history, and geography. In 1819, she appealed to the New York legislature for state aid for women's education. She had come to believe that female education could be equal only if it were publicly supported, as was men's. Not only was Willard's request refused, but a newspaper commented that "they will be educating the cows next." Willard refused to be discouraged and, in 1821, founded the Troy Female Seminary in New York, the first school in the United States to offer a high-school education to women.

A few years later, Scottish-born reformer Frances Wright publicly lectured on the need for public education for all Americans, including women. "Until women assume the place in society which good sense and good feeling alike assign to them," Wright reasoned, "human improvement must advance but feebly." She concluded that, "whenever men establish their own pretensions upon the sacrificed rights of others, we do in fact impeach our own liberties, and lower ourselves in the scale of being."

Advocates of women's education added another dimension to the discussion when they suggested that women needed better training in order to become teachers. Not only were women actually moving into teaching jobs, but a belief in their special qualities as teachers was growing. Supporters of women as teachers emphasized women's innately high character, capacity for affection that would make students anxious to respond to them, and maternal instincts that would allow them to build a greater familiarity and rapport than would be proper for the "other sex."

Other supporters of teacher training for women emphasized the low cost of women teachers. By the 1850s, in an appeal to Congress for appropriations for women's teacher training programs, Catharine Beecher pointed out that "Women can afford to teach for one-half, or even less, the salary which men would ask, because the female teacher has only to sustain herself; she does not look forward to the duty of supporting a family, should she marry, nor has she the ambition to amass a fortune." The argument for women teachers as highly moral and cost-effective may have opened doors for them, but it also created damaging stereotypes that would have to be confronted by later generations.

Women's growing assertiveness led them to work to expand not only their educations but their religious participation. The Second Great Awakening was characterized by female evangelism. Women fostered and organized revivals and directed a militant piety against ungodly and unchurched men. During the Second Great Awakening, women converts outnumbered men by three to two. Women were also prominent in the revival movement in western New York. By 1814, women dominated the churches and religious societies of Utica. According to historian Barbara L. Epstein, women protested against male authority through the acceptable forum of religious zeal. While staying within the bounds of feminine behavior, religious women forced their wills on men by pushing them toward religious activity.

Women also dominated the Sunday schools that were beginning to appear in many churches. By claiming that their inherent virtue qualified them, rather than men, to instruct children in religious values, women essentially seized positions of power within their congregations. Their roles as Sunday-school teachers effectively allowed women to ignore the Pauline doctrine regarding women's silence in church. Through their devoted and selfless commitment to religion, such women created a new and more serious view of women for themselves, their students, and their associates. Their establishment of the image of evangelical womanhood provided both a challenge and an alternative to the frivolous aspect of ladyhood.

As women became the majority of congregants, the clergy responded to their increasing religious participation by continuing to feminize their teachings. For example, in response to mothers' protests against the harsh doctrine of infant damnation due to innate human sin, ministers began to agree that good Christian nurturing could offset original sin. Ministers also supported the concept of superior female morality. They confirmed the growing belief that women exceeded men in piety and purity. In an 1810 sermon, one preacher exclaimed, "We look to you, ladies, to raise the standard of character in our own sex."

In historian Barbara Welter's view, the result of the growing feminization of religion was an emphasis on introspection and morality. Women learned to assess their characters and believe in their strengths—two abilities that propelled them toward independence rather than toward domesticity. The stress that religion placed on brotherhood and equality of men before God became, for many women, a sense of sisterhood and equality of women before God. Women's growing commitment to religious activity was thus at once a protest against their restricted roles and an active attack upon them. Clearly, both the prescription and the practice of American womanhood were complex matters during this era. They proved confusing to white American women. They provided a challenge in adaptation to immigrant women. And they totally bypassed black and American Indian women.

Most black women found their roles and lifestyles dictated by the slave system. They had little control over their domesticity, child-care practices, or even the moral climate in which they lived. They were compelled to perform heavy labor, provide sexual services to white men, and give up the care of their children to women too elderly to work in the fields. Although marriage was an important institution for slave women, it often proved to be unstable through no fault of their own. As one black minister noted, slaves married "until death or distance do you part," a situation that created highly independent wives and mothers who could not count on the presence and aid of men. Black women, who bore an average of four to five children, were also frequently denied the satisfaction of raising their offspring. Mother-child bonds were strong and probably accounted for the fact that less slave women ran away then men. As a result of the instability of the black family under slavery, black women devoted much of their energy to maintaining kinship ties and to creating new kinship networks when slavery destroyed old ones.

Slave women were also laborers outside of their homes. On plantations and farms, black women worked in a wide variety of taxing and often skilled jobs, including those of domestic servants, washwomen, nursemaids, field hands, and artisans. According to one slave woman, women's work was often difficult to distinguish from men's:

> Over there, you would see a road all turned up and you would see men and women both throwing up dirt and rocks; the men would haul it off and the women would take picks and things and get it up. You could any day see a woman, a whole lot of 'em making a road. Could look up and see ten women up over dar on the hill plowing and look over the other way and see ten more. I have done everything on a farm what a man done 'cept cut wheat. I split rails like a man. I used a iron wedge drove into the wood with a maul. I drive the gin, what was run by two mules.

In southern industry, black women worked as heavy labor in cotton and woolen mills, turpentine camps, sugar refineries, food and tobacco factories, hemp manufactories, foundries, saltworks, and mines. They also worked as lumberjacks and ditchdiggers, helping to build levees and lay track for southern railroads. Slave women also worked in southern cities as chambermaids, nursemaids, hairdressers, seamstresses, domestic servants, and vendors.

Yet, in spite of their large economic contributions to the development of the southern economy, black slave women were generally denied pay or other recognition of their labor and were seldom granted any privileges. Slave women faced gender-related difficulties that black men did not. Because the demand for slaves overwhelmed the supply of them after the end of the slave trade in 1809, black women were expected to reproduce as frequently as possible. As one slave woman noted, the more children she had, the more she was worth. Some black women were confined to breeding farms, other "breeders" and "fancy girls" brought prices and were well cared for, while others were expected to continue with their usual tasks while pregnant. In addition, women were not released from domestic tasks or the care of their own families because they labored in the fields. Rather, they were subject to such double burdens as tending cotton while nursing their babies in the fields.

In the "big house" black slave women labored heavily for long hours. Subject to constant surveillance and punishment, they were cut off from their families and friends for many hours of each day. They were also subject to sexual coercion by the white masters with whom they were in constant contact. At the same time, they had to bear the callous treatment of white mistresses who resented their husband's sexual activities. And when children were the product of such unions, slave women were denied the time and resources to care for them properly. Black women subtly rebelled against economic and sexual exploitation by avoiding sexual relationships with both white and black men, aborting unwanted fetuses, and even committing infanticide to save a child from the horrors of the slave system.

Even the slave women who were allowed to practice such skills as nursing, healing, and midwifery for pay seldom derived any benefit from it. One slave woman who was trained as a midwife at the age of thirteen earned substantial sums of money for her owner. In her words:

> I made a lot o' money for old miss. Lots of times, didn't get sleep regular or git my meals on time for three-four days. Cause when dey call, I always went. Brought as many white as culled children. I's brought lots of 'em an' I ain't never lost a case.

In addition to their many other burdens, slave women were expected to care for their families and homes as best they could. Resentful of slave owners' tendency to ignore gender when making assignments to field labor, slave women often sought to preserve their sense of being women by establishing a strict division of labor within their homes. They typically performed most housekeeping tasks and child-care chores themselves despite the heavy demands on their energies by other duties outside of their homes. Thus, slave women were not only involved in the production of goods and services, but they produced and cared for future workers under extremely taxing conditions. They resisted this system that destroyed their families and ignored their gender by attempting to maintain their homes with pride and to tend their families with care. Moreover, they clung to native customs and attempted to instill a respect for their race in their children.

Free black women were only slightly better off. A study of free black women in Petersburg, Virginia, indicates that they held jobs and headed households. Free black women could also, at least theoretically, protest against injustice and use the courts. They formed organizations, published newspapers and books, and joined abolitionist societies. Better than one hundred works of fiction, protest, and autobiography were written by former slaves and free blacks between 1810 and 1860.

Yet free black women were exploited, underpaid, and denied opportunities for education or advancement. The jobs that they held were often exhausting and low-paying, and the households they headed were often not formed by their own choice. In northern cities, free black women, forced by economic necessity to seek employment primarily as domestic servants, were hired by white women who believed them to be docile and passive. White employees required black domestics to live in and treated them much like surrogate slaves. Other black women sewed, or took in laundry, often for the fee of about one cent per shirt. Still others engaged in hairdressing, flower selling, hat cleaning, or other services. Northern mines and factories generally did not hire free black women. Adhering to racist stereotypes of black women as "lazy" and "morally corrupt," white employers and workers refused to accept black women as factory operatives. Other free black women were not able to find jobs at all. In 1827, a black newspaper, *Freedom's Journal,* stated that there were forty-three black women paupers in New York City alone.

Like their slave counterparts, free black women worked diligently to establish meaningful values and activities. Some attempted to improve their educations by forming groups like the "Afric-American Female Intelligence Society" of Boston in 1832. Other free black women, such as Sarah Mapps Douglass of Philadelphia, became teachers themselves. In 1820, Douglass opened a school for free black children and actively participated in the Philadelphia Female Anti-slavery Society, of which she was a founding member. Yet, in 1837, Douglass heatedly described her segregation to a back bench designated for "the people of color" in a Quaker meetinghouse. She concluded that, while some Friends had cleansed themselves "of the foul stain of prejudice," the majority despised her people "for our color."

In a sense, free black women were pathbreakers. They earned wages and even maintained economic independence. Paradoxically, black women were able to work because it was widely understood that black female labor was the cheapest on the market. As women and as blacks, they could now be exploited as "wage slaves."

American Indian women were certainly no better off. With the white population doubling every twenty-five years, it was obvious that Indians would soon be outnumbered and overrun. Thomas Jefferson's prediction that native peoples could live in peace west of the Mississippi River for many years was not to materialize. Instead, white settlers swept across the Ohio and lower Mississippi valleys and began to cross the Mississippi River. They pushed American Indians along ahead of them, frequently destroying them in their haste and determination to settle the West.

As whites invaded native lands, they continued to take advantage of Indian women as guides, sexual partners, and domestic servants. They freely borrowed agricultural tools and methods from native women, but never acknowledged these women's ingenuity and expertise. Whites tended to ignore customary divisions of labor and the traditional crafts of Indian peoples. For example, during the 1830s, the United States Commissioner of Indian Affairs classified the Cherokee as a hunting society because the men hunted. This view totally overlooked the fact that Cherokee women had been adept and productive agriculturalists for centuries. It seemed impossible for white eyes to see women's work as significant, if not crucial. Instead, the Commissioner's office declared that Cherokee women must be taught to spin and weave while the men must be taught to farm. Not only did this prescription slight women's crafts, but it forced men into taking over the growing of crops, long considered to be uniquely within women's realm.

Euro-Americans usually recognized only those native women who helped them to achieve their own objectives. As a case in point, Milly Francis, a Creek Indian woman, received a congressional medal and a small pension for saving a white captive from death at the hands of her people in 1817. By now, it was evident that American Indian women could expect little from white Americans except more pain and exploitation.

Such treatment was extended to Mexican women as well. As whites poured into Texas during the 1830s, they often reacted in a biased fashion to the Mexicans whom they encountered. With heads filled with a negative picture of Mexican character derived from articles, reports, and letters, white settlers leveled harsh criticism against Mexicans. Although the stereotypes were vastly overdrawn, they were indicative of the nativist and racial prejudices of the day. In 1831, one female visitor to Texas wrote that Mexicans were, "generally speaking, timid and irresolute" and also "brutal" and "cowardly." She claimed that even the Comanche Indians liked Americans better than they did Mexicans.

These cruel characterizations of Mexicans seemed to overlook the fact that American settlers were guests in Mexican territory, and as such, it was perhaps less than gracious to so harshly criticize their hosts. In years to come, American disdain for Mexicans would increase, and a growing spirit of Manifest Destiny would convince Americans of their right to add Texas to the Union in 1845, California and environs in 1848, and the Gadsden Purchase in 1853. Although the Mexican frontier would thus become part of the American frontier, assimilation and intermarriage proceeded slowly. The view of Mexicans held by Euro-Americans stood as a barrier between the two groups for many decades.

The westward movement was a much more pleasant experience for white female settlers than it was for the people they displaced. Many women found attractive reasons for relocating to frontier regions that extended to the Mississippi River and beyond by the 1820s. Although their menfolk often made the actual decision, women could appreciate the chance of restored health for a family member in a more favorable climate, the opportunity to recoup a financial disaster sustained by the family, a fortune to be gained from the utilization of natural resources, or the potential of a prosperous future on cheap, available farm land. European women looked toward the American West as a place where they could enjoy landownership, practice religious toleration, or escape tyrannical governments. Army wives chose to follow their husbands to frontier forts. Religious orders of women relocated in the West to serve and educate native peoples. Single women chose to migrate in order to find husbands, procure employment, take up land, or serve as missionaries and teachers.

For many reasons, then, women began the westward trek with husbands, families, and friends in conveyances that ranged from stagecoaches and railroad cars to the legendary Conestoga wagon. Wagons, either the smaller emigrant wagon or the larger prairie schooner, were popular because they contained abundant space for people and possessions. When selected, the wagon was outfitted for the journey. Men equipped it with running gear, trained the horses or oxen that would pull it, and prepared tools, firearms, and stock. Women stitched the wagon cover and readied food, clothing, bedding, and medicines.

While these arrangements progressed, people began to prepare themselves for the coming traumatic separation from the friends and family with whom they had spent their lives. After tearful and often prolonged partings, the migrants were on their way. Once on the trail, they were hardly isolated. Their journals tell of meeting old friends and neighbors and of making new friends. Women visited with other women and exchanged recipes and bits of useful trail lore. One woman's diary contained frequent references to storytelling, music, songs, laughter, and merrymaking.

Although loneliness was not part of the trail routine for women, hard work was. Daily living had to continue despite the trail environment. Women cooked meals over campfires, laid beds out under the stars, and washed clothing in streams. Older children aided women in these tasks, and men sometimes set up tables, started fires, and even cooked. Still, women's chores were extremely heavy. Because of trail conditions, women's work became more intricate and more wearying than it had been before departure. In addition, many trail women were pregnant or nursing infants, which further complicated their numerous trail duties.

Yet women's complaints were not overwhelming. Many women prided themselves on their "housekeeping." Kitturah Belknap, on her way to Iowa in the 1830s, took "good earthen dishes" backed up with tinware and "four nice little table cloths" that she made. She supplemented her family's food by buying fresh produce from farms, baking bread that she set to rise on the warm ground under the wagon during the night, and producing rolls of butter by letting the motion of the lurching wagon operate the churn inside it.

The westward trek was arduous for women. The weather was often frightful, wagons broke down, oxen died, and people fell ill and died. Women were expected to help with men's work, such as driving the wagon or herding stock, at the same time that they tried to protect their children from trail accidents. Some women naturally grew discouraged and turned back. As one explained it: "Some liked the new country, but others returned to their native States."

Most women, however, hung on. They recognized that their efforts were crucial to the success of the migration. Any domestic routines that they would establish, any help that they could offer, any support that they could give were all hedges against the disintegration of the undertaking. In addition, these were farm women who were familiar with most of the tasks that were demanded of them. They approached the trail experience as a time of transition, during which they could hone their skills and prepare their minds for what lay ahead. As one said; "I never thought about its being hard. I was used to things being hard."

When women arrived in their new regions, their reactions were mixed. One recalled that, "when we got to the new purchase, the land of milk and honey, we were disappointed and homesick, but we were there and had to make the best of it." Others remembered being dismayed by native peoples, cold winters, wet springs, hot summers, mosquitoes, and "wild beasts." One woman pragmatically wrote to her mother: "I can't say I like the West as well as I do New England yet I think it is better for me to be here." At the same time, many women were ecstatic at the sight of prairie flowers, green rolling valleys, and flowing rivers. One young woman claimed not to be disillusioned even when she saw the primitive log cabin that was her new home. In "girl fashion," she explained, "I considered it very romantic."

Most women were not so pleased with their first homes, which were anything from the wagon that carried them westward to a corncrib, an abandoned outbuilding, lean-to, tarpaper shack, sod hut, or log cabin. But, despite its condition, women turned their energies to converting their first shelters into homes for their families and workplaces for themselves. Women often complained of frost on the walls, snowflakes on the blankets and table, and ice on the floors. In some regions, wind was the major problem because it carried dust into clothing, cooking utensils, and food. Scorching sun, torrential rains, bugs, and snakes were other enemies of frontier housekeepers. Women endured them all because they realized that their early homes represented the youth of the frontier and marked a stage that every raw frontier community had to tolerate. So they hung quilts as room dividers, papered the walls with newspapers or painted them with lime, and created household furnishings out of packing crates and rope.

With her workplace established, the frontierswoman turned her energies to producing candles, soap, clothing, foodstuffs, and a wide variety of other domestic goods. All of these products demanded ingenuity, expertise, and incredible amounts of time. In addition, women bore many children, educated them, and trained them as domestic or field laborers. They were also expert herbalists who served as apothecaries and morticians to their families and friends. And they brought in all the cash that their families would ever see through the sales of their butter, eggs, knitted goods, and other products.

Despite the fact that these women functioned in their homes as domestic artisans who converted the raw produce of the fields into finished goods, the United States census of the 1830s listed these women as "not gainfully employed." In this industrial economy, only those people who actually received paychecks were considered to be "employed," yet it is impossible to dispute the tremendous significance of women's labor to the frontier economy.

Most frontierswomen found that the worst was over in about two years. They moved into better homes, could buy many items from stores in the new towns that were rapidly springing up, and had friends and neighbors to relieve the initial loneliness. Churches and schools appeared, which gave them other social outlets.

Women were also relieved of field labor as soon as the homestead was established. Sachs has argued that American farm women rejected field work as a means of resisting direction from men. By limiting themselves to the home and garden, women freed themselves of supervision and control. Men retained their authority outside of the home as a result. Thus, the frontier, contrary to popular belief, did not break down the usual division of labor along gender lines. Rather, frontierswomen worked to perpetuate the same labor system within the family that they had always known.

Women also attempted to reestablish domesticity and other feminine values in their new homes. For example, they continued to wear hoop skirts and follow the fashion plates in *Godey's Lady's Book*. They wore sunbonnets to protect their faces from the sun. And they decorated their homes with craftwork and folk art, particularly exquisite quilts that often told a story or recorded family history. For instance, Elizabeth Mitchell of Kentucky used her Coffin Quilt to note family deaths by taking labeled coffins from the quilt's border and moving them into the graveyard in its center.

At the same time, frontierswomen also resisted the dictates of domesticity. They sought education in the country schoolhouses and early women's seminaries. In most regions, coeducation was an accepted practice from the beginning of settlement. Women also rapidly moved into teaching so that most western areas had a higher proportion of female teachers than did eastern states. Women also took up paid employment as railway station agents, team drivers, shepherds, store clerks, prostitutes, lawyers, musicians, artists, authors, journalists, and a wide variety of other jobs. They sometimes voted in local elections and discussed issues such as equality, landownership, and the right of suffrage. In fact, American women would eventually be first granted the vote in several western territories and states.

Until just a few years ago, available information on frontiersmen was vast and varied while that on frontierswomen was sparse and stereotyped. As miner, cowboy, soldier, sodbuster, rancher, or outlaw, the frontiersman captured people's imaginations. On the infrequent occasions when the frontierswoman happened to receive some attention, it was also in romanticized terms. Over the years, frontierswomen have been portrayed as Gentle Tamers, Pioneers in Petticoats, Saints in Sunbonnets, Madonnas of the Prairie, Pioneer Mothers, Light Ladies, Calamity Janes, and Fighting Feminists. On the one hand, the frontierswoman was admired for her tenacity. On the other, she was pitied for her sad fate. At one time, sympathy was expressed for her intrinsic weakness and the domesticity of nature that limited her potential for success on the frontier. At another time, she was commended for her bravery, courage, and fortitude.

What was the reality of frontierswomen? Were they gaunt, pathetic figures in faded calico dresses and tattered sunbonnets? Did they cry and beg to return to their former homes? Or did they bravely face the sun and, with a small child in one hand and a rifle in the other, help to conquer the American West? The truth lies somewhere between the extremes. Some frontierswomen were gaunt, pathetic, and ragged, but others were healthy, hardy, and well-dressed. Some women did hate to leave their homes, but others initiated the idea or migrated on their own. Most of those who stayed on the frontier made incalculable contributions to the settlement of the American West.

Frontierwomen did not display any single characteristic. They exhibited a full spectrum of personalities, talents, abilities, and attitudes. They came from a variety of backgrounds. They followed a large number of careers ranging from homemaker to field hand. In other words, their lives were so multifaceted that they cannot be explained by an image or a stereotype. As one woman said of the fabled sunbonnet, "they were an obstruction to sight and an impediment to hearing." And so it has been with the mystique surrounding the women who wore the sunbonnets. Fortunately, the reality of their lives, roles, and participation in the development of the frontier is finally emerging from its shroud.

Of course, it must be remembered that in reality all American women's lives during the years between 1816 and 1837 were complicated, frequently perplexing, and often full of ambiguity. Many views of women emerged during this era from observers, commentators, and historians who all viewed women through the filter of their own perceptions. For example, in 1835, the writings of a French visitor, Alexis de Tocqueville, presented American women as protected, elevated, and superior beings. To him, the American family was like a miniature democracy, with the man as its head and the woman and children as its citizens. De Tocqueville insisted that, "although the women of the United States are confined within the narrow circle of domestic life, and their situation is in some respects one of extreme dependence, I have nowhere seen woman occupying a loftier position."

Only two years later, another European traveler presented an opposing assessment of American women. According to English writer Harriet

Martineau, women's intellects were confined, their morals crushed, health ruined, weakness encouraged, and strength punished. She condemned public chivalry as an "indulgence" given to women "as a substitute for justice." Marriage was to her "a poor institution" in which "one sex overbears the other." She lamented the shameful treatment of female workers and black slave women. In Martineau's eyes, "the Americans have, in their treatment of women, fallen below, not only their own democratic principles, but the practice of some parts of the Old World." Because America did not extend the principles of the Declaration of Independence to all of its citizens, Martineau found it a disappointing and hypocritical country.

Did the majority of American women fit De Tocqueville's or Martineau's description? Did they see the system in which they lived as beneficent or degrading? Did they adhere to the model of True Womanhood as closely as possible or subvert it at every opportunity? Had the Industrial Revolution and the westward movement brought progress or setback to the images and realities of their lives? All of these questions are clearly impossible to answer with any assurance.

It is clear, however, that numerous women were beginning to exert their talents and time to modify both American society and the model of True Womanhood. Apparently dissatisfied with many of the changes that had occurred in America during the Industrial Revolution, these women were in the forefront of what was soon to become a national reform movement. When the nation's worst economic crisis to date, the Panic of 1837, temporarily interrupted industrialization, the nation was already turning its attention to restructuring a society fraught with problems. Women enthusiastically originated and participated in the increasing numbers and types of reform activities. What remains to be seen is how these women divided their energies between reshaping American life in general and redefining the model of womanhood in particular to stretch the limits of the female "sphere."

SUGGESTIONS FOR FURTHER READING

Boylan, Anne M. "Evangelical Womanhood in the Nineteenth Century: The Role of Women in Sunday Schools." *Feminist Studies* 4 (October 1978): 62–80.

Brownlee, W. Elliot. "Household Values, Women's Work, and Economic Growth, 1800-1923." *Journal of Economic History* 39 (March 1979): 199–209.

Clinton, Catherine. *The Plantation Mistress: Woman's World in the Old South.* New York: Pantheon Books, 1980.

———. *The Other Civil War: American Women in the Nineteenth Century.* New York: Hill and Wang, 1984. Chapter 2.

Cott, Nancy F. *The Bonds of Womanhood: "Woman's Sphere" In New England, 1780–1835.* New Haven: Yale University Press, 1977.

Dewhurst, C. Kurt, Betty MacDowell, and Marsha MacDowell. *Artists in Aprons: Folk Art by American Women.* New York: E. P. Dutton, 1979.

Dublin, Thomas. *Women at Work: The Transformation of Work and Community in Lowell, Massachusetts, 1826–1860.* New York: Columbia University Press, 1979.

———. *Farm to Factory: The Mill Experience and Women's Lives in New England, 1830–1860.* New York: Columbia University Press, 1981.

Dudden, Faye E. *Serving Women: Household Service in Nineteenth-Century America.* Middletown, CT: Wesleyan University Press, 1983.

Dysart, Jane. "Mexican Women in San Antonio, 1830–1860: The Assimilation Process." *Western Historical Quarterly* 7 (October 1976): 365–375.

Ellison, Mary. "Resistance to Oppression: Black Women's Response to Slavery in the United States." *Slavery and Abolition* 4 (May 1983): 56–63.

Epstein, Barbara Leslie. *The Politics of Domesticity: Women, Evangelism, and Temperance in Nineteenth-Century America.* Middletown, CT: Wesleyan University Press, 1981.

Gordon, Jean. "Early American Women Artists and the Social Context in Which They Worked." *American Quarterly* 30 (Spring 1978): 54–69.

Gordon, Linda. "The Long Struggle for Reproductive Rights." *Radical America* 15 (Spring 1981): 74–88.

Gutman, Herbert G. *The Black Family in Slavery and Freedom, 1750–1925.* New York: Pantheon Books, 1976.

Hagler, D. Harland. "The Ideal Woman in the Antebellum South: Lady or Farmwife?" *Journal of Southern History* XLV (August 1980): 405–418.

Harley, Sharon. "Northern Black Female Workers: Jacksonian Era." In *The Afro-American Woman: Struggles and Images,* edited by Sharon Harley and Rosalyn Terborg-Penn, 5–16. Port Washington, NY: Kennikat Press, 1978.

Hine, Darlene. "Female Slave Resistance: The Economics of Sex." *Western Journal of Black Studies* 3 (Summer 1979): 123–127.

James, Edward T., ed. *Notable American Women, 1607–1950: A Biographical Dictionary.* Cambridge, MA: Belknap Press, 1971.

Jensen, Joan M., and Darlis A. Miller. "The Gentle Tamers Revisited: New Approaches to the History of Women in the American West." *Pacific Historical Review* 49 (May 1980): 173–214.

Jensen, Joan M., and Sue Davidson, eds. *A Needle, a Bobbin, a Strike: Women Needleworkers in America.* Philadelphia: Temple University Press, 1984.

Jones, Jacqueline. "'My Mother Was Much of a Woman': Black Women, Work, and the Family Under Slavery." *Feminist Studies* 8 (Summer 1982): 235–269.

Kaufman, Polly Welts. *Women Teachers on the Frontier.* New Haven: Yale University Press, 1984.

Kessler-Harris, Alice. *Out to Work: A History of Wage-Earning Women in the United States.* New York: Oxford University Press, 1982.

Lebsock, Suzanne. "Free Black Women and the Question of Matriarchy: Petersburg, Virginia, 1784–1820." *Feminist Studies* 8 (Summer 1982): 270–292.

———. *The Free Women of Petersburg: Status and Culture in a Southern Town, 1784–1860.* New York: W. W. Norton & Co., Inc., 1983.

Lecompte, Janet. "The Independent Women of Hispanic New Mexico, 1821–1846." *Western Historical Quarterly* 12 (January 1981): 17–35.

Lerner, Gerda. "The Lady and the Mill Girl: Changes in the Status of Women in the Age of Jackson." *American Studies* 10 (Spring 1969): 5–15.

———. ed. *Black Women in White America: A Documentary History.* New York: Vintage Books, 1973.

Matthews, Jane D. "'Woman's Place' and the Search for Identity in Antebellum America." *The Canadian Review of American Studies* 10 (Winter 1979): 289–304.

Melder, Keith. "Women in the Shoe Industry: The Evidence from Lynn." *Essex Institute Historical Collections* 115 (October 1979): 270–287.

Miller, Darlis. "Cross-Cultural Marriages in the Southwest: The New Mexico Experience, 1846–1900." *New Mexico Historical Review* 57 (October 1982): 335–360.

Myres, Sandra L. *Westering Women and The Frontier Experience, 1800–1915.* Albuquerque: University of New Mexico Press, 1982.

———. "Mexican Americans and Westering Anglos: A Feminine Perspective." *New Mexico Historical Review* 57 (October 1982): 317–333.

Riley, Glenda. "Women in the West." *Journal of American Culture* 3 (Summer 1980): 311–329.

———. "'Not Gainfully Employed': Women on the Iowa Frontier, 1833–1870." *Pacific Historical Review* 49 (May 1980): 237–264.

———. *Frontierswomen: The Iowa Experience.* Ames: Iowa State University Press, 1981.

———, ed. *Women in the West.* Manhattan, KS: Sunflower University Press, 1982.

Ryan, Mary P. *Womanhood in America: From Colonial Times to the Present.* New York: New Viewpoints, 1979, Chapters 2 and 3.

Sachs, Carolyn E. *The Invisible Farmers: Women in Agricultural Production.* Totowa, NJ: Rowman and Allanheld, 1983.

Sterling, Dorothy. *We Are Your Sisters: Black Women in the Nineteenth-Century.* New York: W. W. Norton & Co., Inc., 1984.

Suitor, J. Jill. "Husbands' Participation in Childbirth: A Nineteenth-Century Phenomenon." *Journal of Family History* 6 (Fall 1981): 278–293.

Van de Wetering, Maxine. "The Popular Concept of 'Home' in Nineteenth-Century America." *Journal of American Studies* 18 (April 1984): 5–28.

Welter, Barbara. *Dimity Convictions: The American Woman in the Nineteenth Century.* Athens, OH: Ohio University Press, 1976.

When Sarah Josepha Hale became the editor of Godey's Lady's Book *in 1837, she attempted to enlarge the concepts of domesticity, woman's sphere, and women's moral guardianship of the home to include a variety of endeavors and interests not customarily associated with women's roles.* From Godey's Lady's Book, Philadelphia, Pennsylvania.

CHAPTER 4

Reshaping American Life and Values:
The Reform Era
1837–1861

B ETWEEN 1837 and 1861, the peak of the reform era, many women were deeply involved in the national crusade to reshape and improve American life and institutions. In the course of their activities, they also changed the model of the American woman. When many female reformers came to believe that it was necessary to crusade directly for modifications in the status of women, the first American feminist movement was born. As a result, the traditional image of womanhood experienced the first overt onslaught on its form and influence since the founding of the American colonies in 1607. Although it survived, its foundations were definitely shaken and the stage set for future attacks.

Women's widespread efforts to enlarge their lives are illustrated in the careers of many specific women who pursued a wide variety of approaches and arguments. One of these was editor and writer Sarah Josepha Hale, who dedicated her talents to reshaping American ways of thinking regarding women. In 1836, Hale left Boston to become the editor of *Godey's Lady's Magazine*. Since her husband's death in 1823, Hale had built a sound reputation as a poet, novelist, and editor dedicated to the cause of "female improvement." In the first issue of her *Ladies' Magazine* in 1828, she assured her male readers that her purpose was to encourage women to become more competent in their domestic duties and more agreeable as companions. She intended to achieve these ends by working for the improvement of "female education," which, in turn, would increase women's effectiveness as the moral and purifying forces of America. This approach proved to be appealing to both female and male readers. As a result, her competitor, Louis Godey, bought Hale's *Ladies' Magazine* and persuaded her to join him in Philadelphia.

As editor of *Godey's*, Hale became one of the primary proponents of the concepts of women's sphere and the moral powers of women. In her first issue in January 1837, she explained that the mission of *Godey's* was to "carry onward and upward the spirit of moral and intellectual excellence in our own sex, till their influence shall bless as well as beautify civil society. These principles we shall guard with scrupulous care, and watch that nothing be introduced to undermine those sacred relations of domestic life, in which the Creator has placed the sceptre of woman's empire." She followed this statement with a plethora of copy defining and developing her ideas regarding the improvement of women's status within their sphere. Throughout the 1830s, 1840s, and 1850s, Hale employed argument, exhortation, poetry, moral romance, and a variety of other techniques to achieve her objective.

The theme that ran throughout Hale's editorship of *Godey's* was that women were the moral guardians of society. While men engaged in necessary, and often compromising, business practices and public affairs, women served as the moral keepers of home and family. In 1847, Hale expressed this division of function in verse: "He must work—the world subduing/Till it blooms like Eden bright/She must watch—his faith renewing/From her urn of Eden light." Yet, while Hale maintained that women's place was in the home, she also promoted the expansion of the female sphere through improved education, simplified clothing styles that would allow increased activity, and women as teachers, authors of "moral" literature and poetry, missionaries, and medical practitioners. Hale's approach to widening women's sphere was so nonthreatening that she was revered and loved by generations of American readers of all ages.

Of course, Hale did not stand alone in promoting such thinking about women. Many other editors and authors contributed their interpretations and perspectives to the emerging model of the moral American woman. Legions of women writers wrote books that became immediate bestsellers during the 1830s, 1840s, and 1850s, but have languished on library shelves ever since. Domestic novels, as they were called because of their homey themes, frequently went through multiple and worldwide editions. These authors far outsold writers like Herman Melville and Nathaniel Hawthorne. In fact, Hawthorne was reportedly so disgusted with their success that he referred to them as that "damned mob of scribbling women."

One of the most eminent of these women writers was Harriet Beecher Stowe. Coming from a family of reformers and deeply interested in social reform herself, Stowe directed her early writings toward the issues of temperance, higher wages for seamstresses, and improved educational opportunities for women. Hale encouraged Stowe, and thus many of Stowe's first stories appeared in *Godey's*. She later became involved in the abolitionist movement and wrote several novels. In 1852, she became the most visible female author with *Uncle Tom's Cabin*.

Another domestic novelist of the period was Caroline Lee Hentz. She, too, published her occasional first stories in *Godey's* during the 1830s, but because of her husband's lack of business acumen, turned to writing fulltime to support her family. By the 1850s, Hentz was well-known for such novels as *Ernest Linwood* (1856). While she seemed to uphold all the usual ideals of women's moral powers and domestic sphere, the underlying theme of Hentz's work was what one commentator termed "mutilation of the male." Hentz's male characters were typically ill, imbecilic, or morally crippled, while her female protagonists were strong, decisive, all-suffering, and highly moral. A contemporary of Hentz, E. D. E. N. Southworth, removed males from the scene entirely. In such novels as *The Deserted Wife* (1851) and *The Discarded Daughter* (1852), Hentz sent men off to war, the West, or in pursuit of a pretty young woman. The women whom they left behind were self-dependent, energetic, and capable of supporting themselves and their children or siblings, often achieving fame and fortune in the process. When the abject husband returned, he was always forgiven by his magnanimous wife or daughter. That men could not function without the strength and morality of women was clearly the overriding message of both Hentz and Southworth.

A less vitriolic writer was Lydia B. Sigourney, known as "the Sweet Singer of Hartford." She, too, was forced by economic necessity to follow a literary career, which lasted over half a century and produced over fifty works. Her name became a byword for a generation of readers who fed upon the romanticized, didactic poems and stories that she began to produce in the mid-1830s. Like the other domestic writers, Sigourney lauded the traditional virtues of home and family in such works as *Whispers to a Bride* (1850) and *The Daily Counsellor* (1859) while flouting them in her own career and by subtleties in her writings. Eliza Leslie and Catherine M. Sedgwick, neither of whom ever married, also gained popularity by idealizing domesticity, although they rejected it in their own lives. Leslie's works, such as *Mr. and Mrs. Woodbridge and Other Tales* (1841), reiterated homely and wifely virtues, but Sedgwick, particularly in *Married or Single?* (1857), was an outspoken champion of the unmarried woman.

Elizabeth Fries Lummis Ellet took yet another approach to women's roles. She was interested in reconstructing the history of women to demonstrate that women had been prominent nurturers and guardians of American democracy. She also argued that women fulfilled a variety of social functions, did jobs considered to be "men's work," and contributed significantly to the settlement of the frontier. Her best known work, *The Women of the American Revolution*, which appeared in two volumes in 1848, was in its fourth edition by 1850.

Perhaps these women writers were so popular because they were not avowed reformers or feminists. At least on the surface, they preached all of the accepted views regarding women and did not deprecate the customary view of the family and women's place. They supported a perception of women that emphasized their moral guardianship of home and family. Yet, at the same time, these writers presented women as active, influential people. A study of almost two hundred domestic novels, short stories, and essays shows that these writers imparted a contradictory message. Their portrayals of domesticity were riddled with deep discontent. They characterized men as sinful, obsessed with a desire for wealth and social position, and in need of reform. Women were superior beings, responsible for their families and increasingly for guarding against the evils that existed in society as well.

This assignment of influence to women had wide implications. As moral keepers of society, women could conceivably undertake numerous endeavors. For example, the moral guardian theory justified the following positions: mothers must have education to mold their children correctly; women must write "morally improving" novels; women must understand politics to influence male legislators wisely; women must teach school to inculcate children with virtue; and women must form charity organizations to aid the poor and destitute. In short, morally superior women should dominate any function or social situation that would benefit from morality.

The possibilities of the moral guardian theory were almost unlimited. This theory in essence made it easier for women to stay in their own "sphere," because it embraced more of the everyday world. At the same time, values now known as "female," such as morality, virtue, and honesty, were increasingly being held up to all American people as standards to which they should aspire. The growing acceptance of women as moral guardians, which the works of the domestic novelists fostered, resulted in a feminization of American cultural values. This in turn gave women a measure of potency and prestige. Women quickly learned to wield their new position in order to protest and to enlarge the idealized model of what women should be.

Education was a primary focus for many women who desired enhanced status and increased opportunities. Catharine Beecher was especially active in attempting to reform women's education. Throughout the 1820s, Beecher ran the Hartford Female Seminary with her sister, Mary. During these years, she proposed that schools for women be endowed, argued that teachers' assignments be limited to a few fields, and advocated the training of young women in domestic science and teaching. In the 1830s, Beecher established the Western Female Institute in Cincinnati, where she collaborated with William H. McGuffey on his famous "readers," joined the temperance movement, and wrote extensively about women's domestic sphere, although she herself had decided not to marry. Beginning in the 1840s, Beecher supported herself by public lecturing and writing on the cause of women's education. She crusaded for teachers to be sent to the West and for normal schools to be established in frontier regions. She was responsible for organizing missionary societies to send female teachers westward and founded a number of women's schools, such as the Dubuque Female Seminary in Iowa, throughout the West.

Through her active and vigorous career, Beecher never strayed from her conviction that women were by nature domestic creatures. Her schools trained women as teachers before marriage and as homemakers after. Her curriculum stressed health, home economics, English, and arithmetic. Beecher avoided "higher" subjects such as mathematics and philosophy because she believed that they would weaken the female constitution and interfere with a woman's desire and ability to bear children. In her many books, such as the extremely popular *A Treatise on Domestic Economy* that appeared in 1841, Beecher offered household hints and recipes, and encouraged women to abandon stays, corsets, and other unhealthy, but fashionable, practices. Neither a feminist nor a suffragist, Beecher devoted her career to elevating the prestige and proficiency of women as teachers and homemakers.

Mary Lyon of Massachusetts held a slightly different view of women's education. Dissatisfied with her own meager training, Lyon decided in 1834 to found the first women's college in the United States. She wrote: "My heart has so yearned over the adult female youth in the common walks of life, that it has sometimes seemed as if there was a fire shut up in my bones." Indeed, she pursued with a fiery zeal her plan for "a residential seminary to be founded and sustained by the Christian public." She personally appealed to women for "five or ten dollars of hard-earned money, collected by the slow gains of patient industry." Although as an unmarried woman she was criticized for traveling alone, she persevered, and in 1837, her college, Mount Holyoke, enrolled its first student. The three-year course of study included Latin, science, and anatomy at a cost of sixty dollars a year for tuition, room, and board. When Mary Lyon died in 1849, Mount Holyoke had attained a reputation as an outstanding teacher-training institution.

Almira Lincoln Phelps was another educator who urged women to widen the female sphere. In 1841, Phelps and her attorney husband took charge of the Patapsco Female Institute in Baltimore. Here she provided a role model of a woman of attainment for her students. She wrote several standard botany textbooks and many literary pieces. She became the second woman to be admitted to the American Association for the Advancement of Science. After her husband's death in 1849, Phelps ran the school by herself until her retirement at sixty-three. Her mission throughout her career was to help young women find their way to an independent identity and to help them prepare for achievement. She taught them that marriage was not crucial to a productive life and that there were many ways of eluding the limitations of "women's sphere" without admitting it.

Although all of these educational experiments were aimed at middle- and upperclass women, a few did concern themselves with indigent and delinquent women. The Lancaster (Pennsylvania) Industrial School for Girls offered moral instruction and vocational training for girls between the ages of seven and sixteen. The school also provided medical care, a temporary home, and an employment service. Unlike most other women's schools, Lancaster's purpose was to save the daughters of the poor from vice, rather than to urge fundamental changes in women's roles.

Along with revised thinking about women's education came innovative ideas concerning women's health. Catharine Beecher was one of the first to perceive that women's roles as wives and mothers demanded a robust physical condition, stamina, and endurance. She designed an appropriate exercise program for female students in her schools and regarded herself as the inventor of calisthenics during the 1840s. But Emma Willard, Sarah Josepha Hale, Mary Lyon, and Almira Phelps also sought to combat the American woman's poor state of health through exercise. They regularly prescribed activities to improve posture, gracefulness, and general health.

All of these educators, however, operated on the principle that women's bodies could sustain only a limited amount of moderate exercise. They were progressive in that they introduced the idea of exercise for women, but they were restrictive in that they promoted a firm belief in female weakness that bedeviled women's sports programs both then and now. Women were, for example, encouraged to ride horses, but only in "proper" riding dress and sidesaddle. *Godey's Lady's Book* stressed this idea, urging women always to preserve their feminine grace and delicacy while riding. Racing and riding to the hounds was definitely frowned upon, but, by the 1850s, women were allowed to compete in "female equestrian" events at county fairs.

Other acceptable sports for women during the 1840s and 1850s were pedestrianism or foot racing. In 1852, one American woman, Kate Irvine, even competed in a British race in which she covered 500 miles. Most ladies' journals recommended moderate walking and sedate dancing as acceptable exercises. They warned, however, that women proceed with caution, for when the body is "too much exercised, it is apt to produce ganglions on the ankle joints of delicate girls, as wind galls are produced on the legs of young horses who are too soon or too much worked."

Evidently, modifications in women's education were limited by prevailing beliefs. Even when women won the right to become teachers, they soon found that little liberation occurred. By 1860, one quarter of American teachers were women, while in Massachusetts nearly four fifths of teachers were female. Despite their numbers and importance, women teachers still worked under the direction of men, earned low wages, and had little opportunity for alternative employment. Women who sought an education were usually confronted with an unimaginative traditional curriculum. Unfortunately, although some changes were gradually taking place in women's education, most people still agreed with French commentator Jean-Jacques Rosseau: "The whole education of women ought to be relative to men. To please them, to be useful to them, to make themselves loved and honored by them, to educate them when young, to care for them when grown, to counsel them, to console them, and to make life sweet and agreeable to them—these are the duties of women at all times, and what should be taught them from their infancy."

Women's growing resistance to this notion of their roles was demonstrated not only by their attempts to reshape educational philosophy but also by their entry into the temperance movement. Taking their moral responsibilities very seriously, thousands of women joined the American Temperance Society's crusade during the 1820s. They either became members of men's temperance societies, where they soon found their participation strictly circumscribed, or they formed women's societies, in which they could vote, hold office, and set policy. These women's groups occasionally accepted black women as members, but frequently black women worked for the temperance cause within black associations. During these early years, women were engaged primarily in moral suasion to bring about temperance among drinkers.

Gradually, temperance women began to learn of the oppression and abuse that many wives and daughters suffered at the hands of drunken husbands. In addition, they began to recognize that women and children were economically dependent on men, and that alcoholic husbands could destroy their families. Thus, women began to see the problem of alcoholism as male and the solution as female. Yet they felt thwarted because, although they could indeed exercise their moral powers, they could not influence the political realm. As a result, when the temperance movement turned from moral suasion to legal prohibition of alcohol in the 1840s, women felt totally left out of the very cause that they now saw as their own.

Women temperance advocates initially responded to the change in policy by resisting the abandonment of moral suasion as a technique. But in 1846, when Maine passed the first statewide law to ban the manufacture and sale of alcoholic beverages, women were forced to accept legal prohibition as their goal. But how were they to bring about legal prohibition if they could not vote or hold office? This dilemma was resolved by women's decision to resort to increased female pressure that often included confrontation and extralegal force. Women joined the Daughters of Temperance in unprecedented numbers; by 1848, it was one of the largest organizations for women, with a membership of 30,000. They held women's temperance meetings, and major gatherings such as the Women's Temperance Convention that met in New York in 1852. They petitioned legislatures for prohibition legislation. They formed bands that prayed and sang hymns outside, or sometimes inside, saloons. And between 1852 and 1859, groups of women entered saloons and physically destroyed the liquor stock. In essence, respectable and influential women became vigilantes who brandished weapons ranging from petitions to hatchets. Their actions, including the violent assaults on saloons, were supported by their communities and groups of temperance men who saw women as protecting their homes and children in the only ways open to them.

Women's widespread participation in the temperance movement affected women more than it did the consumption of alcohol. Many of them became ardent feminists in response to their absolute lack of political power. A temperance journal, *The Lily*, edited by Amelia Bloomer, began as a newspaper dedicated to "temperance and literature," but by 1852, its new masthead stated that it was "devoted to the interests of women." Women who began their careers as reformers in the temperance crusade frequently ended them in the women's rights movement. Many of them also experienced an increasing enmity toward men, whom they saw as oppressors blocking them from their political rights, and often as morally weak alcoholics as well. At the same time, these women began to see themselves not as submissive domestic beings, but as aggressive, effective reformers. In general, the temperance movement caused large numbers of women to question their place and to challenge domestic ideology.

Women also sought identity and resisted domesticity through religious and moral reform activities. These groups accepted the domestic nature of women, yet counseled women to become assertive participants in shaping the cultural values of their communities. In other words, they offered women the opportunity to deviate from their roles without appearing to do so and to exercise a degree of influence, especially over amoral, or perhaps immoral, men.

For instance, evangelical religions granted women a measure of importance through religious conversions and membership in women's auxiliaries to missionary, tract, and Bible societies. They also offered women an increased voice in church affairs and no longer expected them to be the obedient followers of authoritarian ministers. Moreover, the hope of human perfectability was now held out to women in place of a former emphasis on their inherent evil as daughters of Eve. Several religious sects, notably Shakerism, Spiritualism, Christian Science, and Theosophy, particularly attracted women members because they additionally deemphasized the masculine nature of God, denied the need for a traditional male clergy, and argued that marriage and motherhood were not the only acceptable female roles.

Other similar groups emphasized the positive influence of women and the necessity for women to implement it. Female reform societies urged their members to exert active control over the sexual mores of their friends and neighbors. In 1834, a group of women reformers founded the New York Female Reform Society dedicated to the credo that "it is the imperious duty of ladies everywhere and of every religious denomination, to co-operate in the great work of moral reform." The society published a journal called *The Advocate* to denounce "sin" in all forms. It hired several ministers to aid the needy in hospitals, jails, almshouses, and brothels. And members personally stood vigils and prayed outside of brothels.

During the 1830s, such female reform societies proliferated rapidly and encompassed large numbers of women. In 1835, the Boston Female Moral Reform Society was founded by seventy women who soon brought in hundreds more women through rural auxiliaries. By 1837, the New York society counted 250 auxiliaries and 15,000 members. Other local societies in New York often included several hundred members each. In 1840, when the New York group organized into the national American Female Moral Reform Society, its auxiliaries numbered 555.

Female reform societies used many innovative techniques, especially "visiting." Women reformers sang hymns and prayed at brothels, almshouses, and jails. They talked with prostitutes, the ill, and the poverty-stricken. And they solicited data and cases relating to sexual abuse and other ills. In addition to visiting, moral reformers petitioned state legislatures and lobbied for reform legislation. They also opened homes as refuges for women in need. In New York, this took the form of a House of Reception, a home for prostitutes. In Boston, a Home for Unprotected Girls, a Refuge for Migrant Women, and an Asylum for the Repentant were opened.

Other women attempted to improve American society by participating in Utopian experiments dedicated to alternate forms of labor and products. Brook Farm, outside of Boston, drew the support of the Transcendentalist, Margaret Fuller. Scottish-born reformer, Frances Wright, founded her own agricultural commune, Nashoba, in Tennessee. Other societies experimented with alternate forms of marriage. Oneida, founded in upstate New York in 1847, practiced complex marriage in which all members cohabited with each other and cared for the children as a group. On the other hand, the Shakers, founded by Mother Ann Lee, tried to free women from the handicaps of marriage and childcare by practicing celibacy. Women's voluntary associations were also becoming very active in America, especially in urban areas that faced such growing evils as poverty, crime, and prostitution. Female benevolence accounted not just for simple charity efforts, but also for the creation of complex, influential institutions and organizations. Sarah Josepha Hale's Boston Seaman's Aid Society was an example. Originally designed to help the bereft widows of seamen support themselves, it grew into a non-profit business, vocational training program, school, and home. Similarly, the Providence (Rhode Island) Employment Society began in the 1830s by trying to help exploited seamstresses and soon turned into a small garment business that paid fair wages and provided good working conditions. Such voluntary associations were usually formed as corporations with boards of directors, treasurers and other officers, and public relations programs.

Women's voluntary organizations not only dispensed charity, but drew women out of their homes, trained them in a large variety of business positions, and helped to turn women's morality into a paid vocation. Susan B. Anthony and other critics lamented the dirty work of society being left to women. "Men like to see women pick up the drunk and falling. . . . That patching business is 'woman's proper sphere,'" Anthony complained. But other women recognized the transforming power of voluntary associations on women. In 1841, writer and abolitionist Lydia Maria Child argued that such organizations "have changed the household utensil into a living energetic being." In another situation, the Utopian community of Oberlin, Ohio, encouraged women to enhance their powers through advanced education. This philosophy led in 1833 to the first coeducational college in the nation, Oberlin College.

Not all women who resisted the prevailing model of womanhood did so through such generally acceptable areas as literature, education, temperance reform, and religion. Some were willing to attack male bastions such as medical practice directly. They were disgusted with the philosophy of male midwives illustrated by the professor of midwifery who, in 1848, stated: "I hope the day is far distant when the spectacle shall be seen in our hospitals of troops of women waiting in succession for a public examination of their genitalia, in the presence of large classes of medical practitioners and students of medicine. I regard this public sentiment as to the sanctity of the female modesty and chastity as one of the strong safeguards of our spontaneous public probity—for woman, and man's respect and love for her, are truly at the basis, and are the very cornerstone, of civilization and order." He later responded in outrage to an explicit newspaper advertisement: "Who wants to know or ought to know that the ladies have abdomens and wombs but us doctors. When I was young, a woman had no legs even, but only feet, and possibly ankles: now forsooth, they have utero-abdominal supporters, not in fact only, but in the very newspapers!"

For thousands of women who relied on patent medicines heavy with opium, morphine, or alcohol, rather than seek treatment from unenlightened male physicians, modification of the medical establishment seemed absolutely necessary. In 1835, Harriot K. Hunt began practicing as a "female physician" in Boston after having completed an apprenticeship. Hunt was derided and, in her words, "entirely shut out from the medical world." Despite the obstacles, she practiced for over four decades, always educating herself as medical colleges were closed to women.

Elizabeth Blackwell was the first woman to successfully challenge this exclusion policy. In 1847, she applied to many medical schools, but was rejected by every one. Finally, the students of Geneva College in New York voted to accept her application as a joke. Unaware of the spoof, Blackwell entered Geneva in November, 1847, and began a long, lonely course of study. She was ostracized by the local people as queer and immoral and was barred from classroom demonstrations that involved human anatomy.

Upon receiving her medical degree in 1849, Blackwell sailed for England to seek further training. After many rejections, she finally found a less-than-suitable place as a student midwife in Paris. Here she lost the sight of one eye from disease, thus ending any possibility of a career as a surgeon. In 1850, she was admitted to St. Bartholomew's Hospital in London, where she was allowed to practice all branches of medicine except gynecology and pediatrics.

In 1851, Blackwell returned to New York. Shortly after her arrival, she wrote to her sister Emily that "a blank wall of social and professional antagonism faces a woman physician and forms a situation of singular and painful loneliness, leaving her without support, respect, or professional counsel." Despite discrimination, Blackwell opened a private dispensary that, in 1857, was incorporated as the New York Infirmary and College for Women. This hospital was conducted largely by women. Blackwell's sister Emily and Maria Zakrzewska, both of whom had earned medical degrees with her encouragement, helped Blackwell. Together, they treated patients, trained nurses, and repelled outraged townsfolk who occasionally even threw rocks through the windows.

After 1859, Blackwell lectured in England on medicine as a profession for women. Her name was placed on the British Medical Register, and she was welcomed in the very hospitals that had earlier refused to admit her. She finally settled in England, her place of birth, where she founded the National Health Society in 1871 and began to lecture on gynecology in 1875. She was not only the first woman doctor in the United States, but was one of the first physicians to work in public health and to stress preventative medicine.

As more women moved into medical practice during the mid-nineteenth century, they tended to see their constituencies as women and children. They also differed from male doctors in their emphasis on holistic treatments. Although women doctors were not necessarily feminists, they were often more sympathetic to women's growing demand for birth control information than were male doctors.

Changes in the American economy and an emphasis on Republican Motherhood made large families increasingly undesirable. A decline in the birth rate from an average of 7 in 1800 to 5.4 in 1850 demonstrated women's willingness to use birth control methods, such as coitus interruptus and an improved rubber condom, a result of the development of vulcanization of rubber in 1843. A few outspoken women, such as reformer Frances Wright, publicly advocated the practice of birth control. By the 1840s, there was a dramatic rise in the abortion rate, especially among married women. These trends culminated in the first explicit demand for birth control information by the women's rights movement in the 1840s. They issued a call for "Voluntary Motherhood," arguing that women who chose to bear children would be better mothers than those who were denied the choice.

The early birth control movement manifested a growing desire of many women to exercise control over their bodies and lives. It was becoming evident that numerous women did not wish to be confined to a life exclusively dedicated to wife- and motherhood, nor were they willing to accept their dependency on men. As a result, many different types of women began to speak out on their own behalf.

During the reform era between 1837 and 1861, a number of working women began to question the dominant ideology of domesticity and True Womanhood. One of these, Harriet Farley, a former mill operative at Lowell, even became an avowed women's rights advocate. In 1850, Farley wrote: "It has been impossible for me to consider so long the 'Rights and Duties of Mill-Girls' without opening my eyes to the vista just beyond the rights and duties of woman." She deplored the socialization of "masculine" men and "feminine" women that ignored the common ground between the two genders. She argued that agitation and education were necessary to achieve revision of these practices, and strongly supported the actions of women's rights conventions in creating public awareness of the issues involved. Farley maintained that "every thing that is really strengthening, elevating, enlarging, a woman wants—a woman needs." In her view, women could support themselves without losing their womanhood. "I have seen that they do not become less worthy and interesting when they become more useful and independent," she observed.

Unlike Farley, the majority of employed women during this period dealt with their frustrations and problems in less philosophical and more immediate ways. Their campaigns for working women's rights focused on higher wages, shorter hours, and improved working conditions. The Panic of 1837 caused a depression that lasted five years. Wages fell and unemployment spread. Bread riots were common in New York and other major cities. By 1845, most women were back to work but still earned less than two dollars per week. By 1850, there were 181,000 women employed in manufacturing and untold thousands more working as pieceworkers, domestic servants, and prostitutes. Unemployed women workers were forced to seek assistance from benevolent women's societies and other charity organizations. In New York City, one of the earliest of these was the "Mother Society," devoted to helping poor blacks and unemployed black women.

Most working women during the 1840s and 1850s were convinced that some type of organization was needed to correct the many problems that they faced. But society in general, and male union members in particular, frowned upon their participation in unions. Unwilling to accept the reality of women's employment, these people hoped that women workers would soon return to their "proper" places in the home. Working men also tended to fear women because they accepted low wages. These men did not yet realize that organizations of both women and men might establish fair wages for all workers.

Prejudice did not prevent women workers from joining men's unions, forming their own organizations, and participating in strikes. In 1845, the shoebinders at Lynn established a Producers Cooperative. In 1860, 500 men and 1,000 women held a huge rally during a strike. In the middle of a terrible blizzard, the meeting attracted 1,800 women who cheered the reading of a special poem, "The Song of the Shoemakers Strike." Some 20,000 more workers throughout New England joined this labor protest, known as "The Revolution in the North." It is unclear whether the strike brought about any actual gains, but it did provide the shoebinders with the organizational experience to found the Daughters of St. Crispin some years later.

During the late 1840s and 1850s, women workers in the clothing, shoe, wool, straw hat, printing, and other industries repeated these early attempts at organization and walkouts many times. Household workers and home pieceworkers had little opportunity to organize, strike, or otherwise to protect themselves from exploitation. Many made ends meet by taking aid from charitable societies and hiring out their children. Others turned to prostitution. In 1858, it was estimated that there were 6,000 prostitutes in New York City, one for every 64 adult males. Over half of these women had earned one to two dollars a week as seamstresses, dressmakers, hat trimmers, milliners, tailoresses, servants, and factory workers before becoming prostitutes. Sixty-three percent of them were born in other countries.

This latter statistic points at the tremendous problems immigrant women had in finding employment. Usually lacking industrial skills, forced to work at less than subsistence wages, and often unable to speak English, these women were exploited unmercifully by employers. Many of them became pieceworkers or domestic servants at unbelievably low wages. During the 1840s, one quarter of a million women, or one tenth of the adult female population, worked as domestics. The majority of these workers were Irish immigrants. Many other Irish women worked in the needle trades or as prostitutes. Stranded in urban areas by their lack of funds, Irish and large numbers of other immigrant women were unable to migrate to rural areas where they might put their agricultural skills to use. Chinese women were in a more difficult situation. Imported after 1840 primarily as prostitutes, Chinese women were a profitable commodity. Families often sold their daughters into servitude or were duped into parting with them. Other Chinese families survived only because of the meager wages earned in America. This sordid practice was encouraged by employers who did not want to pay Chinese laborers adequate wages to support a family or encourage permanent Chinese settlement. By the 1850s, Chinese societies known as *tongs* regularly supplied West Coast brothels with Chinese women. Chinese prostitution created miserable lives for the women involved, exacerbated anti-Chinese sentiment, and contributed to the devaluation of women and their labor.

Problems of laboring women were not quite as pressing in farm work. Those women, both immigrant and native born, who did migrate to western agricultural regions from the 1830s onward were quick to seize the limited opportunities that they found. Despite landholding policies that favored men, women could own land and participate in agriculture. Often these were widows, women with disabled husbands, and single women. By the early 1860s, one observer noted:

> We have heard of women in Western New York, Ohio and Michigan, that not only carry on farms but do the outdoor work, as tilling, reaping, etc. There are two sisters in Ohio who manage a farm of 300 acres: and two other sisters, near Media, Pennsylvania that conduct as large a farm. Mrs. D. owns a farm, and does not disdain to graft fruit trees, superintend their planting, gather fruit, send it to market, etc.: and she realizes a handsome profit.

Young women worked on farms as hired laborers during the three decades preceding the Civil War. These hired girls were often newly arrived immigrant women who did not disdain field work. The number of women working as "hired hands" increased as specialization developed. Wheat, corn, and dairy farms all demanded hired labor, both female and male. In 1857, the *Illinois Farmer* stated: "We want a supply of young women from the butter regions of Eastern States to come here and also from the Dairy Districts of England, Scotland, Ireland, and Germany." Black, immigrant, and poor women in particular were recruited for field work, but it was considered appropriate work for all women during periods of labor shortages.

In the South during these years, women were even more active in agricultural work. Historian Keith L. Bryant, Jr. maintains that white women on small tobacco, cotton, and subsistence farms regularly joined men in planting crops, weeding, and harvesting. Women of the middle-class yeomanry played a significant economic role in the family and frequently participated in making economic decisions. In addition, they transformed the raw materials of the fields into finished goods and provided cash income through the sale of their surplus products. Southern women gained property rights in several states during the 1850s, and common practice often protected their ownership of land, looms, cattle, and furniture. Yeoman women usually chose their own mates and often determined the number of children that they would bear. Some abandoned abusive, negligent, or lazy husbands, while many others served as teachers and exhorters. These middle-class southern women were important economic and moral forces whose assertiveness precluded patriarchy in their families.

Of course, the black slave women who provided similar labor on the larger farms and plantations were not in such enviable positions. Their situations did demand immediate attention from reformers. As property themselves, slave women could not own anything. They usually had no right to choose their mates or the number of children they bore. They had no control over their bodies being used for sexual or breeding purposes. They could not desert abusive husbands but might be torn from loving husbands through sale. The threat of physical punishment forced them immediately to accept a new spouse after the sale or death of a mate in order to keep producing children.

One of the few considerations slave women received was an occasional lightened work load while pregnant. One Virginia planter warned his overseers that "breeding wenches you must be Kind and Indulgent to, and not force them when with child upon any service or hardship that will be injurious to them." When not pregnant, however, slave women were expected to maintain an exhausting work schedule. They worked at jobs and performed all the usual domestic chores for their own families. In the fields, slave women sowed, hoed, and picked cotton, hoed and milled corn, and worked in lumbering, construction, and roadbuilding. They were expected to take part in all necessary tasks from plowing to building fences.

In 1853, an observer in South Carolina saw male and female slaves carrying manure containers on their heads to fields where they applied it by hand to the earth around cotton plants. In North Carolina, he observed women hoeing, shoveling, and cutting down trees to create roadbeds. Slave women were also sometimes hired out to cotton and woolen mills, sugar refineries, and tobacco factories. In 1860, about 5,000 slave women were so employed. Only about 5 percent of black slave women attained the relatively privileged status of house servant, serving as household slaves, nursemaids, and wet nurses. Aged slave women also worked hard at such tasks as sewing, weaving, spinning, canning, and caring for babies and young children whose mothers were in the fields. In addition, these aged "grannies" often served as nurses and midwives.

Slave women frequently rebelled against their heavy work loads. "She'd git stubborn like a mule and quit." Or she "chopped" the overseer across his head with her hoe or ran away into the woods to hide as a "truant." One Florida woman even chopped her overseer to death after a reprimand. Some women became concubines and mistresses to escape heavy labor. Others would "sham," that is, claim aches and disabilities due to their menstrual cycle or pregnancy. Another more subtle rebellion was the slave woman's adherence to the traditional division of labor within her home. By maintaining the customary roles and tasks of wife and mother, the slave woman could mock her owner's treatment of her as a man in the fields or foundry. Also, by acting as the force that held the family together in the face of daily adversity or that formed new kinship ties in times of crisis, a slave woman defied her owner's casual attitudes toward the institutions of marriage and family among slaves. By preserving her family from the dehumanizing aspects of slavery, black women were engaged in the ultimate revolt against the system.

By 1860, the population of the South included 7,033,973 whites, 258,000 free blacks, and 3,838,765 black slaves. Even though the constitutional ban on importing slaves went into effect in 1808, the slave system in the South had increased, primarily through smuggling and breeding. The latter method created an additional evil for black women, who were sold as "breeding wenches" and were expected to produce as many children as possible. Other slave women were sexually exploited by their masters. In Linda Brent's *Incidents in the Life of a Slave Girl*, edited by Lydia Maria Child in 1861, a tale of cruelty and licentiousness emerged. The author claimed that her master told her that "I was his property; that I must be subject to his will in all things." Such evils were further exacerbated by whites, whose fears of revolts grew as the numbers of slaves increased. They tightened the codes that restricted the behavior of their chattels and expanded the patrols that enforced such codes.

The dismal situation of slave women was described by Frances Kemble, a distinguished English actress who married a Georgia planter. Of her time spent on a plantation in 1838 and 1839, Kemble wrote: "It appears to me that the principal hardships fall to the lot of the women." Black slave women continually appealed to Kemble to lighten their work, soften their punishments, and extend their time of rest after childbirth to the customary four weeks. She felt overwhelmed by their stories, especially a particularly dismal one involving a woman who had borne sixteen children, fourteen of whom were dead, and had been lashed by "a man with a cowhide [who] stands and stripes" slaves. Kemble wrote: "I give you the woman's words. She did not speak of this as of anything strange, unusual, or especially horrid and abominable: and when I said: Did they do that to you when you were with child? she simply replied: Yes, missis." Outraged, Kemble added: "To all this I listen—I am Englishwoman, the wife of the man who owns these wretches, and I cannot say: That thing shall not be done again. I remained choking with indignation and grief long after thay had all left me to my most bitter thoughts."

Kemble's reactions to the slave system reflected the attitudes of many other plantation mistresses. Although some southern women did defend slavery as sanctioned by the Bible and protective of supposedly childlike blacks, Harriet Martineau claimed in the mid-1830s that she "never met with a lady of southern origin who did not speak of slavery as a sin and acurse the burden which oppressed their lives." Plantation wife Mary Boykin Chestnut also believed that most planters' wives were abolitionists at heart. And Maria J. McIntosh, daughter of an illustrious Georgia family, publicly aired her antislavery views in 1850 in a volume entitled *Woman in America*.

These white southern women had good reasons to hate slavery. They feared revolt, resented their husbands' sexual liaisons with black women, rebelled against their own heavy work loads in supervising and training black workers, and experienced guilt about oppressing black people. But the southern lady was hedged in by custom and economic dependence on her planter husband. She seldom dared to voice antislavery sentiments for fear of reprisal or abandonment. Moreover, as historian Catherine Clinton points out, southern women's social status and financial security depended on the continuation of the slave system, a factor that helped silence them on the issue. Circumscribed by the Cult of White Womanhood, the plantation woman confided her thoughts to her diary rather than to her spouse. In 1858, Georgian Ella Thomas recorded her conviction that "Southern Women are all at heart abolitionists" in her journal. She added: "I will stand to the opinion that the institution of slavery degrades the white man more than the Negro and exerts a most deleterious effect upon our children. . . . The happiness of homes is destroyed but what is to be done?"

While southern men engaged in "male" pursuits, such as business affairs, horse racing, cock fighting, gambling, drinking, and hunting, women kept their thoughts to themselves and worked alongside other women and with slaves. Contrary to the Magnolia Myth—the portrayal of leisured, hoopskirted southern belles—southern women devoted their time and energy to overseeing the house and its servants, conducting massive entertaining, providing medical care and schooling for all the people on the plantation, and supervising cooking, food processing, and the production of clothing.

These women did not support the pre–Civil War patriarchal system; they simply tolerated it when necessary. They strained against its dictates when possible. Some planter-class females employed the concept of Republican Motherhood to argue for improved educational opportunities. Their planter fathers and husbands concurred in the establishment of female academies because of their belief that educating their women would help to maintain the "tone" of the planter class. Women cherished their right to better educations, yet recognized that intellectual development would end with marriage, casting them into roles much like those that their mothers filled.

Besides modifying their views of women's education, antebellum Southerners also altered divorce laws. Women who sought divorce had to appear docile and submissive while substantiating their claim that they had been wronged by an adulterous, drunken, abusive, neglectful, or felonious husband. But once they proved their cases, these women were treated as capable beings and awarded substantial alimony payments, property, and control of their children. Women of means took advantage of the new laws and the more liberal attitudes they reflected. Between 1800 and 1860, twenty-one women in Alabama sued for divorce as opposed to seven men. Eleven of the wives were successful, while only two of the husbands obtained divorces. In Louisiana, sixteen wives sought divorces as compared to six husbands. Seven of the women were successful, while only one of the men was granted his request.

Evidently, many southern women of both the yeoman and planter classes challenged White Womanhood when and where they could during the 1840s and 1850s. Because they functioned in a conservative agrarian society, southern women were not as effective in breaking down barriers as were their northern counterparts, who had the advantage of operating in an industrial, relatively progressive world. Accordingly, not only the attack on women's sphere but the assault on the slave system had to come primarily from northern women.

One of the first northern women to assail the slave system was author Lydia Maria Child. Widely known for her editorship of *The Juvenile*

Miscellany, a children's magazine, and her authorship of *The Frugal Housewife*, a household hint book, Child published an early antislavery tract in 1833. Entitled *An Appeal for that Class of Americans Called Africans*, Child's book asked for justice and equality for black Americans. She pointed out that the "Negro woman is unprotected by either law or public opinion" and that she "must be entirely subservient to the will of their owner." After her readers turned against her for her unfeminine involvement in political matters, Child became the editor of the *National Anti-Slavery Standard* and devoted the rest of her career to the cause of abolitionism.

About the same time that Child's book appeared, a Quaker teacher, Prudence Crandall, accepted a black student into her Canterbury Female Boarding School in Connecticut. Local authorities warned Crandall that, if the young woman stayed, they would "ruin her school." She bravely replied, "Let it sink, then. I shall not turn her out." When all of Crandall's white students withdrew, she converted her school, with the help of abolitionist editor William Lloyd Garrison, into the High School for Young Colored Ladies and Misses, which opened in April 1833. A storm of protest erupted in the town of Canterbury. One group of irate citizens declared: "The Government of the United States, the nation with all its institutions, of right belong to the white men, who now possess them."

Crandall attempted to carry on with her school but was jailed during the summer of 1833 under a newly passed law that forbade the teaching of blacks in the state of Connecticut. Her case was aired around the world by the abolitionist press, and she was finally freed on a technicality. She returned to her school and to the continued harassment of townspeople who threw manure into her well, smashed the windows, threatened the students, and set fire to the building. After mob violence in September 1834, Crandall gave up. Recently married to an abolitionist minister, Crandall and her husband moved to Illinois. She maintained a lifelong interest in temperance reform and women's rights until her death in 1890.

Although these initial attempts to help blacks were abortive, they did alert many women to the need to form antislavery societies. Beginning in 1832, the formation of the New England Antislavery Society, the Connecticut Female Antislavery Society, and others in many states and regions marked the entry of women into the largely male abolitionist movement. Over one hundred societies had emerged by 1838. Because these women viewed slavery as a moral wrong, they felt compelled to exercise their moral powers against it. The Boston Female Antislavery Society declared: "As wives and mothers, as daughters and sisters, we are deeply responsible for the influence we have on the human race. . . . We are bound to urge men to cease to do evil and learn how to do good."

They also felt a growing sense of identification with black women. In

1837, abolitionist Angelina Grimké told a women's antislavery convention that black slave women were their "sisters" and "to us as women they have a right to look with sympathy for their sorrows, and effort and prayer for their rescue." They believed that if one woman was sexually degraded, then all women suffered and that if one mother was devalued, then all mothers lost stature. Women also felt a kind of kinship with slave women because of the restrictions on their lives as chattel. And abolitionist women hoped that, if they helped to free the slaves, liberation would be extended to white women as a logical and just outcome of their efforts.

At first, women's abolitionist societies were engaged in fund-raising and exhortation. They soon moved to more aggressive tactics, including organizing petition campaigns, holding national conventions, and speaking on the public platform. They increasingly resented the limitations placed on their activities due to their gender. In 1837, one woman's convention proclaimed: "The time has come for woman to move in that sphere which providence has assigned her, and no longer remain satisfied in the circumscribed limits which corrupt custom and a perverted application of Scripture have encircled her."

Women's increasing involvement in the abolitionist cause received national attention in the mid-1830s because of the activities of two southern-born women, Angelina and Sarah Grimké. Raised in Charlestown, South Carolina, as proper young ladies, both Grimkés grew up detesting slavery and resenting the restrictions inherent in White Womanhood. In 1821, at age twenty-eight, Sarah moved to Philadelphia and joined the Society of Friends. Angelina followed Sarah to Philadelphia and into the Quaker fold in 1829. Angelina soon joined the Philadelphia Female Anti-Slavery Society, noting in her diary, "I am confident not many years will roll by before the horrible traffic in human beings will be destroyed."

In 1836, Angelina's *Appeal to the Christian Women of the South* was published by the American Anti-Slavery Society. Copies of the pamphlet were publicly burned in the South, and the author was warned not to return to her home there. In that same year, Sarah also wrote a tract entitled *Epistle to the Clergy of the Southern States*. Both women began to lecture against slavery. Their willingness to lecture to mixed audiences of both women and men caused a great deal of public indignation. Undaunted, Angelina wrote a second pamphlet in 1837, *An Appeal to the Women of the Nominally Free States*.

The Grimké's lecturing and political reform activities created a women's-rights controversy. In 1837, a group of Congregationalist ministers in Massachusetts issued a "Pastoral Letter" protesting the sisters' unfeminine conduct. The letter said in part: "We invite your attention to the dangers which at present seem to threaten the female character with widespread and permanent injury. The appropriate duties and influence of women are clearly stated in the New Testament. The power of woman is her dependence, flowing from the consciousness of that weakness which God has given her for her protection."

Abolitionist leaders feared that the antislavery crusade would be jeopardized by the controversy and begged the Grimkés to ignore it. But the sisters replied that they could "not push abolitionism forward until we take the stumbling block out of the road." In 1838, Sarah stated their position in her pamphlet, *Letters on the Equality of the Sexes, and the Condition of Woman*. She minced no words in presenting the case: "I ask no favors for my sex. I surrender not our claim to equality. All I ask of our brethren is that they take their feet from off our necks, and permit us to stand upright on the ground which God has designed us to occupy." Shortly thereafter, Angelina married abolitionist reformer Theodore Dwight Weld. The newlywed couple and Sarah settled in New Jersey, where they continued to work for the causes of antislavery and women's rights.

Thousands of women followed the Grimkés' courageous example and joined the abolitionist movement during the 1840s and 1850s. Because they could not vote, they chose instead to petition Congress to pass laws restricting slavery. Petition-gathering was hard work that required travel and met with both scorn and apathy . Yet these women persevered and collected hundreds of thousands of signatures that Congress could not ignore. In addition to petitioning, abolitionist women lectured, wrote pamphlets, and helped slaves to escape to freedom via a network known as the Underground Railroad.

The most famous "conductor" of the Underground Railroad was Harriet Tubman. Born a slave in Maryland, Tubman fled to Philadelphia in 1849. In 1850, she returned to guide her sister and her two children to freedom and, in 1851, helped a brother and his family to escape. In all, Tubman is believed to have made nineteen trips into slave territory and freed as many as 300 people. Known as the "Moses of Her People," Tubman had a price of $40,000 on her head.

Tubman was not the only black woman to work for the liberation of slaves. Because they were often barred from white women's groups that believed in abolitionism but not equality, black women took matters into their own hands. Maria Miller Steward, a Connecticut free black, began to lecture publicly on behalf of her people during the early 1830s—a time when Frances Wright was one of the few woman brave enough to mount the public lecture platform and black lecturers were virtually unknown. Sarah Parker Remond, a free black woman from Salem, Massachusetts, lectured on the American antislavery cause in many European countries during the late 1850s and 1860s. She also pursued her own education and, in 1868, earned a medical degree in Italy. Ellen Craft, a fugitive slave, carried tales of the American slave system to England during the 1850s and 1860s.

One of the most well-known black female abolitionists was Charlotte Forten of Philadelphia. A teacher and author, Forten was also a founder of the Philadelphia Female Anti-Slavery Society. She was particularly active and effective in educating former slaves on the Sea Islands immediately after the Emancipation Proclamation in 1863. Her name became Grimké in 1878 when she married Francis James Grimké, a natural slave son of a brother of the abolitionist reformers, Angelina and Sarah Grimké.

Harriet Grimké Purvis, one of Charlotte's daughters, was also an active abolitionist. She and her husband were abolitionist leaders who used their Philadelphia home as a station on the Underground Railroad. In 1838 and 1839, Harriet served as a delegate to the Anti-Slavery Conventions of American Women. She continued to actively work for the causes of black Americans and women's rights until 1875.

Harriet's sister, Sarah, contributed poems and essays to the antislavery newspaper, *The Liberator,* composed a widely-sung antislavery song, "The Grave of the Slave," and tirelessly organized antislavery sewing circles and charity fairs. In 1837, she wrote the Grimké sisters that prejudice against her had made her "embittered." She felt that blacks were "innocent victims of prejudice for you are all well aware that it originates from dislike to the color of the skin much as from the degradation of Slavery." She added that she was trying to develop a "spirit of forebearance" for those who were racially biased.

Teacher Sarah Mapps Douglass was another leading black abolitionist. As early as the 1820s, she opened a school for black children in Philadelphia. In 1832, when the Pennsylvania legislature considered a bill that would have required all blacks to carry passes, Douglass became a political activist. "One short year ago, how different were my feelings on the subject of slavery!" she exclaimed. But, when racism indirectly threatened her own freedom, she determined "to use every exertion" in her power "to elevate the character of my wronged and neglected race." As a result, she became deeply involved in the Philadelphia Female Anti-Slavery Society and taught at the Institute for Colored Youth, where she was instrumental in training many of Philadelphia's public school teachers. After the Civil War, Douglass served in a leadership position with the Pennsylvania branch of the Freedman's Aid Commission and continued her innovative teaching career.

Other black female abolitionists were Frances Ellen Watkins Harper, a well-known lecturer, author, and reformer; Mary Ann Shadd Cary, a teacher, journalist, and lawyer; Maria W. Stewart, a lecturer, writer, and teacher; and Sarah Parker Remond, a speaker and author. Despite racism and sexism, these and other black women fought for the improvement of black Americans during the 1830s, 1840s, and 1850s. Discriminated against by white women's abolitionist societies, black women formed their own organizations dedicated to the cause of black freedom or joined racially integrated groups as "colored" members. They soon realized that an aversion to slavery on the part of white women did not mean that they would extend equality to black women. Black women were not represented in the National Convention of Female Anti-Slavery Societies and other groups.

Sojourner Truth was probably the most famous black woman reformer and lecturer of this period. Born a slave in New York and originally named Isabella, she fled from her owner in 1827, a year before slaves were freed in that state. In 1829, she arrived in New York City with two of her children and obtained work as a domestic servant. She became a preacher and was especially active in the effort to turn the city's many prostitutes to religion. In 1843, she took the name Sojourner Truth and set out on foot to preach throughout New England. She became an enthusiastic supporter of the abolitionist movement in 1846. She toured the Midwest lecturing against slavery in spite of threats and physical attacks. In Indiana, she bared her breast to disprove the allegations that she was really a man in disguise. In 1850, after experiencing constant discrimination as a female reformer, she took up the cause of women's rights. In 1852, at a women's rights meeting in Akron, Ohio, she delivered her famous "Ain't I A Woman" speech in which she pointed out that chivalry and True Womanhood were not very meaningful concepts to most women, especially black, laboring, and poor women. After emancipation, Truth argued adamantly for rights for black women as well as for white because she was convinced that "if colored men get their rights and not colored women theirs . . . the colored men will be masters and it will be just as bad as it was before."

Sojourner Truth was far from alone in her frustrations. Many antislavery women, as well as women who supported temperance, moral reform, and other causes, chafed at the limitations they encountered. They had no political influence because they could not own property, vote, or hold office. They were condemned for speaking in public and disdained for entering the halls of Congress with their petitions. How were they to function as effective reformers without some weapons or power? And how were they to wield their moral force? If they were the moral guardians of society, then they must be able to exercise their powers. Women's experience with powerlessness reinforced lessons that they had been learning for over half a century. Since the early 1800s, women's voluntary associations, especially in the newly emerging urban areas of America, had been trying to deal with such problems as alcoholism and prostitution. They had come to recognize the value of reforms that would increase the rights of women. Now, numerous abolitionists and other women reformers added the issue of women's rights to their reform platforms between 1837 and 1861. For some, gaining rights was a practical matter—they simply wanted to proceed with their reforms. For others, achieving their rights was an ethical issue that would allow them to carry out their moral responsibilities to the nation.

The problems posed by women reformers came to a head in 1840, when the national antislavery organization split into male-only and male-female factions over the "woman question." The integrated group sent female delegates to a world antislavery convention in London in 1841. Here, the women were seated behind a curtain and denied the right to vote. When they walked out in indignation, they were joined by a number of sympathetic men. As a result of this upsetting incident, Lucretia Mott and Elizabeth Cady Stanton agreed that a women's protest meeting was needed in America. But it was not until 19 July 1848 that the first women's rights meeting was held in Seneca Falls, New York.

The chairperson of the Seneca Falls meeting was James Mott, Lucretia's husband. Elizabeth's husband, Henry Stanton, had fled in embarrassment. The meeting attracted approximately 300 people, including about 40 men. After many speeches, the delegates paraphrased the Declaration of Independence in a plea for equality and expanded rights for women, including the right to vote. It read: "We hold these truths to be self-evident: that all men and women are created equal: that they are endowed by their Creator with certain inalienable rights: that among these are life, liberty and the pursuit of happiness. The history of mankind is a history of repeated injuries and usurpations on the part of man toward woman, having in direct object the establishment of an absolute tyranny over her."

Although the demands issued at Seneca Falls in 1848 were met with unsparing ridicule in the press, many other similar conventions followed in both eastern and western states. In 1850, James Gordon Bennett of the *New York Herald* asked: "What do the leaders of the women's right conventions want? They want to be members of Congress, and in the heat of debate subject themselves to coarse jests and indecent language." Many people were sincerely puzzled by advocates of women's rights, especially when Amelia Bloomer, a temperance reformer, women's rights editor, and suffragist in Seneca Falls, began to wear a reform dress composed of a short skirt and Turkish-style pantaloons during the winter of 1850–1851. Bloomer and the other women who adopted the costume were expressing their desire for better health, freedom of movement, and even equality by freeing themselves from the dictates of fashion. But, due to the controversy that the Bloomer outfit created, most women had abandoned it by the end of the decade.

Women's rights may have appeared to be a foolish and trivial issue to some people, but for its female and male advocates it was serious and far-reaching in its implications. Seeing the ideal family as a partnership rather than a patriarchy, women's rights supporters campaigned for legal changes that would allow married women to own property. As early as 1829, the *American Monthly Magazine* argued that the present restrictive laws made husbands greedy and wives mean and concealing. In 1839, the state of Mississippi passed the first Married Women's Property Law.

Soon, many women's rights advocates began to promote modification of women's property laws, particularly a Jewish woman of Polish birth named Ernestine Rose. First a temperance and abolitionist reformer, Rose had become committed to women's rights by the 1840s. In New York, Rose circulated petitions and spoke for the newly introduced women's property bill. When it was finally passed in 1848, it was limited in scope but did mark the beginning of alterations in women's ownership of property. Shortly afterward, Pennsylvania passed a similar bill, largely because of the urgings of journalist and newspaper editor Jane Swisshelm.

Proponents of women's rights during the 1840s and 1850s were also eager to gain political privileges for women. They were outraged that the widely touted "democracy" that developed during the Age of Jackson applied only to white males and not to females. To these reformers, suffrage meant more than simply the right to cast a ballot. They saw women's entry into the public arena as the path to the larger goal of equality with men. They drew on the techniques learned through the abolitionist and other reform campaigns and appealed to activists in those areas for support.

The very women who seemed so intent on the extension of equality only occasionally encouraged black women to join in their crusade or discouraged their participation altogether. Although many black women seem to have considered antislavery a more pressing cause, some did become feminists. For example, abolitionist and journalist Mary Ann Shadd Cary was also a feminist. Although the involvement of black women in the women's rights and feminist movements has been generally overlooked, there is evidence that they were active participants.

In the process of defending their demands, women's rights leaders developed an intricate ideology during the 1840s and 1850s. It was derived from three sources. First, existing doctrines of the American Revolution contributed ideas of equality, human perfectibility, and the right of citizens to participate in their own governance. In 1848, the Seneca Falls delegates utilized the Declaration of Independence.

Second, the philosophies of British reformers fed into the American women's rights crusade. In 1792, Mary Wollstonecraft, an English author, published her *Vindication of the Rights of Women*. This book was one of the first arguments for the equality of women and was widely read in America. In the 1830s, Frances Wright's lectures offered valuable insights into the topics of equality, improved education, divorce, and birth control. And Frances Kemble's speeches recounting her life on a Georgia plantation, also published as a book entitled *Journal of a Residence on a Georgian Plantation* in 1863, supplied a firsthand account of the evils of the slave system and the oppression of slave and white southern women.

Third, American writers and speakers offered a variety of perspectives and philosophies. Margaret Fuller, known as the "high priestess" of the Transcendentalist movement, addressed the issue of equality. As editor of the Transcendentalist journal, *The Dial,* during the 1840s, Fuller maintained that women should be allowed to expand their strengths and interests, just as men did. In 1845, Fuller's *Woman in the Nineteenth Century* developed the case for equality further. She stated: "I would have Woman lay aside all thought, such as she habitually cherishes, of being taught and led by men. I would have her free from compromise, from complaisance, from helplessness, because I would have her good enough and strong enough to love one and all beings, from the fullness, not the poverty of being." Fuller concluded: "Now there is no woman, only an overgrown child."

Elizabeth Cady Stanton concentrated her efforts on gaining the ballot for women. As an organizer of the Seneca Falls meeting in 1848, a founder of the Woman's Loyal League in 1863, and a candidate for Congress in 1866, Stanton believed that liberation lay in political participation. She disdained the idea of woman's sphere: "The talk of sheltering woman from the fierce storms of life is the sheerest mockery, for they beat on her from every point of the compass, just as they do on man, and with more fatal results, for he has been trained to protect himself, to resist, to conquer." During the 1840s and 1850s, Stanton also campaigned on behalf of abolitionism, temperance, education, and property rights for women. But because she was blocked by her father and husband and was burdened by the care of her children, she often had to rely on others to carry her messages.

Susan B. Anthony became Stanton's closest collaborator. Henry Stanton reportedly told Elizabeth, "You stir up Susan and she stirs up the world." Anthony did indeed prove herself to be an effective orator and an efficient organizer for temperance, abolitionism, and women's rights during the 1840s and 1850s. A Quaker schoolteacher and manager of the family farm, Susan B. Anthony, never married, was free to travel and speak. After meeting Elizabeth Cady Stanton in 1850, Anthony came to her for ideas and often helped her with the children and household chores in order to free her for a few hours of thought. Like Stanton, Anthony emphasized the right to vote. "Suffrage involves every basic principle of republican government, all our social, civil, religious, educational, and political rights," she maintained. "It is therefore germane to discuss every invidious distinction of sex in the college, home, trades and professions, in literature, sacred and profane, in the canon as well as in the civil law."

Lucy Stone also contributed to the ideology of women's rights. After attending Oberlin College in the 1840s, Stone became an abolitionist speaker and survived a drenching with a hose and a blow from a hurled prayerbook, among other indignities. She soon came to deplore the idea of Civil Death and the limitations that it placed on women. When she married Henry Blackwell in 1855, Stone kept her family name and entered into a well-publicized marriage contract with Blackwell. Their agreement read: "While acknowledging our mutual affection by publicly assuming the relationship of husband and wife, yet in justice to ourselves and a great principle, we deem it a duty to declare that this act on our part implies no sanction of, nor promise of voluntary obedience to such of the present laws of marriage, as refuse to recognize the wife as an independent, rational being, while they confer upon the husband an injurious and unnatural superiority, investing him with legal powers which no honorable man would exercise, and which no man should possess." Coming from a reforming family and himself committed to women's rights, Blackwell seemed to take the ensuing public derision in stride.

Lucretia Mott also came to women's rights through abolitionism. As a Quaker, Mott possessed a strong sense of self-worth that she could not reconcile with the degrading treatment she received as a female reformer. And as an official minister in the Society of Friends, she had a deep religious belief in justice and equality for all people. During the 1850s, she turned her Philadelphia home into an Underground Railroad "station" and, in addition to caring for six children, traveled extensively to lecture on abolitionism and women's rights. She frequently employed Biblical evidence to argue that the inferior status of women was neither natural nor divinely ordained. In 1849, Mott decried women's long-term bondage. Woman "has been so long subject to the disabilities and restrictions, with which her progress has been embarrassed, that she has become enervated, her mind to some extent paralyzed; and like those still more degraded by personal bondage, she hugs her chains." Rather than promoting woman suffrage, Mott concentrated on a new view of women as responsible, self-sustaining individuals.

The energy and ideas of these women's rights leaders helped create a dynamic and visible movement by the 1850s. Hundreds of women's rights meetings were held each year, and the "woman question" was widely and hotly debated. But there were many problems. Women's rights appealed primarily to white middle- and upperclass women. Consequently, the participants were neither numerous nor representative of the female population as a whole. Issues important to working, immigrant, poor, black, and American Indian women were ignored in favor of other larger concerns, such as equality and suffrage. In addition, women's rights advocates lacked effective means to pursue their objectives. Limited to speaking, writing, and petitioning, they often had difficulty getting their points across. To complicate matters further, few Americans were ready to take the matter of women's rights seriously. Finally, other national events tended to overshadow women's rights. The burgeoning settlement of the West, the Mexican War, 1846–1848, the Gold Rush in 1849, unprecedented industrial expansion, King Cotton and slavery, the Fugitive Slave Law of 1850 and the Underground Railroad, reformism, and a literary flowering known as the American Renaissance drew attention away from women's issues between 1837 and 1861.

Still, the groundwork of an American feminist movement was in place. In some ways, it was very rudimentary. Attention was focused on specific issues of women's rights rather than on the development of a more comprehensive feminist platform and consciousness. And, in rather simplistic terms, women's righters frequently identified men as the enemy rather than examining the structure of their society. Yet issues had been pinpointed and discussed, the public had been exhorted to increase its awareness of the ills afflicting women, and the accepted model of womanhood had been seriously challenged. In addition, women had learned organizational and speaking skills, attracted a number of male supporters, and forced legislators to accept their petitions. Although domesticity was still preached as the highest standard for American women, the emergent women's rights crusade had encouraged resistance to its actual acceptance on many fronts.

In 1861, the tremendous crisis of the Civil War would shatter American society, destroying institutions, revising customs, and reshaping the national scene as it progressed. Its effects would be felt by all Americans, particularly blacks and women. That the war radically changed the situation of blacks is a well-known fact. But, even though the war's impact on women is neither as well documented nor as widely recognized, it was significant and fascinating.

SUGGESTIONS FOR FURTHER READING

Albert, Judith Strong. "Margaret Fuller's Row at the Greene Street School: Early Female Education in Providence, 1837–1839." *Rhode Island History* 42 (May 1983): 43–55.

Basch, Norma. "Invisible Women: The Legal Fiction of Marital Unity in Nineteenth-Century America." *Feminist Studies* 5 (Summer 1979): 346–366.

———. "Equity vs. Equality: Emerging Concepts of Women's Political Status in the Age of Jackson." *Journal of the Early Republic* 3 (Fall 1983): 297–318.

Bednarowski, Mary Farrell. "Outside the Mainstream: Women's Religion and Women Religious Leaders in Nineteenth-Century America." *Journal of the American Academy of Religion* 48 (June 1980): 207–231.

Berg, Barbara J. *The Remembered Gate: Origins of American Feminism.* New York: Oxford University Press, 1978.

Berkin, Carol Ruth, and Mary Beth Norton, eds. *Women of America: A History.* Boston: Houghton Mifflin Company, 1979, 177–202.

Belding, Robert E. "The Dubuque Female Seminary." *The Palimpsest* 63 (March/April 1982): 34–41.

Brenzel, Barbara. "Lancaster Industrial School for Girls: A Social Portrait of a Nineteenth-Century Reform School for Girls." *Feminist Studies* 3 (Fall 1975): 40–53.

Bryant, Jr., Keith L. "The Role and Status of the Female Yeomanry in the Antebellum South: The Literary View." *Southern Quarterly* 18 (Winter 1980): 73–88.

Burnham, Dorothy. "The Life of the Afro-American Woman in Slavery." *International Journal of Women's Studies* 1 (July/August 1978): 363–377.

Campbell, John. "Work, Pregnancy, and Infant Mortality Among Southern Slaves." *Journal of Interdisciplinary History* 14 (Spring 1984): 793–812.

Censer, Jane Turner. "'Smiling Through Her Tears': Ante-Bellum Southern Women and Divorce." *American Journal of Legal History* 25 (January 1981): 24–47.

Clinton, Catherine. "Equally Their Due: The Education of the Planter Daughter in the Early Republic." *Journal of the Early Republic* (Spring 1982): 39–60.

———. *The Other Civil War: American Women in the Nineteenth Century.* New York: Hill and Wang, 1984. Chapters 2–4, 6–8.

Conrad, Susan P. *Perish the Thought: Intellectual Women in Romantic America, 1830–1860.* New York: Oxford University Press 1976.

Davis, Angela. "Reflections on the Black Woman's Role in the Community of Slaves." *The Black Scholar* 3 (December 1971): 3–15.

Douglas, Ann. *The Feminization of American Culture.* New York: Alfred A. Knopf, 1979.

DuBois, Ellen Carol. *Feminism and Suffrage: The Emergence of an Independent Women's Movement in America, 1848–1869.* Ithaca: Cornell University Press, 1978.

Eckhardt, Celia Morris. *Fanny Wright: Rebel in America.* Cambridge, MA: Harvard University Press, 1984.

Foner, Philip S., and Josephine F. Pacheco. *Three Who Dared: Prudence Crandall, Margaret Douglass, Myratilla Miner-Champions of Antebellum Black Education.* Westport, CT: Greenwood Press, 1984.

Friedman, Jean E., and William G. Shade, eds. *Our American Sisters: Women in American Life and Thought.* Lexington, MA: D. C. Heath and Company, 1982. Part II.

Ginzberg, Lori D. "Women in an Evangelical Community: Oberlin, 1835–1850." *Ohio History* 89 (Winter 1980): 78–88.

Greene, Dana. "'Quaker Feminism': The Case of Lucretia Mott." *Pennsylvania History* 48 (April 1981): 143–154.

Groneman, Carol. "Working-Class Immigrant Women in Mid-Nineteenth Century New York: The Irish Woman's Experience." *Journal of Urban History* (May 1978): 255–273.

Hardesty, Nancy A. *Women Called to Witness: Evangelical Feminism in the 19th Century.* Nashville: Abingdon Press, 1984.

Hersh, Blanche G. *The Slavery of Sex: Feminist-Abolitionists in Nineteenth Century America.* Urbana: University of Illinois Press, 1978.

Hirata, Lucie Cheng. "Free, Indentured, Enslaved: Chinese Prostitutes in Nineteenth-Century America." *Signs* 5 (Autumn 1979): 3–29.

Hoffman, Nancy. *Woman's "True" Profession: Voices from the History of Teaching.* Old Westbury, NY: Feminist Press, 1981.

Hudson, Winthrop S. "Early Nineteenth-Century Evangelical Religion and Women's Liberation." *Foundations* 23 (April/June 1980): 181–85.

James, Edward T., ed. *Notable American Women, 1607–1950: A Biographical Dictionary.* Cambridge, MA: Harvard University Press, 1971.

Jones, Jacqueline. "'My Mother Was Much of a Woman': Black Women, Work, and the Family under Slavery." *Feminist Studies,* 8 (Summer 1982): 235–269.

Kelley, Mary. "The Sentimentalists: Promise and Betrayal in the Home." *Signs* 4 (Spring 1979): 434–446.

———. *Private Woman, Public Stage: Literary Domesticity in Nineteenth-Century America.* New York: Oxford University Press, 1984.

Kerber, Linda K., and Jane DeHart Mathews, eds. *Women's America: Refocusing the Past.* New York: Oxford University Press, 1982. Part IIa.

Lauer, Jeanette C., and Robert H. Lauer. "The Language of Dress: A Sociohistorical Study of the Meaning of Clothing in America." *The Canadian Review of American Studies* 10 (Winter 1979): 305–323.

———. "The Battle of the Sexes: Fashion in 19th Century America." *Journal of Popular Culture* 8 (Spring 1980): 581–89.

Lerner, Gerda. *The Grimké Sisters from South Carolina: Pioneers for Woman's Rights and Abolition.* New York: Schocken Books, 1971.

———. ed. *Black Women in White America: A Documentary History.* New York: Random House, 1973.

———. "The Political Activities of Antislavery Women." 112–28 In *The Majority Finds Its Past,* edited by Gerda Lerner, 112–28. New York: Oxford University Press, 1979.

Morantz, Regina Markell, and Sue Zschoche. "Professionalism, Feminism, and Gender Roles: A Comparative Study of Nineteenth-Century Medical Therapeutics." *Journal of American History* 67 (December 1980): 568–588.

Nelson, Margaret K. "Vermont Schoolteachers in the Nineteenth Century." *Vermont History* 49 (Winter 1981): 5–30.

Rosenberg, Rosalind. *Beyond Separate Spheres: Intellectual Roots of Modern Feminism.* New Haven: Yale University Press, 1982.

Ryan, Mary P. "The Power of Women's Networks: A Case Study of Female Moral Reform in Antebellum America." *Feminist Studies* 5 (Spring 1979): 66–85.

———. *Womanhood in America from Colonial Times to the Present.* New York: New Viewpoints, 1979. Chapter 3.

Scott, Anne Firor. "Almira Lincoln Phelps: The Self-Made Woman in the Nineteenth Century." *Maryland Historical Magazine* 75 (September 1980): 203–216.

Sklar, Kathryn Kish. *Catharine Beecher: A Study in American Domesticity.* New York: W. W. Norton and Company, 1973.

———. "The Founding of Mount Holyoke College." In *Women of America: A History,* edited by Carol Ruth Berkin and Mary Beth Norton, 177–202. Boston: Houghton Mifflin Company, 1979.

Terborg-Penn, Rosalyn. "Discrimination Against Afro-American Women in the Women's Movement, 1830–1920." In *The Afro-American Woman: Struggles and Images* edited by Sharon Harley and Rosalyn Terborg-Penn, 17–27. Port Washington, New York: Kennikat Press, 1978.

Tyrrell, Ian R. "Women and Temperance in Antebellum America, 1830–1860." *Civil War History* 28 (June 1982): 128–52.

Vertinsky, Patricia. "Sexual Equality and the Legacy of Catharine Beecher." *Journal of Sport History* 6 (Spring 1979): 38–49.

Walsh, Mary R. *"Doctor's Wanted: No Women Need Apply": Sexual Barriers in the Medical Profession, 1835–1975.* New Haven: Yale University Press, 1977.

Walters, Ronald C. "The Erotic South: Civilization and Sexuality in American Abolitionism." In *Procreation or Pleasure? Sexual Attitudes in Amerian History* edited by Thomas L. Altherr, 87–98. Malabar, FL: Robert E. Kreiger Publishing Company, 1983.

Weiner, Nella Fermi. "Of Feminism and Birth Control Propaganda, 1790–1840." *International Journal of Women's Studies* 3 (September/October 1980): 411–430.

White, Deborah Gray. "The Lives of Slave Women." *Southern Exposure* 12 (November/December 1984): 32–39.

———. *Ar'n't I a Woman? Female Slaves in the Plantation South.* New York: W. W. Norton & Co., Inc., 1984.

Woloch, Nancy. *Women and the American Experience.* New York: Alfred A. Knopf, 1984. Chapters 5–8.

After Harriet Tubman escaped from slavery in 1849, she became known as the "Moses of Her People" for her successful activities with the Underground Railroad. During the Civil War, Tubman was the only black person to serve with the Union armies as a scout and a spy. Courtesy of the Library of Congress, Washington, D.C.

CHAPTER 5

"Womanly Strength of the Nation": The Civil War, Reconstruction, and the Gilded Age 1861–1890

*I*N April 1861, the American nation split into two warring factions, the United States of America and the Confederate States of America. Two major questions were at issue: the continuation and extension of the black slave system and the political unity of the northern and southern states. During four long years of hostilities lasting until 1865, the South lost some 265,000 lives and the North, 364,000. Industrialization made widespread and efficient slaughter possible for the first time. Rather than glorious or romantic, the Civil War was destructive and terrifying. Its impact changed the course of American history in many ways.

The Civil War and its aftermath not only shook American society and government to its foundations but had a marked influence on the lives and roles of American women. The model of womanhood, already somewhat unstable as a result of the many attacks by reformers, experienced further blows during the years of war and reconstruction. Yet the resiliency of the image was remarkable. Although it tottered a bit, it did not collapse and fall.

From the very beginning of the Civil War, women were drawn into the war effort by requests for huge amounts of foodstuffs, bandages, and other sanitary goods, which were being rapidly consumed primarily by ill-supplied military hospitals. During the spring of 1861, women began to congregate in homes, hotels, and churches to preserve fruits, roll bandages, sew shirts, and organize charity fairs and other fund-raising events to collect money with which to buy supplies.

These women's groups quickly began to organize into aid societies and sanitary commissions. As early as April 1861, 3,000 New Yorkers met in Cooper Union to form the New York Central Association of Relief. Similar types of organizations appeared in many states, in which women served as officers and on the boards of directors and finance committees. By the end of 1861, there were approximately 20,000 women's aid societies in the United States and the Confederacy.

These women's groups sent tremendous quantities of supplies to the front. Organized in 1862, the Weldon, Pennsylvania, society contributed $17,000 in goods in one year. In one month in 1863, the Center Ridge, Alabama, group sent "422 shirts, 551 pairs of drawers, 80 pairs of socks, 3 pairs of gloves, 6 boxes and a bale of hospital stores, 128 pounds of tapioca and $18 for hospital use." During these years, other local societies began to establish "refreshment saloons" in the North and "wayside homes" in the South to aid passing military personnel. Two Philadelphia saloons had dispensed more than $80,000 in supplies and served more than 600,000 meals by the beginning of 1864.

Frequently, representatives from women's groups traveled to the front to aid the administration of supply distribution. They attempted to organize the efforts of different women's groups, preventing duplicated deliveries on the one hand and shortages on the other. They also routed supply wagons away from roads used by troops and munitions. Annie Turner Wittenmyer of Keokuk, Iowa, served in this way as forwarding agent for aid societies throughout the state and, in 1862, was appointed as a State Sanitary Agent. Appalled by the black coffee, greasy bacon, and hardtack served to patients in the military hospitals, Wittenmyer began to campaign for "diet kitchens" that would serve healthful rations. In 1864, her first kitchen was established, and by the end of the war these kitchens had become an accepted feature of military hospitals. Near the end of the war, she turned her attention to the problem of war orphans and in 1865 persuaded the federal government to give several new buildings and many hospital supplies to the newly organized Iowa Orphans Home Association in Davenport, Iowa.

Besides supplying the troops and hospitals, women also nursed the wounded and dying. Nurses were often trained in the field since few nursing schools existed at that time. By the end of 1861, Dr. Elizabeth Blackwell had established a training program for nurses and applied for the position of Superintendent of Women Nurses. Dorothea Dix was given the job instead, partly because of the hostility against Blackwell as a female doctor. Dix recruited only women who were at least thirty years of age and "plain in appearance," a policy that caused great bitterness among younger women who were eager to contribute their services to the war effort.

Mary Ann Bickerdyke was a particularly well-known war nurse. Called "Mother" Bickerdyke, this Quaker woman gained a reputation as a tireless worker and fearless administrator in the nineteen battlefield hospitals in which she served between 1861 and 1865. A coworker of Bickerdyke's claimed that she was not afraid of anybody, including the high-ranking generals. "But Lord, how she works!" she marveled.

Another Civil War nurse, Hannah Ropes of Massachusetts, kept a diary during her service in 1862–1863 in a Washington hospital that offers insight into the life of the female nurse. In August 1862 she wrote: "We have just cleaned and dressed over a hundred men from the Harrison's Landing—poor, worn fellows!" A month later, she described a young man who was shot through the lungs yet survived the night. "We considered him the greatest sufferer in the house, as every breath was a pang," she commented. As a strong abolitionist, she explained that she could endure the hardships associated with nursing because "this is God's war. . . . The cause is that of the human race, and must prevail."

Mary Livermore, another Massachusetts war nurse, fought long and hard against the terrible conditions that she found in the military hospitals. After a tour of military hospitals in 1863, she instituted a letter-writing and canvassing campaign in Illinois to raise needed supplies. Her description of one of the hospitals in which she served graphically presents the difficult conditions: "It was a miserable place. . . . The cots were placed inside the tents, on unplanked ground. . . . The hospital swarmed with large green flies, and their buzzing was like that of a beehive. . . . Many of the patients did not lift their hands to brush away the flies that swarmed into eyes, ears, noses, and mouths."

The writings of Phoebe Yates Pember, a hospital matron near Richmond, indicated that conditions were no better in the Confederate hospitals. Railing especially against drunken surgeons, Pember also recorded incompetency, laziness, and discrimination against her as a woman administrator. By 1863, wartime prices were so high in Richmond and her salary so meager that, at night, she wrote for magazines or did copy work for the War Department to supplement it.

As a result of such dreadful conditions, yet another Civil War nurse, Clara Barton, eventually began to crusade for the establishment of the American Red Cross in the 1870s. Her wartime experiences convinced her of the need for a national, ongoing relief organization that would be able to offer aid during wars and other national disasters. The Civil War had taught her about corruption, lack of supplies, and carnage so great that, in her words, "I wrung the blood from the bottom of my clothing before I could step."

For their Herculean efforts, army nurses received compliments from many people ranging from wounded soldiers to President Lincoln himself. In 1892, the United States Congress finally granted them formal recognition of their inestimable services by giving them a pension of twelve dollars a month.

Women's contributions to medical hospitals also resulted in the establishment of several institutions dedicated to the training of women doctors. Neither the Union nor the Confederacy commissioned women physicians at the outbreak of the war. In 1861, Mary Walker applied to the Union government as a medical doctor but was denied a commission until 1864. Although such women as Elizabeth and Emily Blackwell and

Maria Zakrzewska practiced in the North and others such as Louisa Shepard and Elizabeth Cohen practiced in the South, there was widespread resistance to women doctors. During the war, however, many people began to recognize the medical competency of these doctors and to support the idea that women should have access to medical training. Such arguments for the active role of women in medical practice led to the founding of the Chicago Hospital for Women and Children and the New York Medical College for Women, both in 1863.

Women offered their talents on many other fronts as well. Some went to the fighting front as soldiers. Disguised as men, about 400 women fought in the Civil War between 1861 and 1865. Sarah Emma Edmonds of Michigan claimed that she served as a male nurse, spy, mail carrier, and soldier for two years, while Amy Clarke of Mississippi enlisted with her husband and continued to fight after he was killed at Shiloh.

Other women served as spies, couriers, guides, scouts, saboteurs, smugglers, and informers. Elizabeth Van Lew of Richmond posed as an eccentric known as "Crazy Bet." Under this guise, she rescued Union prisoners from the Richmond prison and operated as a spy. General Grant reportedly said that she was the best spy in his command. Harriet Tubman, the only black person to serve as Union scout and spy, was also known for her great fortitude and cleverness. The Washington society hostess, Rose Greenhow, was said to be very proficient at relaying intelligence to Confederate leaders in code until her house arrest in late 1861 and her dispatch to Richmond. Her efforts reportedly helped the South win the First Battle of Bull Run in July 1861. Belle Boyd also gained prominence as a Confederate spy and courier in Virginia before she was betrayed and arrested in July 1862.

Women were especially effective as couriers and smugglers since hoopskirts, bustles, and false hairpieces could conceal anything from messages to pistols. Both northern and southern soldiers soon overcame their modesty and by late 1861 began searching these good Victorian ladies thoroughly. Louisa Buckner of Virginia was one of the many women arrested after such a search. She had more than one hundred ounces of quinine intended for a Confederate hospital concealed in her skirt. Still, many ingenious women slipped through the lines with goods hidden in false-bottom trunks, parasols, and their crinolines.

Women were also important on the home front during the war years. They kept the farms and plantations going while their menfolk were off fighting. They took jobs in arsenals and munitions factories. They were more visible than ever in mills and other industrial employment. They invaded the offices of the Union and Confederate governments to become clerks who were often called "Government Girls." And they entered the teaching profession by the thousands in both the North and South.

The wartime situation was particularly hard on southern women. In

April 1861, when Lincoln's naval blockade cut off the primarily agrarian South from its sources of war supplies, women turned their homes into crude factories to produce what goods they could with limited materials. In addition, they had to deal with the terror of war in their own backyards. They frequently pursued a "scorched earth policy," that is, they burned their own crops and killed their own stock to keep them out of Yankee hands. In 1864, a Virginia woman wrote to her soldier husband: "Chrismus is most here again, and things is worse and worse. . . . Everything me and the children's got is patched. . . . We haven't got nothing in the house to eat but a little bit of meal. I don't want you to stop fighten them Yankees till you kill the last one of them, but try and get off and come home and fix us all up some and then you can go back and fight them a heep harder. . . . We can't none of us hold out much longer down here . . . my dear, if you put off a-comin' 'twon't be no use to come, for we'll all hands of us be out in the garden in the old graveyard with your ma and mine." By the end of the war in April 1865, the want and poverty throughout the Confederacy was incredible.

To stave off the specter of starvation during the latter years of the war, some desperate southern women began pillaging and rioting for bread, especially in New Orleans and Atlanta. Many others supported themselves and their children by taking positions in white schools or by joining the "missionary" teachers flocking in from the North to teach in schools established for freed blacks after the Emancipation Proclamation of January 1863. Others became sewing women or salespeople. Still others took jobs with the Confederate Army that ranged from clerk to engineer. Although many of these women were formerly members of a "genteel elite," wartime conditions and economic need clearly took priority over the standards of White Womanhood that at one time would have prevented them from pursuing some means of sustenance and support.

While the war situation was pushing white women in both the North and South into pursuits that were not consistent with the tenets of either True or White Womanhood, the formal, organized campaign for women's rights had largely disbanded. The last major women's rights convention met in 1861. Many women's rights leaders believed that the abolition of slavery and the end of fighting had to be the center of attention. Others took a more practical approach to the issue. In 1861, suffragist Martha Wright wrote to Susan B. Anthony that it was unwise to argue for women's rights "when the nation's whole heart and soul are engrossed with the momentous crisis and nobody will listen."

On 9 April 1865, the Civil War finally came to a halt at Appomattox Courthouse, Virginia. It had been a long, exhausting, and destructive conflict. The United States suffered tremendous property damage, extensive loss of lives, and a blow to its national spirit that would take generations to even begin to heal. Throughout the war, the nation's women were loyal supporters of military efforts in both the North and the South. In addition, women's rights leaders put their own pursuit of justice for women aside to support the emancipation of black slaves. They hoped that when the war ended, women's gargantuan efforts on all fronts would be recognized with extended rights and opportunities. Some even thought that women might be granted the right to vote at the same time that former black slaves were given citizenship and suffrage.

To many advocates of enlarged roles for women, a major revision of the stereotyped American woman seemed to be near at hand. They hoped that the decades following the conclusion of the war would witness the beginning of the end of the model American woman, the fading of traditional notions of female domesticity and passivity. During Reconstruction (1865–1877) and the Gilded Age, which followed, ideas about American women would indeed undergo many modifications, but not drastic ones.

In 1865, women leaders who foresaw changes for women as an immediate result of the war met with disappointment. They were dismayed to learn that proponents of abolitionism were much more concerned about the permanent freedom of former slaves than with the status of women. Abolitionist leaders feared that raising women's rights issues in 1865 would complicate, or even prevent, the passage of legislation to protect blacks. Although the Thirteenth Amendment, which abolished slavery was ratified in December 1865, additional protective and civil rights legislation for blacks was under consideration. Its supporters argued that one step should be taken at a time and that women's turn would come eventually. Even black leader Frederick Douglass, who had been sympathetic to women's rights, told them in 1865: "This is the Negro's hour."

When Congress passed the Fourteenth Amendment in 1866, its provisions extended political privileges to white and black men but not to women. The amendment supported the continued disenfranchisement of women by specifically defining citizenship rights as "male," the first time that this word had appeared in the Constitution. Women's rights leaders were outraged. Reformer Frances Gage scathingly wrote: "Can any one tell us why the great advocates of Human Equality . . . forget that when they were a weak party and needed all the womanly strength of the nation to help them on, they always united the words 'without regard to sex, race, or color?' Who ever hears of sex now from any of these champions of freedom!" And Stanton direly predicted, "If that word 'male' be inserted, it will take us a century at least to get it out."

Women's deep concern over their political exclusion erupted at the first major women's rights convention held since the beginning of the war. Meeting in New York City in 1866, delegates unanimously decided that they must push for suffrage for both blacks and women as their primary goals. They duly organized the American Equal Rights Association to work toward these two objectives. In 1866 and 1867, the new organization lobbied and petitioned to have race and gender restrictions deleted from state constitutions. In 1867, the association supported two suffrage bills in Kansas, one for black men and one for women. When abolitionist leaders failed to support the Kansas woman-suffrage bill, the association decided that it was time to part company with their former allies. They became determined to form a new group devoted exclusively to gaining the vote for women.

Suffrage leaders found, however, that many disagreements existed in their own ranks regarding how woman suffrage might best be achieved. As a consequence, two opposing groups emerged. In 1869, Stanton and Anthony formed the National Woman Suffrage Association in Washington. It excluded men from membership and concentrated its efforts on getting Congress to pass an amendment granting women the right to vote. The NWSA published a newspaper coedited by Stanton and Anthony called *The Revolution*. The newspaper's masthead read: "Men, Their Rights and Nothing More, Women, Their Rights and Nothing Less." In addition to working for the immediate enfranchisement of women, the NWSA supported equal pay for equal work, child-care centers for working mothers, and more equitable divorce laws.

Also in 1869, Lucy Stone, Mary Livermore, and Julia Ward Howe, author of the "Battle Hymn of the Republic," organized the American Woman Suffrage Association in Boston. Unlike the NWSA, the AWSA encouraged men to join and focused their efforts on gaining woman suffrage state by state. The AWSA published a newspaper called *The Woman's Journal,* designed to counteract the "radicalism" of *The Revolution.*

When these two rival organizations formed in 1869, public opinion on the issue of extended rights for women was difficult to determine. In 1867 and 1868, Kansas woman-suffrage amendments had failed. In 1868, a woman-suffrage amendment introduced in Congress had also floundered. But, in 1869, Wyoming Territory granted women the right to vote, followed in 1870 by Utah Territory. Although these latter actions were encouraging, they did not precipitate a landslide toward woman suffrage. In all likelihood, as historian Gerda Lerner has noted, "All feared that the hand that rocks the cradle might, given suffrage, also rock the boat." Although the NWSA and the AWSA, which merged in 1890, worked energetically for twenty years, woman suffrage would not be achieved during that period.

In the years immediately following the war, several individual women's rights advocates also joined the fray for woman suffrage. An articulate and dramatic woman, Victoria Claflin Woodhull, became the nation's first female stockbroker in 1870, ran for President in 1872, and frequently lectured on women's rights. Along with her equally colorful sister, Tennessee Claflin, she attracted a good deal of attention to the suffrage movement, but she also convinced a lot of people that woman suffragists were highly eccentric.

The Quaker Anna Dickinson was also seen by many Americans as something of a "character." During the Civil War, Dickinson lectured eloquently not only on antislavery but on political and military affairs. She shocked people by campaigning on behalf of political candidates in 1863. After the war, dressed now in elegant gowns accented by extravagant jewelry, Dickinson lectured on injustices to women. Known as the "Queen of the Rostrum" to some, Dickinson exhibited the "worst possible taste" in the eyes of others. Yet, in spite of the controversy that continually swirled around them, Woodhull and Dickinson did draw attention to the cause of woman suffrage while demonstrating that women could effectively enter such "male only" areas as finance and politics.

Evidence suggests that a number of southern women were also interested in women's rights during the postwar years. Although they were not generally as outspoken as their northern counterparts, women such as Sarah Ida Fowler Morgan of South Carolina did make public their women's rights stance. Through editorials in the Charleston *News and Courier* during the 1870s, Morgan examined the "woman question" in great detail. Writing under the pseudonym, "Mr. Fowler," Morgan supported employment, singlehood, and equality for women. But instead of focusing on woman suffrage, she believed that the women's movement should be dedicated to economic independence for women.

Many female reformers in the South and the North rejected the idea of woman suffrage entirely. They feared the evils that women's political participation might introduce into American homes and families. When Catharine Beecher and Harriet Beecher Stowe collaborated in the writing of *Principles of Domestic Science* in 1870, they chose not to support woman suffrage for these reasons. Instead, they wrote: "The authors of this volume while they sympathize with every honest effort to relieve the disabilities and sufferings of their sex, are confident that the chief cause of these evils is the fact that the honor and duties of the family state are not duly appreciated, that women are not trained for these duties as men are trained for their trades and professions, and that, as the consequence family labor is poorly done, poorly paid, and regarded as menial and disgraceful." The sisters outlined woman's "profession" as "the care and nursing of the body in the critical periods of infancy and sickness, the training of the human mind in the most impressible period of childhood, the instruction and control of servants, and most of the government and economies of the family state."

The Beecher sisters' traditional portrayal of American women in the late 1860s and 1870s probably reflected many Americans' views of women. Numerous commentators felt that women should return happily to their homes after the war and focus their full attention on their families. Yet, at the same time, many things had begun to subvert the domestic ideal. Women had learned a tremendous variety of new skills as a result of the war. They had, for example, learned to speak in public, to handle finances, and to serve as executive officers of large organizations through such groups as women's aid societies and the Women's Loyal League. In addition, women moved into formerly "male" jobs, where they proved that they could do heavy labor. They became the arbiters, decision makers, and disciplinarians in their families, which now lacked male heads. And they mastered such new technological devices as washing and sewing machines, which not only reduced the amount of time required to maintain their households but helped to elevate the professional status of housekeepers. Although many women returned to their homes as rapidly as possible at the war's end in 1865, they found it difficult to resume passive, submissive roles.

As a consequence of all the wartime adaptations, American society had gradually come to permit, even to encourage, women's increased entry into a wide variety of endeavors during the 1860s and 1870s. One of these was literature, long a stronghold for achievement-oriented women. But now female authors wrote on such previously taboo subjects as politics and war. Mary Abigail Dodge wrote many outspoken essays of opinion and propaganda under her pen name, Gail Hamilton. In "A Call to My Country-Women," written in 1863, she urged women to aid the war effort. Julia Ward Howe employed poetry to arouse her readers' love of country, the most famous of which was her poem "Battle Hymn of the Republic," written in 1861 and set to music in 1862.

Other women served as newspaper correspondents who shared their wartime experiences and observations with thousands of interested readers. One of these was Charlotte Forten, a black teacher in Georgia, who contributed essays on "Life in the Sea Islands" to *Atlantic Monthly* in 1864. Still other women authors were responsible for an outpouring of books, pamphlets, and tracts designed to raise funds or shape public opinion. And yet other women published personal diaries, reminiscences, and novels written during the war years and afterward.

During the 1860s, several "serious" women authors emerged. Emily Dickinson of Amherst, Massachusetts, wrote many of the 1,775 poems that she would produce in her lifetime during this decade. Although she was little known in her own day, Dickinson is now hailed as the first serious American woman poet because her focus was not on domesticity, but on the larger issues of life, death, immortality, and religion. Dickinson was encouraged in her work by another author of the day and a crusader for American Indian rights, Helen Hunt Jackson. A prolific essayist, poet, and novelist in her own right, Jackson later became known for *Ramona: A Story* (1884), a book championing American Indian women.

Another well-known woman writer of the time was Louisa May Alcott, an author of magazine fiction and novels. In *Little Women*, Alcott portrayed Jo, the central character, as a restless, searching feminist. Interested herself in alternative roles for women, Alcott had one of the novel's characters advise her daughter: "Don't shut yourself up in a bandbox because you are a woman, but understand what is going on, and educate yourself to take part in the world's work, for it all affects you and yours."

While these authors were expanding the scope of women's literary undertakings, other women were taking Alcott's advice to educate themselves and to enter paid employment. Women particularly moved into the schoolroom as teachers. In 1860, women teachers accounted for 25 percent of the nation's teachers. By 1880, women would compose 60 percent of the country's teaching force. In 1865, the *New York Times* commented that teaching was a work "to which intelligent women are preeminently adapted" and "a duty in which many more ought to be engaged."

Women teachers were willing to work for low wages and to accept seasonal employment. As men deserted the teaching profession for better paying jobs in industry or to take up western homesteads, women gladly filled the void. This in turn put pressure upon existing colleges to admit women as students and stimulated the founding of normal schools and women's colleges to train female teachers. Vassar College in Poughkeepsie, New York, opened its doors to a class of 353 women in 1865. The curriculum included philosophy, Greek, Latin, German, French, English, mathematics, astronomy, physics, chemistry, hygiene, art, and music. Smith College and Wellesley College offered similar programs when they opened in 1875.

In the South a similar trend developed. Many middle- and upperclass women who now felt the need to help to support their families entered the teaching profession. By 1883, Alabama's superintendent of public instruction noted that "members of the most elegant and cultivated families in the State are engaged in teaching." This movement of southern women into the classroom resulted in a demand for teacher-training schools. In 1875, a normal school opened in Nashville with thirteen women in its student body and two women on its faculty. Several fine southern women's colleges were also established during the postwar years, including Agnes Scott, Goucher, Randolph-Macon, and Sophie Newcomb.

Women also eagerly enrolled in land-grant colleges, which had been coeducational since their underwriting by the Morrill Act in 1862. The presence of female students often created confusion at such schools as

Iowa State College, which tried to integrate them into a male-oriented curriculum. Iowa State decided to treat all students as equally as possible, a policy that resulted in uniformed women toting rifles and drilling in military science programs.

Changes in women's sports accompanied these educational developments for women. Vassar College provided facilities for gymnastics, bowling, horseback riding, swimming, skating, and gardening. In 1866, several Vassar women formed a baseball club that played every Saturday afternoon. One young woman commented that "the public so far as it knew of our playing was shocked." Croquet was a much more acceptable game for women and provided the first sport in which women and men could participate together.

There were many other fashionable activities for women. Ice and roller skating were favorites. Bowling became popular, and in 1868, *The New York Clipper* told of a woman who had bowled a 290- and a 300-point game in the same evening. In 1874, Mary E. Outerbridge of New York introduced tennis into the United States. Hampered by long skirts, corsets, and large hats, women played tennis with ladylike grace but little agility. Also in the mid-1870s, archery tournaments, probably the first organized sport for women, became very popular.

In the years following the Civil War, there were many other ways for American women to get into good physical shape. Hundreds of handbooks on diet, appearance, hygiene, digestion, and female health rolled off the presses in an attempt to convince wan, corseted women to begin some kind of physical self-help program. One type suggested mechanical aids such as nose pinchers, shoulder braces, and massage rollers. Others were cosmetic or medicinal in nature and promised both beauty and health. Of these, Lydia E. Pinkham's Vegetable Compound, produced by a family business founded in 1875, became the most famous. In addition, intellectual exercises such as hobbies, reading, and "character development" were recommended.

While women were generally interested in improving their health, many were deeply determined to gain control over their own bodies, especially in the matter of reproduction. Evidence indicates that birth control by abortion had increased during the war years; apparently, women wanted to control their childbearing. This desire to limit family size alarmed many people who felt that it was woman's role to bear many children, feared the possible physical complications of abortion, or believed that the population of the United States would be depleted. In fact, as early as 1829, many states had begun to pass legislation restricting abortions. And in 1832, when Charles Knowlton, a Massachusetts doctor, advocated "checks to conception," he was arrested and fined. This did not deter others from continuing to advertise "Female Monthly Regulating Pills," which were supposedly abortants guaranteed to cure "all cases of suppression, irregularity, or stoppage of the mensus." Newspapers also advertised "Preventive Powders" at five dollars a package and a rubber diaphragm called a "Family Regulator, or Wife's Protector," also costing five dollars.

By the 1850s, medical practitioners and concerned citizens were beginning to be alarmed by the low national birthrate. Accordingly, they accelerated their opposition to planned parenthood and birth control. In 1862, an Ohio obstetrician introduced the first statute banning contraception and abortion. By 1865, many people were more worried about the huge loss of population during the Civil War. The American Medical Association thus launched a full-scale campaign against birth control and abortion. In 1873, these events culminated in the Comstock Law which made it a federal crime to send obscene materials, including birth-control information, through the mail.

Although many women continued to bear unwanted children during the 1860s and 1870s to avoid harm from illegal abortions and to escape legal prosecution, thousands of others continued to seek abortions and birth-control information despite the laws. They were encouraged by such feminists as Elizabeth Cady Stanton, who argued that women were entitled to choose how many children they would bear, and by an industrial, urban economy that made the rearing of large numbers of children more expensive and difficult than it had been on farms. Although technology had not yet offered dependable birth control devices, it had created the conditions that helped motivate women to search for them.

Naturally, technology affected women in many other ways as well. For instance, the emergence of the women's dress-pattern industry during the 1860s democratized female fashions. The mass production of paper patterns enabled women to make their own stylish clothes at will. Before the war, the treadle-powered sewing machine had eased the burden of clothing their families but had not convinced women that they could devise their own complicated outfits. But then the Civil War stimulated industry, including pattern production. Ebenezer Butterick began his pattern business in 1867 with 12 workers, a number that jumped to 140 in 1870. The availability of paper patterns made fashion at least theoretically accessible to women of every social class and occupation by the early 1870s.

Technology also offered women such new contrivances for the home as improved lamps and stoves. The mystique of domesticity slowed down the adoption of home technology during the 1860s and 1870s because it preached that only unfeminine, lazy, or incompetent women would use new-fangled machines to care for their families. Maintaining an old-fashioned household was such a matter of pride that many women hesitated to accept the aid of mechanical instruments.

Catharine Beecher was the first reformer to call for the adoption of technology, particularly in the kitchen, where, according to her, women spent over 50 percent of their time. In 1869, Beecher designed a model kitchen based on a ship's galley. It incorporated built-in flour and grain bins, a built-in dish draining board, a cast-iron stove set in an alcove with glass doors to block off the heat, and an indoor sink with two pumps, one for rain water and one for well water.

Other women besides Beecher were interested in technology and its applications. Before the Civil War, fifty-five patents were granted to women, but between 1860 and 1888 nearly 3,000 women applied for patents. It is believed that many other women's inventions were patented under men's names. Butterick's wife, for example, is believed to have created the first paper patterns.

Widespread prejudice and discrimination deterred many women from entering technological and scientific fields and from admitting to any interest in such matters. In 1850, America's first female astronomer, Maria Mitchell, had been elected to the American Academy of Arts and Sciences for her discovery of the comet that received her name, but another woman was not so honored until 1943. A mid-nineteenth century editor remarked: "If an unfortunate female should happen to possess a lurking fondness for any special scientific pursuit she is careful (if of any social position) to hide it as she would some deformity."

In spite of such discouraging attitudes, women attracted to science continued to pursue their interests. A number of women began to form scientific study groups during the mid-1860s. Groups of women interested in educational reform promoted the introduction of more scientific courses into women's curricula. And, in the 1870s, women approached male scientific societies requesting membership. They were, however, granted only the status of corresponding members who were neither expected to attend the meetings nor allowed to vote.

The practice of law was also difficult for women during the 1860s and 1870s. State licensing bodies simply barred women from taking the required examinations. In 1869, however, Arabella Babb Mansfield applied for admission to the bar in Iowa. She was allowed to take the examinations at the order of a judge who was sympathetic to women's rights. One of her examiners noted that Mansfield passed with high honors, giving "the very best rebuke possible to the imputation that ladies cannot qualify for the practice of law." Mansfield never practiced law, choosing instead to teach at Iowa Wesleyan and later at DePaul University in Indiana.

In the same year that Mansfield became the first licensed woman lawyer in the United States, Myra Bradwell applied to the Illinois Supreme Court for a law license. Bradwell had studied law with her husband while founding and editing the very successful *Chicago Legal News*. An avowed suffragist, she had also drafted several bills to expand women's property rights. In 1869, Bradwell took the licensing examination and passed it with credit but was denied a license because she was a woman. She appealed her case to the United States Supreme Court, which tossed the matter back to the State of Illinois. Bradwell was finally granted a license in 1890, four years before her death.

Other women soon became "firsts" in the legal field. In 1871, Phoebe Couzins became the first woman to receive a formal law degree when she graduated from Washington University in St. Louis. She was licensed in Missouri but never practiced law. Instead, she became a leading figure in the national woman suffrage movement. A year after Couzins' graduation, Charlotte E. Ray graduated from the law department of Howard University and was admitted to the District bar. She was the first black woman lawyer in the United States and the first woman admitted to practice in the District of Columbia.

Art was another area that attracted talented and ambitious women. Of course, women continued to produce a tremendous amount of folk art in their homes. Quilts especially reflected current events through the use of such designs as Sherman's March, the Underground Railroad, and the Slave Chain. But when the woman's pavilion at the Centennial Exposition in Philadelphia displayed women's artwork in 1876, almost none of the folk art created by self-taught women artists was included. Neither women's folk art nor, for that matter, very much of women's fine art was accorded serious attention or appraisal at that time. In fact, although women had been instrumental in raising the funds for the Centennial Exposition of 1876, they were denied exhibit space in the main exhibition hall and even had to raise additional money for the woman's pavilion.

Women who wanted to practice the fine arts did receive limited encouragement after the Civil War. It was now acceptable for them to move to cities and other countries for art training and to relocate frequently in search of commissions. Still, over half of mid-nineteenth century women artists chose to remain single rather than attempt to combine their demanding careers with marriage. Another change was the gradual admission of women to life drawing classes with nude models, which put them on a more even footing with men in artistic training. And in 1874, when the Art Students' League was established in New York City, it routinely admitted women. At the same time, art was increasingly being perceived as "feminine." In 1860, *The Canyon* claimed that the arts were in harmony with women's delicate and sensitive natures. The arts themselves were seen as embellishment and refinement, so it was not difficult for Americans to begin to think of them as a part of woman's sphere.

During the 1860s, a number of women sculptors emerged. The most prominent of these was Harriet Hosmer of Watertown, Massachusetts. Hosmer had studied in Rome with respected sculptor John Gibson during the 1850s. During the 1860s, her commissions ranged from London to San Francisco. As a sculptor of international repute, Hosmer enjoyed a rich social life, yet declined to marry. At the age of twenty-four, she had written to a friend: "Even if so inclined, an artist has no business to marry. For a man, it may be well enough, but not for a woman, on whose matrimonial duties and cares weigh more heavily, it is a moral wrong, I think, for she must either neglect her profession or her family, becoming neither a good wife and mother nor a good artist. My ambition is to become the latter, so I wage eternal feud with the consolidating knot." Never an ardent feminist, Hosmer did maintain that "every woman should have the opportunity of cultivating her talents to the fullest extent, for they were not given her for nothing."

Hosmer encouraged the work of Edmonia Lewis, a New Yorker of black and Chippewa Indian parentage. Lewis studied briefly with a Boston sculptor in the early 1860s and then went to study in Rome in 1865. By the 1870s, Lewis had a solid reputation in both the United States and Europe. Her works enjoyed quite a success at the Centennial Exposition of 1876 and demonstrated to many Americans that the artistic production of women could be both interesting and creative.

In the field of music, women composers were also illustrating that, despite such obstacles as lack of opportunities for training, prejudice against publishing their compositions, and the social and economic need to marry, they could produce fine work. By the time of the Civil War, several women composers had achieved public acclaim. Jane Slocum, for example, a young pianist from England, published songs and solo piano compositions into the 1850s. During the 1860s, Faustina Hassae Hodges, daughter of organist Edward Hodges and an organist herself, composed ballads, sacred songs, and piano pieces. One of her songs, "Rose Bush," reportedly sold 100,000 copies. Few American female composers of symphonies and concertos have been identified, but neither were there many American male composers since classical music in America concentrated on European repertory well into the late nineteenth century.

By the 1860s and 1870s, women were not only moving into the arts and professions but into all types of paid employment. Women continued to dominate the needle trades but were now present in growing numbers in retail sales, office work, cigar making, typography, commercial laundries, and various types of mills. Many of the jobs that women filled were "new," that is, they had not previously been filled by men but were created by the growing economy.

Whenever women were hired, wages fell. This was in harmony with the idea that, because woman's place was in the home, she was just an occasional worker interested in "pin money." Actually, numerous women worked to help support their families because many men were disabled or killed during the Civil War or were not paid a living wage. Furthermore, the number of single women who had to support themselves was rising. Yet American employers were still thinking of the ideal woman instead of facing the reality of employed women.

Female workers did not accept the rationalizations offered to them for their low pay, long hours, and terrible working conditions. A number of female workers, like many male workers, came to believe that some form of labor organization might help to improve their situations. Women often turned to men's labor organizations but soon learned that women were usually not welcome. By 1870, thirty-two unions existed in America, but women were barely represented in them, despite the marked increase in the number of women workers since 1860.

Employed women responded to their exclusion from male unions by forming their own groups. For example, the Lady Cigar Makers of Providence, Rhode Island, was organized in 1864. Although women cigar makers accounted for close to 10 percent of all cigar makers, they were denied membership in the national union. Another woman's union, the Collar Laundry Union of Troy, New York, was also founded in 1864. This group was remarkably successful and raised their wages to a level near that of working men. Middle- and upperclass women who continued to be interested in reform after the war organized other types of groups to help working women. Called working women's protective societies, these associations offered services such as legal aid, medical treatment, and advice to employed women.

In addition to the cause of working women, American women were interested in many other reform issues. Although the reform crusade had lost some of its impetus during the war years, it had not totally disappeared. During the 1860s and 1870s, American women worked for many reforms, including civil rights, woman suffrage, and temperance.

This last reform movement particularly attracted thousands of female supporters. Out of local bands of women who either prayed or destroyed stocks of whiskey came the National Woman's Christian Temperance Union, founded in 1874, with Annie Turner Wittenmyer of Iowa as its first president. To Wittenmyer, the crusade was a fulfillment of woman's moral role in the salvation of humankind. In an address in 1877 Wittenmyer stated her position: "We have been called by the Spirit of the Lord to lead the women of the world in a great and difficult reform movement, and thousands in our own, and other lands, are looking to us with hope and expectation. The drink system is the common enemy of women the world over, and the plans we inaugurate, will be eagerly sought after by the women of all civilized nations, and as the success of all moral reforms depends largely upon women, the world will halt, or move in its onward march toward millennial glory, as we halt or march." This organization soon became the largest woman's organization in the nineteenth century.

Women interested in improving American society also continued their interest in helping the black people of America after the war's end in 1865. Many women participated in the effort to aid newly freed slaves by working for the Freedmen's Bureau, in charity organizations, and as missionary teachers in the South. One of the advocates of relief work for freed blacks was Josephine Griffing, who served as the general agent for the Freedman's Relief Association in Washington between 1865 and 1872. This benevolent organization differed from the government-supported Freedmen's Bureau in many ways. The most notable was Griffing's idea that freed blacks ought to be settled throughout northern and western states at governmental expense. She lobbied Congress to accept her plans while she turned her office and home into a settlement house for freed blacks. Griffing's plan, however, helped no more than a few thousand blacks to resettle.

Black women also worked energetically on behalf of black Americans. Fanny Jackson Coppin, born a slave in the District of Columbia, became an outstanding educator of black youth in the 1870s. Because the southern states seldom made any significant provisions for the education of freed slaves, many educated black women moved south as missionary teachers for black charity schools. Typically, they taught children during the day, adults at night, and held Sabbath schools on Sundays.

Missionary teachers were often supported by missionary and other similar societies dedicated to helping black Americans. In 1864, Sara G. Stanley asked for the support of the American Missionary Association so that she could teach in the South. "No thought of suffering, and privation, nor even death, should deter me from making every effort possible, for the moral and intellectual elevation of these degraded people," she asserted. She would receive ten dollars a month plus board for her efforts.

For black women in the South, the Civil War radically changed their lives in some ways but not in others. Marriage was now a legal institution for blacks. This resulted in a widespread move to formalize individual marriages and establish stable families including both parents. Massive marriage ceremonies involved as many as sixty or seventy couples. Former slaves worked diligently to locate spouses or children who had been sold away from them, some traveling from state to state and advertising in newspapers.

Marriage and the family might have been recognized legally, but the economic insecurity of the black family remained. Consequently, a large number of newly freed black women labored in the fields or foundries next to men in order to supplement their families' inadequate incomes. Black men who viewed women's labor outside the home as a badge of slavery watched their wives work in the fields and as domestics. Because sharecropping replaced slavery as the dominant mode of production in the postwar South, black women, despite their desire to escape field work, continued to labor in the cotton, tobacco, and rice fields. Other black women took domestic employment as washwomen, domestics, nursemaids, and seamstresses, jobs they had performed as slaves. By 1877, half of adult black women held jobs, while others worked in the fields with their sharecropper husbands.

Freedom offered some advantages to black women workers. Many could now define their own working hours to some extent or could change employers at the end of a contract term. They could marry and bear children without fearing the loss of family members through sale. They also had the opportunity to appeal to authority when dissatisfied. Formal complaints to agents of the Freedmen's Bureau indicated problems that were nevertheless different from those that arose under slavery. Employers commonly withheld pay to control black women workers and sometimes reacted to them with violence, yet the legal hold of slavery was gone. Women resisted, filed complaints, moved to other plantations, or took other jobs. Wages were low and conditions were difficult, but black women were no longer chattels.

The lives of black women, however, were still circumscribed in many ways. Free black women were denied vocational training and the right to hold certain jobs. While black men were given the right to vote and to hold office in the late 1860s, black women were overlooked. Black men could now own land, but black women seldom had the means to do so.

A large number of rural black women tried to improve their lot by migrating to southern cities. Here they found poor housing, limited job openings, and low wages. In Jackson, Mississippi, and Galveston, Texas, black washwomen protested and went on strike to receive $1.50 per day. Whites arrested the leaders and threatened to require license fees of washwomen. Domestic servants were even worse off. They worked long hours, seven days a week, for which they received low pay supplemented by cast-off clothing and leftover food. Some urban black women tried to escape these evils by selling such goods as spruce beer, peanuts, blueberries, strawberries, and vegetables in local markets. Those women who could raise the necessary capital opened restaurants, grocery stores, and boardinghouses. Despite independence, these urban black women found that their lives were still harsh.

Those black women who migrated to northern cities after the Civil War did not find the opportunities that they had hoped for, either. Like their southern counterparts, they were limited to domestic, menial, and service jobs with long hours and poor pay. In 1871, a northern black woman complained in the Philadelphia *Post:* "Why is it that when respectable women answer an advertisement for a dressmaker, they are invariably refused, or offered a place to cook or scrub, or to do housework: and when application is made to manufactories immediately after having seen an advertisement for operators or finishers, meet with the same reply." These women were further dismayed to learn that, although they paid taxes, their children were denied admission to tax-supported schools because of their race.

Black women, disillusioned with the southern plantation or the urban areas of the South and North, sometimes turned their faces westward during the late 1860s and 1870s. As pioneers and Exodusters (communities of black immigrants, especially in Kansas) they soon discovered that they could not escape racial prejudice. It followed them even into the most progressive of western communities. Once again they were relegated to farm labor and domestic service. In one Iowa town, a black woman who worked as a washwoman for many of the community's white women lived by herself in poverty despite continuous labor and was patronizingly called "Nigger Ellen" by the townspeople. It must have been a harsh blow to learn that even the supposedly egalitarian frontier placed severe limits on the lives of black women.

Southern white women also faced difficult conditions after the Civil War. High-born ladies now learned to perform domestic tasks without the help of servants and to run plantations without the aid of their men who had been disabled or killed during the war. Southern women of all classes were forced to take jobs as clerks, teachers, and industrial laborers to help support their families. The thousands who could not find employment had to depend on rations from northern-based charity groups. Already bitter over the war's destruction of their lifestyles, southern women lived in fear of the black occupation patrols posted in their towns or regions. And when black males were given the right to vote in 1866, many disenfranchised white females were outraged.

Because the labor and any cash income that they produced were now in demand to help keep agricultural enterprises afloat, southern women did seem to gain more respect as farmers after the war. As they moved into the fields and various aspects of farm operations, women proved themselves as workers and managers. One notable female farmer was Frances Butler, the daughter of Frances Kemble and Pierce Butler. When her father died shortly after the war, Butler took over the management of his rice and cotton fields on the sea islands of Georgia. She negotiated labor contracts with black workers, acted as her own overseer, and paid wages without resorting to sharecropping. Many novelists found inspiration in these women. For example, Elizabeth Pringle, writing under the pseudonym, Patience Pennington, dramatized women planters in *A Woman Rice Planter* in 1913.

Western women also participated more fully in farming and home-steading after the Civil War. On the Great Plains, women often managed an isolated claim by themselves while their husbands worked elsewhere to raise the necessary capital for seeds, equipment, and building materials. Others worked alongside their fathers or husbands in "breaking" the claim for cultivation. During the 1870s, one Dakota woman graphically described the demands placed on women settlers: "I had lived on a homestead long enough to learn some fundamental things: that while a woman had more independence here than in any other part of the world, she was expected to contribute as much as a man—not in the same way, it is true, but to the same degree: that people who fought the frontier had to be prepared to meet any emergency: that the person who wasn't willing to try anything once wasn't equipped to be a settler."

Single women also took advantage of the Homestead Act of 1862, which offered a settler a free quarter section of land on the condition that she or he cultivate it for a period of five years. A sample of land office data for Colorado and Wyoming shows that the number of female home-stead entrants ranged from 11.9 to 18.2 percent of the total. The data further indicate that 42.4 percent of women succeeded in placing a final claim on their homestead as opposed to only 37 percent of successful men. Frequently called "girl homesteaders," these women were judged an "interesting segment of the population" by one Dakotan.

Since the opening of the Oregon trail and the discovery of gold in California in the late 1840s, female migrants had entered the mining, lumbering, farming, and ranching areas of the far West. They traveled overland, across the Isthmus of Panama, or "around the horn" of South America. In many cases, women found the hardships of the trip less severe than they had feared. Female migrants traded with American Indians, who often were not as fierce and savage as women had been led to believe. As one woman settler later wrote: "We suffered vastly more from fear of the Indians before starting than we did on the plains." Other women raved about the beauty of the prairies, plains, and mountains, and extolled the "wonders of travel." In other cases, however, women became discouraged, frightened, and determined to return to their former homes as soon as possible.

Some plains and far western women had lifestyles similar to earlier frontierswomen on agrarian frontiers. An army wife of the 1860s enjoyed her rough and erratic life in frontier forts. She traveled about Kansas and Oklahoma in an army ambulance without much discomfort or danger from Indians. She basked in the attention paid her as one of the few women in camp and decided that "there is considerable romance in my manner of living." Some women, however, found themselves thrust into unexpected situations. In 1874, an Arizona army wife wrote: "I concluded that my New England bringing up had been too serious, and wondered if I had made a dreadful mistake following my husband to Arizona. I debated the question with myself from all sides, and decided then and there that young army wives should stay at home with their mothers and fathers, and not go into such wild and uncouth places."

Other western women with unusual lifestyles were those who took jobs in service industries, including dance halls, saloons, and brothels. Many "soiled doves" who provided companionship and sexual services were hardworking laborers and business entrepreneurs. Irish immigrant Mary Josephine Welch, for example, settled in Helena, Montana, in 1867, where she established the Red Light Saloon. Soon known as "Chicago Joe" after her last hometown, Welch brought in women as dollar-a-dance workers in her saloon. These women, known as "hurdy-gurdy girls" after the popular stringed instrument of the day, earned up to fifty dollars an evening. In 1873, however, Montana passed legislation against dance halls in an attempt to attract a stable family population.

Apparently, women's adaptation depended to a great extent on their backgrounds, personalities, philosophies, and occupations. Certainly by the 1860s and 1870s, there were all types of women living in the West. Many were town dwellers who lived in the western settlements that composed the urban frontier. Others were single women in search of employment, husbands, or both. Others were prostitutes who worked the cattle towns and gold camps. Some, like the popular trail guide, Mountain Charley, donned male clothing and assumed male roles. Many were immigrants from Canada, Mexico, Germany, Holland, England, Ireland, Sweden, Norway, and the Orient. Many others were associated with such religious groups as the Church of Jesus Christ of Latter-day Saints, or Mormons, in Utah or the Presentation Sisters in the Dakotas. Others were ardent suffragists, like Abigail Scott Duniway of Oregon. And still others were black, like Mary Ellen "Mammy" Pleasant, a California pioneer and boardinghouse keeper in San Francisco.

Frontierswomen were not only a diverse group but often a politically privileged one as well. The right of suffrage was first granted to women by four western governments. In 1869, Wyoming Territory gave women the right to vote. Supposedly, this occurred because of the urging of Esther Morris and others, who argued that woman suffrage would attract women to Wyoming, thus balancing the population ratio of six men to one woman and introducing a "law and order" faction into rather unbridled Wyoming society. Utah followed with its own woman suffrage law in 1870. Some scholars believe that leaders of the Church of Latter-day Saints wished to insure their political power over the inroads of male non-Mormons, or Gentiles, entering the area. There is some evidence that church leaders were also interested in allowing Mormon women to vote in favor of polygamy, the extremely controversial institution of plural marriage practiced by Mormons at that time.

Largely because of the efforts of Oregonian Abigail Scott Duniway and her suffrage newspaper, *The New Northwest,* Washington Territory passed a woman suffrage measure in 1883, and Idaho in 1896. Although women were thus granted a degree of political participation in these frontier regions, there is little evidence that a revolution in sex roles or women's rights was under way.

Many changes also occurred in the American West for native women. By the 1860s and 1870s, American Indian communities had been disrupted by white settlement, their families torn apart by wars, and the status of women reduced because of the adoption of male-oriented white values. They were increasingly confined to reservations, where their numbers were decimated by malnutrition, famine, and disease. And their children attended reservation schools that attempted to change Indians into pseudowhites by erasing both their culture and their pride in it.

Still, American Indian women of the Plains and other interior tribes did have a measure of choice and control over their lives. White observers often thought that native women were degraded because they performed all domestic and agricultural labor while men engaged in hunting and warfare. Actually, this division of labor extended respect and the right of decision-making to both women and men. Also, Indian women had a degree of control over childbearing. In addition, most Indian cultures stressed the need for both partners to be satisfied in a marriage relationship. Divorce was usually fairly simple to obtain; thus native women could escape abusive, lazy, or intemperate mates without losing their children and personal property as white women usually did.

Furthermore, some American Indian women still exercised a degree of power within their tribes. Occasionally, Plains Indian women served as shamans, medicine people, and warriors. Matrilineal tribes, such as the Mandans of the Dakotas and Tlingits of the Pacific Northwest, vested land in the eldest female of the family who then passed ownership of lands, fields, gardens, houses, and stock through her female descendants. American Indian women also frequently functioned as decision makers and often sat on the council of elders. They participated in decisions that concerned both wars and hunts.

Some Indian women served as spokespeople for their communities by carrying Indian grievances and misgivings to white authorities. The best known of these was Sarah Winnemucca, a Paiute woman from Nevada. In the 1870s and 1880s, Winnemucca served as chief of her tribe and made many futile attempts to save her people from the ravages of white invasion. As a public lecturer dressed in beautiful native garb and the author of *Life Among the Paiutes: Their Wrongs and Claims* (1883), she alerted the nation to the cause of the decimated American Indians.

Winnemucca was far from alone on the lecture circuit during these years. By 1877, when President Rutherford B. Hayes issued the order that removed the army of occupation from the South and technically brought Reconstruction to a close, women were clamoring for all manner of modifications in American society. Women's rights, woman suffrage, civil rights, black rights, temperance, and American Indian rights were some of the issues. Other women who did not mount the lecture platform were also initiating modifications in the prevailing social system by pushing into jobs, professions, and other endeavors previously dominated by men. Clearly, a major theme during the 1860s and 1870s was change in women's roles, rights, and responsibilities. These changes did not dissipate with the end of the Reconstruction era but continued to grow during the period known as the Gilded Age, which spanned the years between 1877 and the early 1890s. The social, political, and economic developments of this period put additional stress on the customary stereotype of the American woman.

Drawing its name from a Mark Twain novel, the Gilded Age was seen as being gilt on the outside and base metal underneath; as being all style and no substance. It was particularly marked by enormous expansion in industrialization, urbanization, and immigration. Although these three trends were not unique to the Gilded Age, they accelerated during the period.

The first of these three developments—increasing industrialization—affected American women in a number of ways. The proliferation of technological devices and convenience goods changed the nature of women's work within the home. At the same time, the rapid expansion of the industrial work force opened a growing number of employment opportunities to women outside of the home. As a result of mass production and early assembly lines, jobs once done by skilled male workers could be performed by unskilled workers willing to work for low wages. Married women were often forced by economic necessity to seek paid employment in order to supplement the marginal wages earned by their husbands. Immigrant daughters were expected to contribute to their families' meager incomes. And an increasing number of single women, many of them migrants from rural areas, needed to provide their own support.

Consequently, by 1890 nearly four million women worked for wages outside their homes. Approximately one out of every seven women was employed. The overwhelming number of these women were single, with slightly over 4 percent married and almost 6 percent widowed. About one million of them were black women concentrated in southern agriculture, domestic labor, and service industries. Only a small number of black women held factory employment.

During the 1880s and 1890s, women's participation in the labor force was characterized by low pay, lack of skills, and segregation in "women's" jobs, meaning those that required minimal training and garnered little respect. In the textile industry, for example, men served as managers and as such skilled operatives as fabric cutters, while women worked as machine operators, trimmers, and finishers. In bakeries, men were bakers and women were packers. In breweries, men were brewers and women were bottle washers.

Unskilled women earned considerably less than did skilled men, but even skilled women earned only about half the wage commanded by their skilled male counterparts. Black women earned only half the pay of white women. Moreover, women flocked to those industries that would employ them—textile, garment, tobacco, printing, and food processing—thus insuring that women's wages would remain low.

A growing number of women sought to redress their poor wages and dismal working conditions by joining labor organizations. By 1895, women accounted for 5 percent of union membership. After 1881, when the Knights of Labor voted to open membership to women, female workers joined formerly male assemblies as well as organized female assemblies. Black women workers also participated in this movement, particularly by forming assemblies of laundresses, chambermaids, and housekeepers. Women's organizational efforts were aided by such paid organizers as Leonora Barry, who lectured, inspected factories, and organized labor assemblies throughout the 1880s.

Women members of the Knights of Labor organized strikes for wage increases, shorter hours, and improved conditions. In 1884, several women's assemblies of textile workers and hatmakers gained the admiration of labor leader Terence V. Powderly by their effective strikes. The Knights of Labor encouraged the efforts of their female members by organizing a woman's department and supporting the causes of equal pay for equal work, woman suffrage, and temperance. Unfortunately, after Barry left her post as general investigator in 1890, many of the union's women-oriented programs were abandoned.

Women were also eligible for membership in the American Federation of Labor (AFL) from its inception in 1881, but it was not until 1888 that its president, Samuel Gompers, urged the organization of women workers. Women soon found union dues too high for their limited wages and the reception given them by male members decidedly cool. Still, in 1888, Elizabeth Morgan became the prime mover in the formation of the Ladies Federal Labor Union, and in 1890, Mary Burke of the Retail Clerks International served as the first woman delegate to an AFL convention. In 1891, the AFL created the office of National Organizer for women; in 1892, bindery worker Mary E. Kenney was appointed to the post.

Despite the moves of organized labor on behalf of women, resistance to the idea of women working remained strong. Male workers feared that women's willingness to work for low wages would devalue their own earning power. Many also clung to the ideology of women as wives and mothers while refusing to recognize the social changes and economic necessities that propelled women into the labor force.

Thus, women saw little improvement in wages, hours, and working conditions. In 1893, Helen Campbell described in *Women Wage-Earners* the conditions encountered by the Massachusetts Bureau of Labor. She wrote that it found "employees packed 'like sardines in a box'; thirty-five persons, for example, in a small attic without ventilation of any kind." Campbell added: "There are no conveniences for women; and men and women use the same closets, wash-basins, and drinking cups. . . . In another case a water-closet in the center of the room filled it with a sickening stench."

Campbell's report also detailed health hazards to women workers. Those who worked as feather-sorters, fur-workers, cotton-sorters, or with other dust-laden materials were prone to lung and bronchial diseases. Caustic soda ate at soap-workers' hands, which became raw and bleeding by the end of the day. Match-workers often had their jaws eaten away by phosphorus. And button and pin workers regularly suffered jammed and caught fingers which were treated at the worker's own expense after the first three injuries.

The situation of black working women was even more dismal. Most were not eligible for union membership because they were seldom involved in the trades or factory labor. Racial prejudice and the accompanying belief that blacks were best at heavy labor confined black women to such menial jobs as laundry workers, scrubwomen, cooks, and tobacco strippers. Black women were prevalent in tenant farming and sharecropping; black women prisoners were used as convict labor in field and road work. In 1890, census figures indicate that 975,530 nonwhite (black, Indian, and Oriental) women were employed. Of these, 30.83 percent were servants, 15.9 percent were laundresses, while only 2.76 percent worked in manufacturing.

Black women were almost totally excluded from office and sales work. These jobs, which had once been the province of white men, were increasingly being filled by white native-born women. In 1870, there were 19,000 female office workers, a figure that had jumped to 75,000 by 1890. Women also rapidly replaced men as telegraph and telephone operators and sales clerks.

Employed women also moved into the profession. Nursing and teaching were becoming female dominated. While their status was slightly higher than that of other working women, nurses and teachers also endured low wages, long hours, and poor working situations. In medicine, such women physicians as Mary Putnam Jacobi and Elizabeth Blackwell continued to work at improving the professional status of female doctors. And in science, women began to establish their right to formal training and membership in professional associations.

Despite overwhelming odds, some black women fought their way into skilled jobs and professions. In 1883, Mary Ann Shadd Cary received a law degree from Howard University and became a successful lawyer in Washington. In 1886, Lucy Craft Laney founded the Haines Institute in Augusta, Georgia, a school particularly dedicated to training blacks as teachers and nurses. And Janie Porter Barret of Virginia became a teacher at Hampton Institute and, in 1890, founded the South's first settlement house for blacks.

Southern white women also invaded the professions that had so long been closed to them. In North Carolina, Cornelia Ann Phillips Spencer became a noted journalist and educational crusader who, in 1891, helped to found the Normal and Industrial School for Women, now the University of North Carolina at Greensboro. Southern women also continued to move into agricultural pursuits and increasingly worked in offices, stores, and factories. By 1890, slightly more than two out of five textile workers in the South were female.

In the West, the majority of women continued to engage in agriculture and domestic production, although a growing number moved into manufacturing, office work, and sales. By 1890, 13 percent of western women worked outside of their homes, as compared to 17 percent nationally. Western women were highly represented in the professions, however, with 14 percent employed in professional areas as opposed to 8 percent overall. Ella L. Knowles, for example, passed the Montana bar examination with distinction in 1889, thus becoming the state's first female attorney. Knowles practiced law in Helena and became active in the Populist party and in the campaign for woman suffrage after 1890.

The second major trend of the Gilded Age—urbanization—also had many effects on women. During the 1870s and 1880s, America's urban population was growing more rapidly than was its rural population. Cities such as New York and Chicago were becoming magnets for immigration from abroad and migration from rural areas, were serving as major marketplaces and centers of manufacturing, and were contributing to an upheaval of ideas and values.

Urban living contributed to women's growing employment, education, and social activism. Urban women also increasingly chose singlehood, divorce, and decreased fertility. The latter trend—shrinking family size—was most pronounced among native born, middle class, well-educated white women who, during the 1880s, bore between two and three children.

During the 1870s and 1880s, the concept of voluntary motherhood was supported by suffragists and moral reformers as well as by women who desired freedom from continual pregnancies and childcare. Because birth control devices were not yet widely disseminated, birth was controlled primarily through abstinence, male continence or the avoidance of ejaculation, and coitus interruptus.

Those who feared women's control over childbirth and its possible ramifications—medical complications and population decrease—responded to the falling birth rate by launching a crusade against planned parenthood and abortion in particular. Such groups as the American Medical Association and the Young Men's Christian Association (YMCA) initiated national programs. The YMCA's agent for the "Suppression of Vice," Anthony Comstock, not only filed complaints against those who sold contraceptives and distributed birth control information, but in 1873, persuaded the Congress of the United States to adopt an act for the "suppression of trade in, and circulation of, obscene literature and articles of immoral use." Called the Comstock Law, this legislation banned "any article or thing designed or intended for the prevention of conception or procuring of abortion" and the "advertisement" of such contraband.

Both black and immigrant urban women were comparatively slow to become involved with voluntary motherhood. Black women's fertility, which had begun to decline somewhat even before the Civil War, continued to drop during the 1880s. This was not, however, a result of the mistaken idea that black families during the 1870s and 1880s tended to be matriarchies. Rather, the majority of black households were two-parent and much more stable than generally believed. A study of black families in Boston in 1880 demonstrated that black families remained intact during moves to the city. Neither did immigrant families disintegrate during migration. After resettlement, immigrants tended to cling to traditional ideas of family size and limited roles for women, at least until the second generation began to introduce modifications. Eventually, these women expanded their domestic roles, sought vocational training and other types of education, and frequently took paid employment. Moreover, the size of their families slowly decreased.

These changes in roles and fertility rates reveal the tremendous impact of the third major development of the Gilded Age—immigration—on non-American-born women. Gradually, immigrant women and their families were forced to consider, and often to adopt, new ways of thinking about women's domestic functions, paid employment, and education. Whether they went to the frontier or settled in urban areas, non-American-born women frequently modified their attitudes and behaviors as a result of the new environment. As they adapted to the language, lifestyles, and values they encountered in America, they began to revise their own ways of thinking and acting. Through informal networks of friends and family, ethnic churches and organizations, and social agencies, they came to understand their new home and often to adopt a freer lifestyle than they had followed in their lands of origin.

At the same time, immigrant women contributed much to their new country. Young single immigrant women joined the labor force in positions ranging from factory operatives to domestics. Besides laboring, immigrant women often thought, wrote, and worked for reform. Irish women were particularly active in reform causes. Charlotte Smith O'Brien campaigned for social services for immigrant women and was instrumental in the establishment of the Our Lady of the Rosary Center in New York in 1830. Irish women religious, including the Sisters of Mercy, the Presentation Sisters, and the so-called "gray nuns," established and provided a myriad of social services. Many other women who immigrated to America during the Gilded Age, including Russian Jew Emma Goldman and Polish Jew Rose Schneiderman, became leading reformers of the following decades.

Clearly, the years spanning the period of 1865 to 1890 were marked by a ferment of change. Neither the postwar upheaval of Reconstruction nor the industrialization, urbanization, and immigration of the Gilded Age reinforced the customary image of the American woman. Although the stereotype of the American woman had not sustained the mortal injuries for which women's rights leaders of the post-Civil War years hoped, it was showing signs of wear. As the Progressive Era began to dawn, it seemed quite likely that the invented American woman was in for yet further modification.

SUGGESTIONS FOR FURTHER READING

Andrews, William D., and Deborah C. Andrews. "Technology and the Housewife in Nineteenth-Century America." *Women's Studies* (1974): 309–328.

Aron, Cindy S. "'To Barter Their Souls for Gold': Female Clerks in Federal Government Offices, 1862–1890." *Journal of American History* 67 (March 1981): 835–853.

Banner, Lois W. *Elizabeth Cady Stanton: A Radical for Women's Rights.* Boston: Little, Brown and Company, 1980.

Beezley, William H., and Joseph P. Hobbs. "'Nice Girls Don't Sweat': Women in American Sport." *Journal of Popular Culture* 16 (Spring 1983): 42–53.

Berch, Bettina. *The Endless Day: The Political Economy of Women and Work.* New York: Harcourt Brace Jovanovich, Inc., 1982.

Berkeley, Kathleen C. "The Ladies Want to Bring About Reform in the Public Schools': Public Education and Women's Rights in the Post–Civil War South." *History of Education Quarterly* 24 (Spring 1984): 45–58.

Berkin, Carol Ruth, and Mary Beth Norton, eds. *Women of America: A History.* Boston: Houghton Mifflin Company, 1979. Part III.

Blocker, Jr., Jack S., ed. "Annie Wittenmyer and the Women's Crusade." *Ohio History* 88 (Autumn 1979): 419–422.

Brown, Minnie Miller. "Black Women in American Agriculture." *Agricultural History* 50 (January 1976): 202–212.

Brumgardt, John R., ed. *Civil War Nurse: The Diary and Letters of Hannah Ropes*. Knoxville: The University of Tennessee Press, 1980.

Bulger, Margery A. "American Sportswomen in the 19th Century." *Journal of Popular Culture* 16 (Fall 1982): 1–16.

Carrell, Kimberley W. "The Industrial Revolution Comes to the Home: Kitchen Design Reform and Middle-Class Women." *Journal of American Culture* 2 (Fall 1979): 488–499.

Clark, E. Culpepper. "Sarah Morgan and Francis Dawson: Raising the Woman Question in Reconstruction South Carolina." *South Carolina Historical Magazine* 81 (January 1980): 8–23.

Clinton, Catherine. *The Other Civil War: American Women in the Nineteenth Century*. New York: Hill and Wang, 1984. Chapter 5. Collier-Thomas, Bettye. "The Impact of Black Women in Education: An Historical Overview." *Journal of Negro Education* 51 (Summer 1982): 173–180.

Cowan, Ruth Schwartz. "From Virginia Dare to Virginia Slims: Women and Technology in American Life." *Technology and Culture* 20 (January 1979): 51–63.

de Graaf, Lawrence. "Race, Sex, and Region: Black Women in the American West, 1850–1920." *Pacific Historical Review* 49 (May 1980): 285–314.

Diner, Hasia R. *Erin's Daughters in America: Irish Immigrant Women in the Nineteenth Century*. Baltimore: Johns Hopkins University Press, 1983.

DuBois, Ellen C. *Feminism and Suffrage: The Emergence of an Independent Women's Movement in America, 1848–1869*. Ithaca: Cornell University Press, 1978. 53–78.

Dunfey, Julie. "'Living the Principle' of Plural Marriage: Mormon Women, Utopia, and Female Sexuality in the Nineteenth Century." *Feminist Studies* 10 (Fall 1984): 523–536.

Dye, Nancy Schrom. "The Louisville Woolen Mills Strike of 1887: A Case Study of Working Women, the Knights of Labor, and Union Organization in the New South." *Register of the Kentucky Historical Society* 82 (Spring 1984): 136–150.

Elbert, Sarah. *A Hunger for Home: Louisa May Alcott and Little Women*. Philadelphia: Temple University Press, 1984.

Epstein, Barbara Leslie. *The Politics of Domesticity: Women, Evangelism, and Temperance in Nineteenth-Century America*. Middletown, CT: Wesleyan University Press, 1981.

Faragher, John Mack. *Women and Men on the Overland Trail*. New Haven: Yale University Press, 1979.

Foster, Lawrence. "Polygamy and the Frontier: Mormon Women in Early Utah." *Utah Historical Quarterly* 50 (Summer 1982): 268–289.

Godfrey, Kenneth W., Audrey M. Godfrey, and Jill Mulvay Derr. *Women's Voices: An Untold History of the Latter-Day Saints, 1830–1900*. Salt Lake City: Deseret Book Company, 1982.

Gordon, Jean. "Early American Women Artists and the Social Context in Which They Worked." *American Quarterly* 30 (Spring 1978): 54–69.

Gordon, Linda. "The Long Struggle for Reproductive Rights." *Radical America* 15 (Spring 1981): 74–88.

———. "Voluntary Motherhood: The Beginnings of the Birth-Control Movement." In *Family Life in America, 1620–2000,* edited by Mel Albin and Dominick Cavaloo, 131–147. New York: Revisionary Press, 1981.

Gutman, Herbert G. "Persistent Myths about the Afro-American Family." *Journal of Interdisciplinary History* 6 (Autumn 1975): 181–210.

Harris, Barbara J. *Beyond Her Sphere: Women and the Professions in American History.* Westport, CT: Greenwood Press, 1978.

Hedges, Elaine. "The Nineteenth-Century Diarist and Her Quilts." *Feminist Studies* 8 (Summer 1982): 293–308.

James, Edward T., ed. *Notable American Women 1607–1950: A Biographical Dictionary.* Cambridge, MA: Belknap Press, 1971.

Jeffrey, Julie Roy. *Frontier Women: The Trans-Mississippi West, 1840–1880.* New York: Hill and Wang, 1979.

———. "Women in the Southern Farmers' Alliance: A Reconsideration of the Role and Status of Women in the Late Nineteenth-Century South." In *Our American Sisters: Women in American Life and Thought,* edited by Jean E. Friedman and William G. Shade, 348–371. Lexington, MA: D. C. Heath & Company, 1982.

Jones, Jacqueline. *Soldiers of Light and Love: Northern Teachers and Georgia Blacks, 1865–1873.* Chapel Hill: University of North Carolina Press, 1980.

Kerber, Linda K., and Jane DeHart Mathews, eds. *Women's America: Refocusing the Past.* New York: Oxford University Press, 1978.

Kessler-Harris, Alice. *Out to Work: A History of Wage-Earning Women in the United States.* New York: Oxford University Press, 1982.

Kohlstedt, Sally Gregory. "In From the Periphery: American Women in Science, 1830–1880." *Signs* 4 (Autumn 1978): 81–96.

Lerner, Gerda, ed. *Black Women in White America: A Documentary History.* New York: Random House, 1973.

Lupton, Mary Jane. "Ladies Entrance: Women and Bars." *Feminist Studies* 5 (Fall 1979): 571–588.

Massey, Mary Elizabeth. *Bonnet Brigades: American Women and the Civil War.* New York: Alfred A. Knopf, 1966.

Morantz, Regina Markell. "Feminism, Professionalism, and Germs: The Thought of Mary Putnam Jacobi and Elizabeth Blackwell." *American Quarterly* 5 (Winter 1982): 459–478.

Painter, Diann Holland. "The Black Woman in American Society." *Current History* 70 (May 1976): 224–227, 234.

Painter, Nell. *Black Migration to Kansas After Reconstruction.* New York: Alfred A. Knopf, 1977.

Pleck, Elizabeth H. "The Two-Parent Household: Black Family Structure in Late Nineteenth-Century Boston." *Journal of Social History* 6 (Fall 1972): 3–31.

Pursell, Carroll. "Women Inventors in America." *Technology and Culture* 22 (July 1981): 545–49.

Richey, Eleanor. "Sagebrush Princess with a Cause: Sarah Winnemucca." *The American West* 12 (November 1975): 30–33, 57–63.

Riley, Glenda. "Farm Women's Role in the Agricultural Development of South Dakota." *South Dakota History* 13 (Spring/Summer 1983): 83–121.

———. *Women and Indians on the Frontier, 1825–1915.* Albuquerque: University of New Mexico Press, 1984.

Roeder, Richard B. "Crossing the Gender Line: Ella L. Knowles, Montana's First Woman Lawyer." *Montana the Magazine of Western History* 32 (Summer 1982): 64–75.

Rogers, Gayle J. "The Changing Image of the Southern Woman: A Performer on a Pedestal." *Journal of Popular Culture* 16 (Winter 1982): 60–67.

Ryan, Mary P. *Womanhood in America From Colonial Times to the Present.* New York: New Viewpoints, 1979. Chapter 4.

Schlissel, Lillian. *Women's Diaries of the Westward Journey.* New York: Schocken Books, 1982.

Scott, Anne Firor. *The Southern Lady: From Pedestal to Politics, 1830–1930.* Chicago: University of Chicago Press, 1970.

Stage, Sarah. *Female Complaints: Lydia Pinkham and the Business of Women's Medicine.* New York: W. W. Norton & Company, 1979.

Sterling, Dorothy, ed. *We Are Your Sisters: Black Women in the Nineteenth Century.* New York: W. W. Norton & Company, 1984.

Terborg-Penn, Rosalyn. "Teaching the History of Black Women: A Bibliographical Essay." *The History Teacher* 13 (February 1980): 245–250.

Walsh, Margaret. "The Democratization of Fashion: The Emergence of the Women's Dress Pattern Industry." *Journal of American History* 66 (September 1979): 299–313.

Wertheimer, Barbara Mayer. *We Were There: The Story of Working Women in America.* New York: Pantheon Books, 1977.

Woloch, Nancy. *Women and the American Experience.* New York: Alfred A. Knopf, 1984. Chapters 9–10.

Unemployed, homeless women line up outside the women's almshouse on Blackwell's Island, New York, in 1903. Courtesy of the Byron Collection, Museum of the City of New York, New York, New York.

CHAPTER 6

"Reordering Women's Sphere":
The Progressive Era
1890–1917

T HE 1890s was an especially difficult decade for the United States. The nation suffered a debilitating depression between 1893 and 1897 that thoroughly shook many Americans' belief in economic opportunity. A number of leaders came to realize that hard work did not automatically guarantee success; rather, governmental welfare and social justice programs were needed to redress the injustices of an imperfect economic system. Unbridled enthusiasm for the pursuit of wealth and the creation of gigantic corporations was increasingly replaced by a concern for trust-busting and consumers' rights.

The malaise that affected many Americans during the 1890s was exacerbated by the increase of labor violence, the multiplication of urban slums, the spread of disease, and the growth of poverty. People began to talk of reform—in industry, education, government, race relations, the family, and women's roles. By the first decade of the twentieth century, reformers calling themselves "progressives" had emerged. The various reform movements that developed during the 1890s and early 1900s were all aimed at renovating American society, politics, and economic life. Young, educated, and middle-class women and men formed the vanguard of the Progressive movement. With the strong faith in progress that led to their name, these reformers committed themselves to a thorough reworking of American institutions and values.

There were few women living in America whose lives were not touched in some way by Progressivism. Untold thousands became active participants in reform efforts. Millions of others found opportunities in such new areas as education and employment. And almost all were encouraged to believe that the traditional image of women as domestic and passive beings, uninvolved in the larger society outside of their own homes, was about to undergo extensive revision. It would only gradually become apparent that the characterization of the American woman as passive, dependent, and domestic would continue.

Thousands of women flocked to the various reform causes. Of course, women had long been involved in reform movements, notably abolitionism, temperance, and women's rights. During the 1890s and early 1900s, however, women became involved in reform activities more than ever before. Women worked individually, joined organizations of men and women, and became members of women's voluntary associations in an effort to right a multitude of wrongs.

Women reformers, for example, enthusiastically entered the Progressive crusade against prostitution. Calling prostitution a "Social Evil" that constituted a moral problem as well as a national menace, reformers called on the government to control it. Unfortunately, making prostitution a criminal offense only drove it underground. The streetwalker replaced the brothel; pimps and crime syndicates took over the organization and marketing of prostitutes. Attempts to abolish prostitution thus failed, leaving other problems in their wake.

Women's efforts to alleviate the evils caused by poverty and urban slums were somewhat more successful. Urbanization and massive immigration had, by the 1890s, created cities rife with tenements, crime, disease, and despair. By 1900, six American cities numbered over a half million people; three of them included over one million. Like most American cities, all six were marked by a notorious inability to solve their proliferating social problems.

The settlement house movement was the primary response of women reformers to urban difficulties. One of the early prime movers was Jane Addams. Born in Illinois in 1860, Addams attended Rockford College and later left medical school in 1883 due to poor health. While traveling in Europe to recuperate, Addams observed a number of social experiments, particularly in England. This led her to return to Chicago and establish Hull-House in 1889 with the aid of her friend, Ellen Gates Starr. In her 1910 autobiography, *Twenty Years at Hull-House,* Addams explained that it was their purpose "to provide a center for a higher civic and social life; to institute and maintain educational and philanthropic enterprises, and to investigate and improve the conditions in the industrial districts of Chicago."

The founders of Hull-House, and of the approximately fifty other urban settlement houses that modeled themselves after it, attempted to achieve their ends by living among the people whom they served, thus experiencing and truly understanding their problems. Settlement-house workers campaigned for better garbage collection, public health programs, and the establishment of branch libraries and museums. They also offered vocational training, child care and kindergartens, youth clubs, and health education and care. In addition, settlement house workers attacked the problem of poverty itself by crusading for such labor reforms as the eight-hour day, the minimum wage, and unionization. They frequently advocated welfare programs, unemployment compensation, and a form of what would later be known as social security.

Settlement houses also gradually became training schools for women activists. Florence Kelley, the leader of the National Consumers League for thirty-two years and a strong opponent of child labor, began her career as a social reformer at Hull-House in 1891. Edith and Grace Abbott, too, started out at Hull-House. Edith later produced a number of classic works on social welfare and served as dean of the School of Social Service Administration at the University of Chicago between 1924 and 1942; Grace headed the United States Children's Bureau from 1921 to 1934.

Similarly, the Henry Street Settlement House on New York's East Side spawned many female reformers. Lillian Wald was one of the first public health nurses and an early settlement worker on Henry Street during the 1890s. She later moved to the forefront of the child welfare movement and in 1904 joined Florence Kelley and others in founding the National Child Labor Committee. In 1912, Wald and Kelley succeeded in getting a children's bureau established in the Department of Commerce and Labor. Its first head was another social worker and reformer, Julia C. Lathrop. Lucy Sprague Mitchell, the founder of the Bureau of Educational Experiment in 1916, was yet another welfare worker who had been influenced early in her career by Wald and the Henry Street Settlement House.

In addition to training women reformers, settlement houses also helped to motivate the woman suffrage movement. Since the lack of the vote placed limits on their political influence, female settlement workers often became committed to woman suffrage. Thwarted in their efforts to attack such problems listed by Addams as "unsanitary housing, poisonous sewage, contaminated water, infant mortality, adulterated food, smoke-laden air, juvenile crime, and unwholesome crowding," these women added the cause of suffrage to their speeches, articles, and petitions. How could women, they reasoned, fully exercise their moral obligations to American society when denied political participation and power?

A similar pattern developed among women determined to abolish alcohol consumption. Seeing alcoholism as a basic factor in the disruption and corruption of American family life, women thronged to the temperance movement. During the 1890s, the Women's Christian Temperance Union (WCTU) became the largest women's organization to that time. By the turn of the century, it counted over 176,000 members, with chapters in every state and county. It owned its own newspapers, office buildings, temperance hotels, and other related businesses. Consequently, the

WCTU provided a practical training ground for female leaders, business executives, speakers, and writers. Through its strong ties with Protestant churches, the WCTU also taught generations of women to believe firmly in the value of their moral sensibilities in an increasingly troubled society.

Under the aggressive leadership of educator and temperance reformer Frances Willard, the WCTU soon added the woman suffrage campaign to its multifaceted program. As president of the WCTU between 1879 and 1898, Willard argued that temperance could not be achieved without political influence. Her slogan—"Do Everything"—thus included not only the support of alcohol-free restaurants, boys' clubs for orphans, industrial schools for girls, homes for alcoholic women, and paid temperance organizers on the local and state levels, but also woman suffrage speakers, literature, and petitions to legislatures.

Willard also understood that the power of women depended on unity. Unlike many other women reform leaders who overlooked black and immigrant women and failed to establish regional branches, Willard urged the WCTU to reach across racial, ethnic, social class, and regional lines. Thus, she attracted women of many backgrounds and persuasions, not only to temperance, but toward woman suffrage as well. The WCTU might have foundered in convincing the majority of Americans of the wisdom of temperance, but it was tremendously influential in raising women's consciousness of their own problems and in directing thousands of its members to the woman suffrage movement.

After Willard's death in 1898, the WCTU moved away from its strong suffrage stance. The liquor interests were already alarmed that women, if given suffrage, would use the vote to establish national prohibition. Like so many other women's reform groups, the WCTU also feared that its advocacy of woman suffrage might be construed as support of feminism, a radical cause to many persons at the turn of the twentieth century.

The suffragists themselves feared alienating the public with their relatively radical positions. When, in 1890, the National Woman Suffrage Association and the American Woman Suffrage Association united into the National American Woman Suffrage Association (NAWSA), Elizabeth Cady Stanton was elected president. She was replaced by Susan B. Anthony in 1892, however; many suffragists feared that Stanton's very controversial *Woman's Bible,* an attempt to show the role of religion in oppressing women, would turn public sentiment against their organization.

During the 1890s and early 1900s, the NAWSA found its efforts severely hampered by active antisuffrage groups. The NAWSA tried to gain support state by state, but between 1896 and 1910, suffrage amendment referendums were held in only six states, and all were defeated. By 1910, women had the right to vote in only four states. And in 1911, the National Association Opposed to the Further Extension of Suffrage to Women organized and soon claimed a membership larger than the NAWSA.

Under the conservative leadership of Anna Howard Shaw between 1904 and 1915, the NAWSA made few gains on behalf of woman suffrage. It rejected militancy as a risk to the public image of the organization and relied instead on the education of women and state suffrage campaigns to advance its cause. Also afraid of drawing public enmity by raising race issues, the NAWSA was hesitant to recruit black women as members. One exception was Adella Hunt Logan of Alabama. A Tuskegee Institute faculty member, Logan wrote one of the most comprehensive arguments in support of woman suffrage in 1905. She insisted that "government of the people for the people and by the people is but partially realized so long as woman has no vote."

More typically, black women were left to form their own suffrage associations. The Tuskegee Woman's Club of Alabama and the Colored Woman's Suffrage Club of Los Angeles are only two examples of black women's suffrage groups active during the 1890s and early 1900s. Black women suffragists tended to see woman suffrage as both a gender and a race issue. In the South, enfranchised black women would be denied the vote as blacks through Jim Crow laws and the activities of white supremacist groups. They argued that they thus needed the vote for themselves as citizens as well as to enhance their efforts to uplift and liberate black Americans. In the view of black reformer and suffragist Anna J. Cooper, black women activists had no choice but to fight for women's rights and black rights at the same time.

White women suffragists were also beginning to claim that they needed the vote in order to help society in general. The argument that women had a right to the vote was gradually replaced by the argument that women needed the vote to become effective reformers and moral caretakers of society. The moderate tone of this appeal would eventually allow many Americans to begin to accept the idea of woman suffrage during the era of the First World War. But during the early years of the twentieth century, suspicion of woman suffrage continued to be rampant, while the wider cause of feminism was even more suspect.

Still, feminist thought did make some difference around the turn of the century. In the research universities that were emerging during the 1890s and early 1900s, female students fought for their right to equal education, the number of women faculty members increased, and research on sex differences began to thrive. Female enrollments in the social sciences climbed dramatically at such schools as the University of Chicago and Columbia University after 1900. At Chicago, psychology graduate student Helen Thompson pioneered intelligence tests of undergraduates that demonstrated that men and women students differed only slightly in intellect. At Columbia, psychology graduate student Leta Hollingworth confirmed that male and female intellectual capabilities were indeed similar.

During the 1890s and early 1900s, other feminist scholars opened many areas for exploration. Sociologist Mary Roberts Coolidge and physician Clelia Mosher conducted studies of sexuality that refuted myths about women's "natural" sexual inhibitions. Emily Putnam, author and the first dean of Barnard College, analyzed women's roles throughout history, most notably in *The Lady: Studies of Certain Significant Phases of Her History* (1910). And lecturer and popular sociologist Charlotte Perkins Gilman explored ideas regarding the restructuring of society to emancipate women.

Gilman was perhaps the best known of these feminist thinkers. Her call for a "reordering of woman's sphere" culminated in her most important work, *Women and Economics,* published in 1898. Gilman's basic thesis was that women's total dependence on men was destructive to the female personality. She argued that the economic independence of women would make them happier and better wives, mothers, and individuals. Recognizing that the economic emancipation of women would require far-reaching changes in social structures, Gilman suggested that communal kitchens and day-care centers be established to provide efficient and professional services to working women. She wrote, "This is the true line of advance, making a legitimate human business of housework; having it done by experts instead of by amateurs; making it a particular social industry instead of a general feminine function." Although Gilman was widely read and was the leading intellectual of the woman's movement of the day, her ideas were not adopted. Seen as extremely radical, they were hotly debated but never implemented.

Yet another "ism" involving a large number of women was even more alarming to many Americans—socialism. A socialist women's movement peaked between 1870 and the First World War. Dedicated to the principles of women's right to labor and to vote, socialist women were primarily foreign-born and white natives. One of these was Russian-born Emma Goldman, who repeatedly crossed the country lecturing on anarchism and women's rights. Another was Minnesotan Kate Richards O'Hare, who also became a major spokesperson for American socialism. An avowed feminist, O'Hare supported such issues as woman suffrage and maternity benefits for working women. Widely known as a lecturer and writer, O'Hare carried socialist and feminist messages across the nation and particularly to the Great Plains.

Western women also committed themselves to reform concerns, frequently on a regional basis. Mary Elizabeth Lease, a controversial speaker for the Farmers' Alliance and the Peoples' (Populist) party during the early 1890s, shocked Kansas, Missouri, and the far West on behalf of the free coinage of silver and other Populist proposals. In 1894, a number of western women took an active role in Coxey's March on Washington, which appealed to the Congress of the United States to aid the unemployed by creating temporary public works jobs. Coxey's protest attained its greatest following in western states where men joined "regiments" as marchers and women served as homeguards, auxiliaries, and suppliers of food and other resources. Although Coxey's "Army" achieved little relief for the unemployed, its large component of women indicated the strong social activism of western women.

Southern women had also entered reform activities of various kinds by the turn of the twentieth century. Although ideas of chivalry and women's place hung on after the Civil War, a number of southern women gradually began to coalesce into what came to be known as the "woman movement." These assertive southern women moved into the missionary societies of the various churches, chapters of the WCTU, school reform associations, and eventually into woman suffrage organizations. One "new woman" of the South was Belle Kearney, a WCTU organizer and, after women achieved the vote in 1920, the first woman senator in the Mississippi legislature. Other examples were Jean Gordon of Louisiana, who battled for a child labor law during the early 1900s, and Mary Partridge, who in 1910 began organizing woman suffrage societies in Alabama. Anne Firor Scott, historian of southern women, maintains that by 1910 "the woman movement in the South was moving out into the open." The "new women" were asking for their rights and were also willing to fulfill their social responsibilities by contributing their resources and energies to reform activities.

Clearly, women's reform efforts permeated many levels of social activity. Leaving little unexamined, women fought an unbelievably wide spectrum of ills. And they themselves came from every social class, ethnic and racial group, and region. The universality of women reformers' origins and interests can be best seen in the women's club movement of the late nineteenth century.

The women's club movement originated with such women as Caroline Severence, a reformer who organized the New England Woman's Club (NEWC) in Boston, and Jane Cunningham Croly, a journalist who founded Sorosis in New York, both in 1868. The club movement was furthered by many other women, including Julia Ward Howe, author of "The Battle Hymn of the Republic," who served as president and the dominant force behind the NEWC between 1871 and 1910, the year of her death.

By 1890, the women's club movement had grown to such proportions that individual clubs joined into a national association called the General Federation of Women's Clubs. This was followed by the rapid growth of both state clubs and state federations of clubs. For instance, in North

Carolina the Woman's Association for the Betterment of Public School Houses formed in 1902, while the North Carolina Federation of Women's Clubs organized under Sallie Sims Southall Cotten in 1901.

Women's clubs focused on cultural and literary activities, the reform of social conditions within their own communities, the opening of new jobs and careers for women, and the achievement of woman suffrage. Their members were devoted to "municipal housekeeping," the idea that women had special talents and moral responsibilities that allowed them to understand and solve civic problems. In fact, club women often saw the community as a larger home in which they functioned. As one commentator explained in 1912: "Woman has a special function in developing the welfare of humanity which man cannot perform. This function consists in her power to make, of any place in which she may happen to live, a home for all those who come there. Women must now learn to make of their cities great community homes for all the people."

The philosophy of the women's club movement was also a type of feminism, often called "domestic feminism"—the enlargement of women's interests and sphere. Because the club movement provided a basis of organized volunteerism by women and legitimized the right of women to engage in civic affairs, it helped women to enter the public arena so long dominated by men. The commitment of these clubs to integrating women into the public sphere was demonstrated in the individual efforts of members as well as their official endorsement of woman suffrage in 1914. Although clubwomen did not yet move beyond suffrage to demand equality, they did make it clear that women's proper place was no longer limited to the home.

White native-born women were not the only ones to organize into clubs. In 1893, the National Council of Jewish Women formed within the Jewish community to promote various types of social services. After 1900, many additional groups organized on behalf of the Zionist movement to establish a Jewish homeland in Palestine. By 1912, this culminated in the founding of Hadassah, the Jewish women's Zionist group dedicated to providing funds for medical and other services to Palestine.

A strong club movement also developed among black women interested in pursuing educational, philanthropic, and welfare activities, especially in southern communities where welfare institutions excluded blacks. Black women's clubs established kindergartens, day-care centers, orphanages, schools, and health-care programs, and provided a plethora of other social services.

Black women's groups also defended blacks against discriminatory treatment, including lynching. Beginning in 1892, a Memphis, Tennessee, newspaper editor, Ida Wells-Barnett, began to organize a national anti-lynching crusade. Wells-Barnett's stand against the sexual abuse of black women by white men and her exhortations to black women to defend their race from violence and abuse led to the founding of the Women's Loyal Union in New York in 1892. It was soon followed by the Women's New Era Club, organized in Boston by Josephine St. Pierre Ruffin.

In 1895, invited to speak to the first national convention of representatives from rapidly proliferating black women's clubs, Ruffin asserted: "All over America there is to be found a large and growing class of earnest, intelligent, progressive colored women, women who, if not leading useful lives are only waiting for the opportunity to do so." She stressed the need for black women to organize and attack community problems and to begin "to make the most of our own, to some extent, limited opportunities."

Because black women's clubs were denied membership in the General Federation of Women's Clubs, Ruffin urged the formation of a national black women's club organization. In 1896, the National Association of Colored Women (NACW) became a reality. By the First World War, the NACW counted 50,000 black women as members in twenty-eight state federations and over a thousand clubs.

Mary Church Terrell, also of Memphis, Tennessee, served as the NACW's first president. Terrell graduated from Oberlin College in 1884 and became a teacher, a suffragist, and an ardent defender of black rights. Under her leadership between 1896 and 1901, the NACW sponsored kindergartens, day nurseries, mother's clubs, homes for the aged, musical clubs, and temperance groups. The overriding concern was the elevation of black Americans. As Terrell stated in 1897: "We wish to set in motion influences that shall stop the ravages made by practices that sap our strength, and preclude the possibility of advancement. . . . We proclaim to the world that the women of our race have become partners in the great firm of progress and reform."

The black women's club movement in Indiana during the 1890s and early 1900s provides a case study of the larger national trend. Although black women in Indiana were a small part of the total population, they created a large number of organizations. Two of the earliest women's clubs in Indiana were the Sisters of Charity (1874) and the Alpha Home Association (1883), both dedicated to helping blacks ravaged by age, illness, and poverty.

During the 1890s and early 1900s, increasing black migration to Indiana and the growth of urban social problems stimulated the organization of many more clubs and societies. In 1903, for example, Lillian Thomas Fox founded the Woman's Improvement Club (WIC) in Indianapolis. Committed at first to the self-improvement of its members, the WIC soon turned its attention to a program designed to eradicate tuberculosis among blacks. In 1911, Anna C. Moore founded the Thursday

Coterie, which took on the rescue of young black girls from prostitution. These Indianapolis groups were replicated in every town and city in Indiana with populations of black women.

Other black women's groups proliferated across the nation. In 1897, Victoria Earle Matthews founded the White Rose Industrial Association of New York to help migrant women from the South to obtain housing, employment, and training. In 1908, Cynthia Lugenia Burns Hope organized the Atlanta Neighborhood Union to provide playgrounds for black children, as well as health and other services to Atlanta blacks. And in 1910, the College Alumnae Club of Washington, D.C., formed to establish reading clubs for children, encourage black girls to attend college, and underwrite a scholarship program.

Like white clubwomen, black clubwomen frequently added woman suffrage to their list of worthy causes. Such leaders as Wells-Barnett and Terrell included suffrage activities among their many reform efforts. Adella Hunt Logan, principal of Tuskegee Institute, argued that black women needed the vote in order to secure a share of public school funds for black schools. Margaret Washington, a president of NACW, reasoned that black women could use suffrage to further social reform. Such groups as the College Alumnae Club also vigorously supported women's right to vote through their publications and public addresses.

Although the goals and ideals of the black women's clubs were similar to those of white clubwomen, the two groups failed to work together to any degree. The General Federation of Women's Clubs did eventually admit black women's groups, but only as segregated local chapters. White clubwomen were bound by the prevailing racial prejudices of the time and had not yet added racial discrimination to their list of problems needing reform. Black women, on the other hand, often found it necessary to strengthen their own organizations and pursue their commitment to the improvement of black Americans rather than to adopt white clubwomen's priorities.

Both white and black clubwomen did inadvertently cooperate in revising the accepted image of women as helpless and passive. Women's impact on their communities' problems, social structures, and power bases demonstrated that women were effective shakers and movers who provided crucial services to a highly industrialized, urbanized, and complex nation.

Yet the effect of clubwomen's activities on the customary image of American women was limited in some ways. Along with women involved in such reforms as settlement houses, temperance, and suffrage, clubwomen cast themselves in the traditional role of moral keepers. Like women of the pre–Civil War era, reformers and clubwomen of the 1890s and early 1900s emphasized their superior womanly virtue, thus continuing to segregate themselves. They presented themselves as a unique group invested with special attributes, a characterization which thwarted the integration of women with men.

In education, women showed a similar tendency to assert their right to participate while clearly identifying themselves as women. By 1910, when approximately 5 percent of college-age Americans attended college, 40 percent were female. A large proportion of these women students attended such women's colleges as Barnard, Bryn Mawr, Mount Holyoke, Radcliffe, Smith, Vassar, and Wellesley. These schools built excellent academic reputations, but at the same time they created a separate sphere for women in education and embodied an ambivalence about women's roles.

Affected by the theory of the day, which claimed that higher education might debilitate women mentally and physically, women's colleges dedicated themselves to educating women without destroying health and femininity in the process. Consequently, women's colleges combined academics, physical and health education, and domestic service and training. These programs produced many successful women, including Alice Freeman Palmer, second president of Wellesley and the first dean of women at the newly founded University of Chicago in 1892. For generations of female college students, she exemplified the educated woman who could combine intellect, service, and domesticity.

Throughout the 1890s and early 1900s, women's schools struggled with the question of whether to perpetuate domestic ideas and values or to break with them. Under the presidency of M. Carey Thomas between 1894 and 1922, Bryn Mawr, a Quaker college, took the lead in challenging concepts of domesticity. Thomas believed that women had the full capability to be serious scholars and had little sympathy for those who sacrificed their careers for "suffocating" marriages. In 1913, Thomas wrote that women "may have spent half a lifetime in fitting themselves for their chosen work and then may be asked to choose between it and marriage." She added that "no one can estimate the number of women who remain unmarried in revolt before such a horrible alternative." To Thomas, marriage was possible only if the partners were equally involved in careers and home.

Many women of this era, like Thomas herself, chose not to marry at all. Instead, a number of them formed long-term relationships with other women. Actress Charlotte Cushman, for example, lived, worked, and traveled with sculptor Emma Stebbins for twenty years. Because these women hedged-in their personal lives with great privacy, it is impossible to determine whether or not these liasons were lesbian in nature. Certainly, many women of the time, including married women, formed close bonds with other women as a result of women's separate sphere, culture, and education.

By 1910, women's colleges had begun to abandon their challenge to the cult of domesticity, although they did maintain rigorous academic programs. By that year, 67 percent of Bryn Mawr graduates were marrying, as compared with 45 percent before 1900. The number of children borne by these women rose while the number who entered graduate schools and professions fell. Women's colleges could not resolve the age-old question of how women could combine career and family, or even if they should attempt to do so at all. A decade after her graduation, a Radcliffe graduate of 1900 succinctly described the dilemma of a college trained woman: "I hang in a void midway between two spheres. A professional career puts me beyond reach of the average woman's duties and pleasures, but the conventional limitations of the female lot put me beyond reach of the average man's duties and pleasures."

Many coeducational colleges and universities faced their own problems as the number of women in their student bodies rose to 50 percent after 1900. Fearing the encroaching feminization of higher education, they limited female admissions, developed special curricula to attract more male students, and relegated women to their normal schools or home economics departments. Along with many other Americans, administrators at these schools feared the low rate of marriage among college trained women as well as the effect that the production of such a female elite might have on women's roles in general.

Despite their hesitations regarding the impact of higher education for women on futures and on society in general, both women's colleges and coeducational institutions strongly supported active sports programs for their women students. Tennis and basketball became the two most popular sports for college women, tennis becoming common during the 1880s and basketball during the 1890s. Basketball was introduced at Smith College in 1892, only a year after its invention, and soon became the first team sport played widely by women. College athletic associations also sponsored field days for women's competition in track and field, field hockey, rowing, winter sports, and aquatics. Golf was also very popular because it was considered to be particularly well-suited to the delicate and genteel nature of turn-of-the-century women.

Louise Pound, a Nebraska woman who earned a Ph.D. degree at the University of Heidelberg in 1900, provides an outstanding example of a woman who thrived on both scholarship and sports. Pound made news in lawn tennis during the 1890s and in golf between 1900 and 1927. She explained that she played for a long time without a set of matched clubs: "Most women at that time would use their husband's clubs cut off. When I got a set of matched clubs in 1931 I cut six strokes off my game." Pound supported basketball at the University of Nebraska, where she became a full professor in 1912. She also organized a female military company replete with 1880 Springfield rifles. A distinguished scholar, beloved teacher, and competent sportswoman, Pound was the personification of the "new woman" ideal of the early twentieth century.

At the same time of these far-reaching changes in white women's education, black female education was undergoing drastic revision as well. Few black women received higher education before 1890, but after that year, a growing number of them sought advanced training, particularly as teachers. In 1890, the number of black women in education began to outdistance that of black men. By 1900, there were 13,524 black women teachers, as opposed to 7,734 black men. By 1910, 22,547 of the nation's 29,772 black teachers were female.

Black women attended such black schools as Wilberforce University in Ohio and such integrated white schools as Oberlin, also in Ohio. By the First World War, there were nearly 100 black colleges and universities that admitted women. Of these, Scotia Academy, Spelman, and Bennett were exclusively for black women. These schools often diverged sharply from their white counterparts in curriculum. Anxious to meet the practical needs of the black community rather than to provide a rigorous, classical education, black women's schools offered training primarily as teachers and homemakers.

Mary McLeod Bethune is one of the most outstanding examples of an educated black woman. A daughter of former slaves, Bethune attended Scotia Seminary in North Carolina and the Moody Bible Institute in Chicago. After teaching in various southern schools during the 1890s, Bethune decided to establish a school for girls similar to Scotia in Florida. With only $1.50 in cash, Bethune collected wooden boxes for benches, begged for other necessities, and sold ice cream and sweet potatoe pies to construction workers. When she opened her school of six students in 1904, Bethune lacked the $5.00 she had promised in payment for her schoolhouse, but she still had "faith in a living God, faith in myself, and a desire to serve."

Bethune's little school soon grew into the widely respected Daytona Normal and Industrial Institute and in 1923 became Bethune-Cookman College. Bethune served as the president of the college until her death in 1955. She was also a leader of the National Association of Colored Women's Clubs and the National Council of Negro Women and became involved in management of the National Youth Administration under President Franklin D. Roosevelt.

In addition to teaching, nursing was another area open to ambitious black women. Although black women had long served as nurses, they were barred from formal training. The first school to establish a nursing course and to accept a black student was the New England Hospital for Women and Children, which graduated the first black trained nurse, Mary E. Mahoney, in 1879. This school followed a quota of one black and one Jewish student per year. As a result of such limitations, black medical educators began to establish black nursing schools. Between 1890 and 1900, a number of black nursing schools were founded. Denied jobs in white hospitals, the Army Nurse Corps, and the Red Cross, black female nurses worked within the black community and as private nurses. In 1908 they formed the National Association of Colored Graduate Nurses—they were excluded from membership in the American Nurses' Association.

Black women also moved into the practice of medicine. Only fifteen years after Elizabeth Blackwell became a doctor in 1849, Rebecca Lee, a black woman, earned an M.D. degree at the New England Medical College. Others followed her lead. In 1897, Matilda A. Evans graduated from the Woman's Medical College of Pennsylvania and opened a practice in Columbia, South Carolina, where she established a hospital for blacks and a black nurses' training school. In 1890, there were 155 black female physicians; a number that grew to 160 by 1900. In 1901, Dr. Eliza Anna Grier, a physician in Greenville, South Carolina, lamented: "There are a great many forces operating against the success of the Negro. These, however, I hope someday will be overcome."

Certainly, many black women were doing their best during these years to combat the negative forces of which Grier wrote. They were proving themselves as writers, entrepreneurs, speakers, actresses, and singers. In 1892, Frances Ellen Watkins Harper published *Iola Leroy, Shadows Uplifted,* thought to be the first novel by a black woman writer. In 1905, Sarah Breedlove Walker invented the Walker method for hair straightening and soon became a millionaire. And during the opening decade of the twentieth century, Gertrude "Ma" Rainey brought the blues to millions of Americans.

White women were also entering the professions, concentrated in teaching, nursing, midwifery, medicine, library and social work, and academic pursuits. During the 1890s and early 1900s, women formed a higher proportion of the professions than they did of the general work force. In 1890, they constituted 36 percent of the professional people but only about 17 percent of those employed. Between 1890 and 1920, the number of professional women increased by 226 percent.

Medicine was especially hospitable to the entry of women. Nursing was a well-established profession by 1900, with a large number of reputable programs being offered. Midwives were trained in European or American schools or by apprenticeship and, in 1910, still attended to approximately 50 percent of all births. Women also became physicians in large numbers. In 1900, nearly 9,000 women held physicians' licenses. In that year, women comprised 10 percent of medical students and, by 1910, 6 percent of medical practitioners.

Despite women's gains as physicians, they failed to dominate any field, including gynecology and pediatrics. Moreover, many of them worried that female solidarity was a deterent to their success. As a result, a number of women doctors rejected association with such women's institutions as the New England Hospital. Others clung to the concept of female solidarity, believing, like reformers and clubwomen, that women had certain desirable qualities to offer to medicine.

The number of women engaged in scientific fields also increased after 1900. In 1906, 149 women were listed in a popular directory of scientists, and 204 women's names appeared in 1910. Between 1900 and 1910, 23 women described themselves as being involved in the new scientific field of home economics. Slightly more women scientists than men earned Ph.D. degrees and held employment in academic institutions.

But, as was the case with women in medicine, women in science also faced continuing problems. They were often stuck in inferior positions and excluded from membership in professional scientific societies. Given the obstacles confronting women scientists during the early twentieth century, it is remarkable that so many, including anatomist Florence Sabin and geologist Florence Bascom, produced significant work.

Whether in medicine, science, nursing, teaching, library or social work, they were paid less than men in the same areas. The discrepancy in teachers' pay well illustrates this point. In 1890 male teachers averaged $33.00 a week and women, $13.00; in 1900 men earned $34.00 and women, $14.00; and in 1910 men received $36.00 and women, $17.00. Yet, for a variety of reasons, women continued to pour into the profession, accounting for 77 percent of all teachers by 1910.

Generally, women found it easier to develop in certain professions deemed more suitable to their sex. Women professionals were more acceptable in places that were extensions of the home, such as hospitals and schools, and offered services that were an extension of domestic duties, such as health care or learning guidance. The career of Ellen Swallow Richards illustrates the fusing of domesticity and career. A holder of a chemistry degree from MIT, Richards became a professor of "sanitary chemistry" and a leader in the new scientific field of home economics. She solved the confusion between home and career by merging the two, much to the acclaim of her male colleagues. She claimed that her hesitancy to "scorn womanly duties," and to regard it "a privilege to clean up," won her strong allies.

The areas of art and literature were increasingly becoming associated with women's supposed cultural sensibilities, a trend that encouraged women artists and writers. By 1910, women accounted for 45.2 percent of artists and art teachers. In 1913, the Armory Show in New York included a piece of crazy quilt in the exhibit, introducing "modern art." The acclaimed work of modern artist Sonia Delaunay, who worked in the abstract style of Orphism, began with a patchwork blanket made for her son in 1912. Women were also illustrators for journals and novels. Alice Barber Stephens was one very popular illustrator, while Frances Flora Palmer was both an expert lithographer and the mainstay of the staff of *Currier and Ives.*

Other women achieved acclaim as painters. Lilla Cabot Perry became a portrait painter and a promoter of impressionism in America around the turn of the twentieth century. Cecilia Beaux was a leading portraitist in New York during the early 1900s, noted for her portraits of famous women. And Mary Cassatt, the most distinguished woman artist of the age, became widely known for her impressionist painting and print-making.

In the field of literature, women also exhibited energy and creativity. They contributed greatly to an emerging style of writing known as regionalism. Marietta Holley of upstate New York, known as the female Mark Twain of her day, used local color and satirical humor to support a number of reform causes, especially feminism. Holley's primary character, Samantha Smith Allen, was an eloquent feminist who romped her way "episodin' and allegorin'" through more than twenty novels and a number of short stories. Maine author Sarah Orne Jewett also wrote of the rural people of her own area. A strong disciple of regionalism, Jewett was known for works concentrating on Maine's rich history, including *The Country of the Pointed Firs* (1896) and *The Tory Lover* (1901). Willa Cather, another regionalist, presented farm and prairie life without a romantic gloss. She is best remembered for her stories of Nebraska life, *O Pioneers* (1913) and *My Antonia* (1918). Less well-known at the time was Kate Chopin, who combined feminist ideas with Creole local color in *The Awakening* (1899) and other novels.

A number of women also moved into the field of journalism. Ida M. Tarbell established herself as a muckraker with her harsh exposé, *The History of The Standard Oil Company* (1904). Elizabeth Seaman worked until 1895 as a famous New York *World* reporter known as "Nellie Bly." And Sophie Loeb publicized the cause of mothers' pensions through her feature articles in the New York *Evening World.*

As the theater became increasingly important in American life, women achieved prominence on the stage. Because women were now a majority of theater audiences, and large numbers of them attended matinee performances unescorted, many actresses played to their female audiences by addressing women's issues. On and off the stage, Mary Shaw supported the causes of women's clubs, feminism, and suffrage. The embodiment of the "American Beauty," Lillian Russell, lent her glamour to exercise for women and woman suffrage. The "American Girl," Ethel Barrymore, used her status as a cult figure to advocate aid for working women and emancipation for women. In the play, *The Twelve Pound*

Look, Barrymore zealously portrayed a woman who chose economic independence over a confining marriage.

Yet in spite of these advances by women into some professions, a number of areas remained essentially closed to them. The ministry, for example, continued to be a male dominated field. One of the few women to penetrate it was Mary Baker Eddy, who founded the Christian Science Church during the 1870s. Eddy was an overwhelming success because she capitalized on what were considered to be womanly attributes—her spirituality and intuition—to build a successful religious sect. When she died in 1910, she left a huge, permanent, and wealthy religious institution behind her.

Law also remained largely closed to women. Although a small number of women attended law schools around the turn of the century, they were excluded from courtroom practice once licensed. By 1910, there were only 1,500 women attorneys, most of whom were forced to find work with governmental agencies, legal journals, and women's organizations. Some, like Sophonisba Breckinridge, the first woman admitted to the bar in Kentucky in the 1880s, entered academic life instead of the law.

Evidently, a certain ambivalence existed regarding women's roles. A number of advances had been made, yet the invented American woman, with her emphasis on home and family, remained a popular image. The tensions were reflected in American attitudes toward women and the family. While many Americans indicated a growing respect for women as diverse individuals, others continued to typecast them along traditional lines.

At the same time, women were both experiencing and implementing changes in the realm of family. Increasingly, women were asserting themselves and demanding sex education. By 1900 the birth rate had fallen to 3.5 children per mother, while the divorce rate had risen to one out of twelve couples in 1900 and one out of nine by the First World War. About two thirds of divorces were granted to women. About 10 percent of women chose not to marry at all. These trends suggest that women were beginning to expect more personal rewards from marriage and family than did their mothers.

Countervailing forces, however, pushed women toward the traditional family status. By 1900, strong anti-abortion laws denied women the right to limit family size through the surgical removal of a fetus. Birth control information was also restricted by state laws and the Comstock law. The media urged women to devote large amounts of time and energy to child rearing. They were also expected to develop their managerial and technical skills because of the switch from servants to home technology. Meanwhile, the emphasis on the maintenance of human relations within the family unit demanded the wife's and mother's constant attention in providing a moral example, solace and support, and instruction for other family members.

In 1900, an essayist in *Harper's Bazaar* extolled the virtues of home life for women:

Today, when hundreds of young women of our best blood and culture in America are standing within the open doors of schools and colleges, eagerly straining their gaze out into the future, hoping to catch a glimpse of the opportunity for a career, it seems to behoove the conservative thinkers among us to suggest to some of them the profession of home life. We American women all take our 'public works' too seriously, toil and strive too unremittingly, give too little heed to the trivial round of home life, which we expect to maintain itself unaided.

In 1912, Charlotte Perkins Gilman opposed this view. She disputed the "naive assumption" that "only men are human creatures, able and entitled to perform the work of the world; while women are only female creatures, able to do nothing whatever but continue in the same round of duties to which they have been so long restricted." To Gilman, women's growth in all areas of life was highly desirable. "As they so rise and broaden," she maintained, "filling their full place in the world as members of society, as well as their partial places as mothers of it, they will gradually rear a new race of men, men with minds large enough to see in human beings something besides males and females."

As the debate raged, the invented American woman changed in appearance and behavior. The "Gibson Girl," created by Charles Dana Gibson for *Life* magazine during the 1890s, was a healthy, sensual, and rebellious young woman. Dressed in a simple shirtwaist and skirt or a one-piece bathing suit, the "Gibson Girl" soon became the prevailing image of the "new woman." Many women cycled, skated, and played golf and lawn tennis. Others loosened their corsets or, as did Alice Roosevelt, smoked in public. When President Roosevelt was criticized for his daughter's behavior, he responded that he could do only one of two things—be President or control Alice. The idea that women were becoming uncontrollable was reinforced by the dance craze of 1912 based on the bunny hug, the turkey trot, and the tango. In 1914, the Massachusetts Vice Commission reported that a sizable number of young women were willing to be picked up by men and to have sexual relations with them.

During the 1890s and early 1900s, another tremendously significant but less visible change was taking place among American women. They were entering the work force in larger numbers than at any previous time in history. By 1900, five million women, or one out of every five, were employed. There were now four times as many women working in industry as there had been in 1870. These women were young, three out of four in industry being under twenty-five. Approximately 75 percent were single. They were also largely white and urban based. In the West, only 13 percent of women worked outside of the home, as compared to 17 percent nationally. In industry women were concentrated in the manufacture of textiles, shoes, hats, gloves, stockings, and collars, but they were also found in such areas as tobacco, canning, bookbinding, meat-packing, and laundries.

Employed women also worked as clerks. In 1870, men accounted for 97.5 percent of clerical laborers. By 1890, women constituted 17 percent of the clerical work force, a figure that jumped to approximately 50 percent by the First World War. Women's entry into clerical labor was eased by the typewriter, which was both new and posed no threat to men's customary occupations. In fact, typing soon became known as "woman's work;" women comprised 80.6 percent of all stenographers and typists by 1910. Another factor that facilitated women's dominance of clerical work was the widespread belief that women's "feminine" qualities, including manual dexterity, attention to minor details, and talents as caretakers, were particularly suited to office work.

Other women worked in sales, particularly in the large department stores that were becoming the symbol of urban consumerism. In 1899, an investigator for the Chicago Consumers' League who posed as a department store clerk revealed that wages were $2.00 to $3.00 a week, supplemented by a 5 percent commission on sales. Total wages averaged $3.00 to $5.00 per week or about $.06 to $.10 per hour. In addition, female clerks were expected to stand constantly without rest breaks and to take only a thirty-minute lunch period. She explained that the clerks were limping by evening and that "many sales were made under positive physical agony."

Yet other working women toiled at such domestic jobs as housekeeper, maid, nursemaid, and dressmaker. Largely immigrant or black, domestics tended to leave their jobs as soon as other employment alternatives appeared. In 1911, a government study discovered that domestics preferred even commercial laundry work over domestic service. One black woman cited more time to herself and better pay as advantages of her laundry job, as did an Irish woman who was also a former servant. In 1870, half of all employed women had worked as domestics; the figure had dropped to under 20 percent by the First World War.

In every area of employment, women struggled with numerous problems. Low pay, long hours, and brutal conditions continued to characterize women's work. In the workplace, women were socialized into dependent female roles by low wages, lack of security, few opportunities for advancement, and paternalistic supervision by male managers. Within the home, women's duties were both heavy and exclusively theirs since male wage earners seldom saw housework as part of their duties. Moreover, poor municipal services to working class areas, tenements, and slums made crucial resources such as water very difficult to obtain, thus exacerbating working women's household drudgery.

By 1900, journalists known as muckrakers were beginning to expose the meager wages and harsh conditions suffered by working women. Investigatory bodies discovered that women tolerated the situation because they had to work to support themselves and to help their families. Garment workers, for example, continued to work as poorly paid and highly exploited piece workers, assembling flowers, shoes, and other goods in their homes. Other workers tolerated sweatships, as the garment factories were known, as well as the tyranny of bosses called sweaters.

Although these evils were made public again and again, little was done to correct them. In 1911, a fire broke out at the Triangle Shirtwaist Factory in New York City. As fire ripped through the lofts, setting piles of material aflame, female workers rushed to the doors, only to find them locked to prevent workers from walking out with goods. Fire escapes and sprinkler systems were nonexistent, although they had been requested during a 1909 shirtwaist workers' strike. As a result, 146 women perished in the fire and by jumping or falling out of ten-story high windows. Labor leader Rose Schneiderman told a mass meeting: "This is not the first time that girls have been burned alive in the city. . . . Every year thousands of us are maimed."

Schneiderman and other labor leaders had long worked for necessary reforms. When such large national unions as the American Federation of Labor (AFL), conservative in their stance toward women in the labor force, were hesitant to recruit them into membership, women formed their own organizations. Working Girls' Clubs began to meet in New York as early as the 1880s in order to address practical issues including wages, insurance, employment bureaus, and lunch programs.

In 1903, these clubs and other similar working women's groups were replaced by the National Women's Trade Union League (NWTUL). Membership combined trade unionists and wealthy women interested in labor problems and feminism. The NWTUL endorsed equal pay for equal work, the organization of workers into unions, the eight-hour day, minimum wages, special legislation to protect women workers, and rights of citizenship for women. Members also hoped to develop a cooperative spirit between working and wealthy women as well as a synthesis between unionism and feminism.

All of these goals were difficult ones to achieve. Under the leadership of such women as Margaret Drier Robins, president of the league between 1907 and 1922, the NWTUL was successful in founding programs to help immigrant women, provide health care for working women, and bring working women together to discuss their grievances. Through its journal, *Life and Labor*, published between 1911 and 1921, the NWTUL informed the public about the situation of employed women. The league also attempted to organize women into unions and to gain them membership and active roles in already existing unions of the AFL. The NWTUL supported strikes and pickets. It lobbied the federal government to conduct investigations and pass labor legislation. And it worked diligently for woman suffrage. But, although its contributions were great, the NWTUL was never able to resolve internal divisions between laboring and "allies" (nonlaboring women) or between unionism and feminism.

One of the most significant accomplishments of the league was the training of rank-and-file labor women who later went on to help promote labor organizations and reforms for women. Rose Schneiderman was one of these. Another was Leonora O'Reilly, a shirtworker and the league's most effective orator, who organized a local trade union of the United Garment Workers in New York City. Yet another was Mary Anderson, a stitcher and the only woman member of the board of the International Boot and Shoe Workers who, in 1920, became the first director of the Women's Bureau of the United States Department of Labor.

Many other aggressive women labor reformers emerged during the early years of the twentieth century. Pauline Newman was a veteran shirtwaist striker who became the first female organizer of the International Ladies' Garment Workers' Union in 1909. Marie Van Vorst campaigned for an end to child labor and exposed the conditions in southern mills in her book *The Woman Who Toils* (1903). Mary Harris "Mother" Jones devoted her life to organizing workers in the coal, western mining, and southern cotton industries until her death in 1930 at nearly one hundred years of age. And Helen Gurley Flynn became a fiery orator for the "Wobblies," or International Workers of the World, after its founding in 1905.

Besides speaking, organizing unions, writing, and lobbying, women labor reformers utilized pickets and strikes. Many protests followed in rapid succession. One of these was the strike of glove-workers against assembly-line techniques in 1898. In 1905, 8,000 laundry workers in Troy, New York, protested against new regulations and machines. In 1909, 20,000 shirtwaist workers left factories in New York and Philadelphia. In 1912, women textile workers striking in Lawrence, Massachusetts, found themselves involved in a violent confrontation with management.

Despite such aggressive tactics, reform for working women came slowly, if at all. Employers responded by using the courts, public opinion, police, blacklists, fines, and dismissal. It was difficult for women to unionize widely enough to combat such techniques. Long hours and heavy home responsibilities kept women from meetings; low wages could not support union dues; and the hostility of male union members intimidated potential women members. Consequently, in 1900, only 3 percent of women factory workers were organized, a figure that had climbed only to 6 percent by 1913.

Many labor reformers came to the conclusion that protective labor legislation was at least a partial answer to women's labor-related problems. During the Progressive Era there was a drive to obtain state laws that would guarantee safe working conditions, reduce health hazards, establish a minimum wage, shorten hours, and compensate workers for on-the-job accidents. By 1912, the NWTUL shifted its priorities from organization to legislation. Labor unions were less enthusiastic about the idea; they believed that organization was the only way to protect workers, male and female.

Gradually, however, state governments were drawn into protecting female laborers through legislation. This not only identified women workers as a distinct group; it also emphasized their physical weakness and child-bearing duties. A few women's groups opposed "women-only" legislation, fearing that "welfare legislation will protect women to the vanishing point." It was evident that the battle lines were being drawn for a large dispute yet to come.

Non-American-born women in particular had difficulty with jobs as well as with other aspects of American life. Between 1910 and 1915, over one-half million non-English-speaking females under the age of thirty entered the United States. Coming from southern and eastern Europe— Poland, Russia, Yugoslavia, Italy, and Lithuania—these women lacked knowledge of their new language and culture. In immigrant communities, unmarried women were expected to help support their families; non-American-born women thus flocked into the labor force, where they became easy targets for the exploitation of unscrupulous employers and others eager to take advantage of their ignorance.

Often victimized by extremely low wages, long hours, piecework in the home, seduction into prostitution, unwanted pregnancies, grinding poverty, and lack of welfare services, immigrant women turned to such organizations as the Immigrants' Protective League of Chicago (directed by Grace Abbott) for help in locating employment and housing, health care, and general guidance. Typically, immigrant women also turned to other women for help, an action that led to the formation of ethnic women's organizations. The largest of these was the Polish Women's Alliance founded in 1898 and dedicated to the education of Polish women. Another was organized in 1910 by Finnish domestics, who pooled their money to rent a communal apartment. This became a local self-help cooperative known as the Finnish Women's Cooperative Home, a venture which numbered 400 shareholders and housed more than forty women by 1920.

The sense of community spirit and self-help among Jewish women in New York was particularly impressive. In 1902, for example, Jewish women formed into groups to boycott and to stage demonstrations against sharp rises in the prices of kosher meats. Lasting almost a month, the kosher meat riots were a form of local political action that illustrated Jewish women's willingness to act on behalf of their economic interest. Women were also a strong constituency in the Educational Alliance of the Jewish community in New York. Julia Richman, a member of the board between 1893 and 1912, worked to Americanize Jews and to uplift Jewish women through the espousal of feminism and other women's causes. Like Richman, Esther Luria, a Polish Jew and writer for the Yiddish socialist press in New York during the Progressive years, strongly supported woman suffrage and the unionization of women workers.

Gradually, non-American-born women became Americanized. Young employed women provided a bridge between their traditional mothers and the larger world into which the daughters daily ventured. In addition, women who could not understand English could understand and enjoy the new silent picture films increasingly available in urban areas. Drawing audiences that were largely immigrant and working class, these films acculturated old and new generations of women, who learned from them how to dress, act, and think in more modern ways.

Of course, not all non-American-born women settled in cities. Scandinavian women frequently settled on the Great Plains frontier around the turn of the twentieth century in hopes of establishing homesteads. Mexican-American women migrated into Texas and the Southwest as wives, migrant farm workers, and industrial laborers during this period. And Asian women settled primarily on the West Coast. By the turn of the twentieth century, the number of Chinese women entering the United States had declined to approximately 107 per year, while the number of Japanese women increased (a large number of them immigrated as "picture" brides) and contributed stability to Japanese society in California.

Wherever they settled, non-American-born women were confronted with new clothing styles, language, cultural practices, and ways of thinking about the family, women's roles, and control of children. They found their old culture and values disdained by their new communities. Rapid assimilation seemed the only key to acceptance by American society.

These pressures were also directed at American Indian women. Largely relegated to reservation lands by the beginning of the Progressive Era, native women were generally overlooked by reformers, scholars, and the general public. Those teachers, reformers, and missionaries who did dedicate time to reservation service usually preached the necessity of assimilation, the abandonment of native ways. Even missionaries sympathetic to the Indians, like Elaine Goodale Eastman, teacher on the great Sioux reservation in the Dakota territory until 1891 and writer on Indian causes until her death in 1953, ultimately agreed that the "melting pot" process had to be applied to the American Indian.

The governmental policies designed to hasten the acculturation of American Indians had far-reaching effects on native women. For instance, one major plan around 1900 was to transform Sioux Indians in the Dakotas into self-sufficient farmers. Anglo in design, the plan excluded Sioux women from their essential, traditional roles in agriculture, demanding instead that native men fill them. Indian men received plots of land, tools, stock, and annuities from the government, an ownership pattern that destroyed women's political and economic power within their tribal groups. Sioux women adapted to the situation by producing textiles and other commodities for sale in the off-reservation marketplace. They combined traditional techniques of quillwork and beading with newer skills, including quilting, crocheting, and lacemaking. Consequently, they earned meager incomes over which they exercised full control.

The egalitarian balance of power in native families was subtly disrupted as the control over the household's provisions and means of production shifted to the males. Sioux women also lost political power in the community when white emissaries of the federal government made it very clear that they had no interest in dealing with women. On the other hand, Indian women did retain autonomy over their work activities and production. They also continued to exercise their right to leave an unsatisfactory marriage at will, a practice that appalled and upset white missionaries and teachers.

Clearly, Sioux Indian women experienced drastic changes in their roles, family structure, and social power during the Progressive Era. In some instances, they preserved their independence by adaptation—such as shifting production from agriculture to market goods. In other cases, they clung only precariously to their former prestige—for instance, their important roles in ceremonies and dances—only to see those rituals gradually eroded by the influence of white culture and government. Others solved the problem of diminishing power by marrying soldiers, agents, traders, and other white men, thus, ironically, joining the group whose policies were responsible for the dramatic changes in their lives.

By the time that Progressivism began to wane, it was evident that the various groups and types of women residing in America had undergone significant changes in roles, lifestyles, values, and expectations. They now participated in the public world in large numbers. Many were well-educated and achievement-oriented; by 1914, there were 9,000 women listed in *Who's Who*. As a consequence of their involvement in reform crusades, the campaign for woman suffrage and other feminist causes, the women's club movement, women's education, the industrial and agrarian work force, and the development of all sectors of the economy and regions of the country, women could no longer be characterized as passive, dependent, and easily relegated to a private, domestic sphere. More than in any other time, women of the Progressive Era asserted themselves as willing, able, and rightful participants of the world.

Yet, at the same time, the enlargement of women's roles was closely tied to the fact that women were female. The argument for the expansion of women's sphere still derived its strength, just as it had with the moral guardian theory of the post–Civil War period, from the idea that women played a very special role in society because of their female morality, virtue, and ability to "keep house," whether at home or in the community, the office, or politics. Although women's "sphere" had definitely expanded by 1914, it was still a bounded space. Thus, it continued to be segregated and limited in many ways.

How to resolve this separation of female and male, private and public, and domestic and political would prove to be an ongoing debate for many Americans during the years of the First World War. The war itself would serve as a catalyst for further discussion and change. America's momentous decision to enter the world fray in 1917 would prove to have a huge number of unexpected ramifications on the status and activities of American women.

SUGGESTIONS FOR FURTHER READING

Albers, Patricia. "Sioux Women in Transition: A Study of Their Changing Status in a Domestic and Capitalist Sector of Production." In *The Hidden Half: Studies of Plains Indian Women,* edited by Patricia Albers and Beatrice Medicine, 175–234. Washington, D.C.: University Press of America, 1983.

Antler, Joyce. "Feminism as Life-Process: The Life and Career of Lucy Sprague Mitchell." *Feminist Studies* 71 (Spring 1981): 134–157.

Baker, Paula. "The Domestication of Politics: Women and American Political Society, 1780–1920." *American Historical Review* 89 (June 1984): 620–647.

Banner, Lois W. *Women in Modern America: A Brief History.* San Diego: Harcourt Brace Jovanovich, Publishers, 1984.

Barker-Benfield, G. J. *The Horrors of the Half-Known Life: Male Attitudes Toward Women and Sexuality in Nineteenth Century America.* New York: Harper and Row, 1976.

Basen, Neil K. "Kate Richards O'Hare: The 'First Lady' of American Socialism, 1901–1917." *Labor History* 21 Spring 1980: 165–199.

Berch, Bettina. *The Endless Day: The Political Economy of Women and Work.* New York: Harcourt Brace Jovanovich, Inc., 1982.

Berkin, Carol Ruth, and Mary Beth Norton, eds. *Women of America: A History.* Boston: Houghton Mifflin Company, 1979. Part III.

Berrol, Selma. "When Uptown Met Downtown: Julia Richman's Work in the

Jewish Community of New York, 1880–1912." *American Jewish History* LXX (September 1980): 35–51.

Blair, Karen J. *The Clubwoman As Feminist: True Womanhood Redefined, 1868–1914.* New York: Holmes & Meier Publishers, Inc., 1980.

Blocker, Jack S., Jr. "Separate Paths: Suffragists and the Women's Temperance Crusade," *Signs* 10 (Spring 1985): 460–476.

Bordin, Ruth. *Women and Temperance: The Quest for Power and Liberty, 1873–1900.* Philadelphia: Temple University Press, 1981.

Brownlee, W. Elliot. "Household Values, Women's Work, and Economic Growth, 1800–1930." *Journal of Economic History* 39 (March 1979): 199–209.

Buhle, Mari Jo. *Women and American Socialism, 1870–1920.* Urbana: University of Illinois Press, 1983.

Campbell, Barbara Kuhn. *The 'Liberated' Woman of 1914: Prominent Women in the Progressive Era.* Ann Arbor: UMI Research Press, 1979.

Collier-Thomas, Bettye. "The Impact of Black Women in Education: An Historical Overview." *Journal of Negro Education* 51 (Summer 1982): 173–180.

Connolly, Mark Thomas. *The Response to Prostitution in the Progressive Era.* Chapel Hill: University of North Carolina Press, 1980.

Cookingham, Mary E. "Combining Marriage, Motherhood, and Jobs before World War II: Women College Graduates, Classes of 1905–1935." *Journal of Family History* 9 (Summer 1984): 178–195.

Davies, Margery W. *Woman's Place Is at the Typewriter: Office Work and Office Workers, 1870–1930.* Philadelphia: Temple University Press, 1982.

Degler, Carl N. "What Ought To Be and What Was: Women's Sexuality in the Nineteenth Century." *American Historical Review* 79 (December 1974): 1467–1490.

Dewhurst, C. Kurt. Betty McDowell, and Marsha MacDowell. *Artists in Aprons: Folk Art by American Women.* New York: E. P. Dutton, 1979.

Drachman, Virginia G. "Female Solidarity and Professional Success: The Dilemma of Women Doctors in Late Nineteenth-Century America." *Journal of Social History* 15 (Summer 1982): 607–619.

Dye, Nancy Schrom. "Creating a Feminist Alliance: Sisterhood and Class Conflict in the New York Women's Trade Union League, 1903–1914." *Feminist Studies* 2 (1975): 24–38.

———. "Feminism or Unionism? The New York Women's Trade Union League and the Labor Movement." *Feminist Studies* 3 (1976): 111–125.

Epstein, Barbara Leslie. *The Politics of Domesticity: Women, Evangelism, and Temperance in Nineteenth-Century America.* Middletown, CT: Wesleyan University Press, 1981.

Ewen, Elizabeth. "City Lights: Immigrant Women and the Rise of the Movies." *Signs* 5 (Spring 1980): 545–565.

Eastman, Elaine Goodale. *Sister to the Sioux: The Memoirs of Elaine Goodale Eastman, 1885–1891.* Lincoln: University of Nebraska Press, 1978.

Friedman, Jean E. and William G. Shade, eds. *Our American Sisters: Women in American Life and Thought.* Lexington, MA: D. C. Heath and Company, 1982. Part III.

Garcia, Mario T. "The Chicana in American History: The Mexican Women of

El Paso, 1880–1920: A Case Study." *Pacific Historical Review* XLIX (May 1980): 315–338.

Golden, Claudia. "The Work and Wages of Single Women, 1870 to 1920. *Journal of Economic History* XL (March 1980): 81–88.

Harley, Sharon. "Anna J. Cooper: A Voice for Black Women." In *The Afro-American Woman: Struggles and Images,* edited by Sharon Harley and Rosalynn Terborg-Penn, 87–96. Port Washington, NY: Kennikat Press, 1978.

Harris, Ann Sutherland, and Linda Nochlin. *Women Artists, 1550–1950.* New York: Alfred A. Knopf, 1979.

Hayden, Dolores. "Charlotte Perkins Gilman and the Kitchenless House." *Radical History Review* 21 (Fall 1979): 225–247.

Haller, Jr., John S. "From Maidenhood to Menopause: Sex Education for Women in Victorian America." In *Procreation or Pleasure? Sexual Attitudes in American History,* edited by Thomas L. Altherr. Malabar, FL: Robert J. Krieger Publishing Company, 1983.

Hine, Darlene Clark. *When the Truth is Told: a History of Black Women's Culture and Community in Indiana, 1875–1950.* Indianapolis: National Council of Negro Women, 1981.

———. "From Hospital to College: Black Nurse Leaders and the Rise of Collegiate Nursing Schools." *Journal of Negro Education* 51 (Summer 1982): 222–237.

Hyman, Paula E. "Immigrant Women and Consumer Protest: The New York City Kosher Meat Boycott of 1902." *American Jewish History* LXX (September 1980): 91–105.

Ichioka, Yuji. "*Amerika Nadeshiko:* Japanese Immigrant Women in the United States, 1900–1924." *Pacific Historical Review* XLIX (May 1980): 339–357.

Jones, Beverly W. "Mary Church Terrell and the National Association of Colored Women, 1896 to 1901." *Journal of Negro History* LXVII (Spring 1982): 20–33.

Jacoby, Robin Miller. "The Women's Trade Union League and American Feminism." *Feminist Studies* 3 (1976): 126–140.

James, Edward J. ed. *Notable American Women: A Biographical Dictionary.* Cambridge, MA: Belknap Press, 1971.

Katzman, David M. *Seven Days a Week: Women and Domestic Service in Industrializing America.* Urbana: University of Illinois Press, 1981.

Kenneally, James J. "Women and Trade Unions, 1870–1920: The Quandary of the Reformer." *Labor History* 14 (Winter 1973): 42–55.

Kennedy, Susan Estabrook. *If All We Did Was to Weep at Home: A History of White Working Class Women in America.* Bloomington: Indiana University Press, 1979.

———. "'The Want It Satisfies Demonstrates the Need of It': A Study of *Life and Labor* of the Women's Trade Union League." *International Journal of Women's Studies* 3 (July/August 1980): 391–406.

Kerber, Linda, and Jane DeHart Mathews, eds. *Women's America: Refocusing the Past.* New York: Oxford University Press, 1982. Part IIb.

Kessler-Harris, Alice. *Out to Work: A History of Wage-Earning Women in the United States.* Oxford: Oxford University Press, 1982.

Kleinberg, Susan J. "Technology and Women's Work: The Lives of Working

Class Women in Pittsburgh, 1870–1900." *Labor History* 17 (Winter 1976): 58–72.

Leloudis, II, James L. "School Reform in the New South: The Woman's Association for the Betterment of Public School Houses in North Carolina, 1902–1919." *Journal of American History* 69 (March 1983): 886–909.

Lerner, Gerda. *The Majority Finds Its Past: Placing Women in History.* Oxford: Oxford University Press, 1979. Chapter 6.

———. ed. *Black Women in White America: A Documentary History* New York: Vintage Books, 1973.

Litoff, Judy Barrett. *American Midwives: 1860 to the Present.* Westport, CT: Greenwood Press, 1978.

May, Elaine Tyler. "The Pressure to Provide: Class, Consumerism, and Divorce in Urban America, 1880–1920." In *The American Family in Social-Historical Perspective,* edited by Michael Gordon, 154–168. New York: St. Martin's Press, 1983.

Melosh, Barbara. *"The Physician's Hand": Nurses and Nursing in the Twentieth Century.* Philadelphia: Temple University Press, 1982.

Mohr, James C. *Abortion in America: The Origins and Evolution of National Policy, 1800–1900.* New York: Oxford University Press, 1978.

Neverdon-Morton, Cynthia. "The Black Woman's Struggle for Equality in the South, 1895–1940." In *The Afro-American Woman: Struggles and Images,* edited by Sharon Harley and Rosalyn Terborg-Penn, 43–57. Port Washington, NY: Kennikat Press, 1978.

Pratt, Norma Fain. "Culture and Radical Politics: Yiddish Women Writers in America, 1890–1940." In *Decades of Discontent: The Women's Movement, 1920–1940,* edited by Joan M. Jensen and Lois Scharf, 131–152. Westport, CT: Greenwood Press, 1983.

Reitano, Joanne. "Working Girls Unite." *American Quarterly* 36 (Spring 1984): 112–134.

Roeder, Richard B. "Crossing the Gender Line: Ella L. Knowles, Montana's First Woman Lawyer." *Montana the Magazine of Western History* 32 (Summer 1982): 64–75.

Rosen, Ruth. *The Lost Sisterhood: Prostitution in America, 1900–1918.* Baltimore: Johns Hopkins University Press, 1982.

Rosenberg, Rosalind. *Beyond Separate Spheres: Intellectual Roots of Modern Feminism.* New Haven: Yale University Press, 1982.

Rossiter, Margaret W. "Women Scientists in America before 1920." *American Scientist* 62 (May/June 1974): 312–323.

Rothman, David J., and Sheila M. Rothman, eds. *On Their Own: The Poor in Modern America.* Reading, MA: Addison-Wesley Publishing Company, 1972.

Schwantes, Carlos A. "Western Women in Coxey's Army in 1894." *Arizona and the West* 26 (Spring 1984): 5–20.

Scott, Anne Firor. *Making the Invisible Woman Visible.* Urbana: University of Illinois Press, 1984.

———. "On Seeing and Not Seeing: A Case of Historical Invisibility." *Journal of American History* 71 (June 1984): 7–21.

————. "The 'New Woman' in the New South." *South Atlantic Quarterly* 61 (Autumn 1962): 473–483.

Seller, Maxine Schwartz, ed. *Immigrant Women*. Philadelphia: Temple University Press, 1981.

Sklar, Kathryn Kish. "Hull House in the 1890s: A Community of Women Reformers," *Signs* 10 (Summer 1985): 658–677.

Smith-Rosenberg, Carroll. "The Female World of Love and Ritual: Relations between Women in Nineteenth Century America." *Signs* 1 (August 1975): 1–29.

Sterling, Dorothy, ed. *We Are Your Sisters: Black Women in The Nineteenth-Century*. New York: W. W. Norton & Company, 1984.

Strong, Bryan. "Ideas of the Early Sex Education Movement in America, 1890–1920." In *Procreation or Pleasure? Sexual Attitudes in American History*, edited by Thomas L. Altherr, pp. 127–144. Malabar, FL: Robert J. Krieger Publishing Company, 1983.

Tentler, Leslie Woodcock. *Wage-Earning Women: Industrial Work and Family Life in the United States, 1900–1930*. Oxford: Oxford University Press, 1979.

Terborg-Penn, Rosalyn. "Nineteenth Century Black Women and Woman Suffrage." *Potomac Review* 7 (Spring/Summer 1977): 13–24.

Towne, Marion K. "Charlotte Gilman in California." *Pacific Historian* 28 (Spring 1984): 5–17.

Walsh, Mary Roth. *"Doctors Wanted—No Women Need Apply": Sexual Barriers in the Medical Profession, 1835–1975*. New Haven: Yale University Press, 1977.

Wein, Roberta. "Women's Colleges and Domesticity, 1875–1918." *History of Education Quarterly* 15 (Spring 1974): 31–47.

Wertheimer, Barbara Mayer. *We Were There: The Story of Working Women in America*. New York: Pantheon Books, 1977.

Winter, Kate H. *Marietta Holley: Life With "Josiah Allen's Wife"*. Syracuse: Syracuse University Press, 1984.

Woloch, Nancy. *Women and the American Experience*. New York: Alfred A. Knopf, 1984. Chapters 9–12.

Yost, Nellie Snyder. "Nebraska's Scholarly Athlete: Louise Pound, 1872–1958." *Nebraska History* 64 (Winter 1983): 476–490.

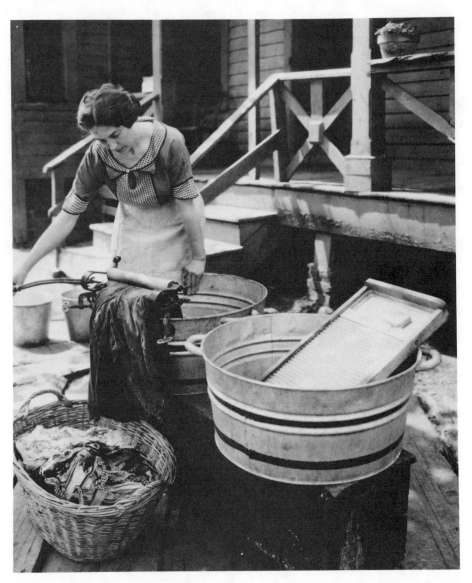

Even during the twentieth century, women's work continued to be domestically ori-ented and extremely taxing. Taken in Hinsdale, Illinois, in 1919, this photograph shows that home technology was often rudimentary, dependent on "elbow grease" as a power source. Courtesy of the State Historical Society of Wisconsin, Madison, Wisconsin.

CHAPTER 7

The "New Woman":
World War I and the 1920s

AFTER President Woodrow Wilson's futile attempts to preserve American neutrality and to keep the country out of the war raging in Europe, Congress declared war against Germany in April 1917. Jeannette Rankin of Montana, the only woman in Congress, was the one congressperson who voted against the war in hopes of a peaceful solution to world problems. Outraged at Germany's aggressive actions, most of the other representatives and senators swiftly voted in favor of American intervention.

For women, the years between 1917 and 1929 seemed to offer unparalleled opportunities. The war itself drew women out of their homes in unprecedented numbers; the postwar years witnessed the final successful push for woman suffrage; and the spirit of the 1920s encouraged women to express themselves as independent, sexual, and political individuals. Yet, while the period between America's entry into the war in 1917 and the dramatic end of the era with the stock market crash in 1929 appeared to be one of tremendous liberation for women, many of the changes were only superficial ones. Although American women fought on many levels against the stereotypes and traditional images that circumscribed their lives, they once again learned that reform comes with excruciating and exasperating slowness. With the force of history and tradition behind it, the invented American woman did not crumble and fall as a result of the onslaught against it; rather, it underwent only limited modifications.

Women were not drawn into the war effort immediately. Throughout the summer of 1917, the Department of Labor stated that no additional female laborers would be needed because there were plenty of men available for war industries. One of the department's slogans was "Plenty of Work for Men." Labor leaders also supported this claim.

Women did engage in war-relief work, such as war-bond drives. They conserved resources and foodstuffs needed for the war effort and maintained homes and farms, just as they had in previous wars. Many women volunteered their energies to the Red Cross to provide medical supplies and other services to the military. Other women joined the United States Army Corps of Nurses. Yet others worked with governmental agencies or with one of the myriad of women's voluntary associations that organized to aid the war effort. Women also created meatless, wheatless, and butterless meals. They knitted their own socks and sweaters and cut their skirts short to save material.

But women were not expected, at least initially, to replace men in industrial jobs. One commentator pointed out that this thinking was fallacious, since every man at the front required twenty workers at home producing war supplies. He added that there would not be enough men both to fight and work. His predictions were soon confirmed as volunteering, the draft, and a rapid decline in European immigration sharply reduced supplies of available male workers. The first draft alone, held on 20 July 1917, called 1,347,000 men away from home.

Employers attempted to fill the resulting job vacancies with experienced female workers. When this source was quickly exhausted, they turned to mobilizing unemployed women. During the fall of 1917, the United States Employment Service also attacked the problem by launching a governmental campaign to recruit women workers for war-industry jobs. A survey by the Women's Bureau of the United States Department of Labor of over five hundred war plants showed 14,402 women employed before the first draft, 19,783 after the first draft, and 23,190 after the second draft.

The labor of women was seen as a national necessity by the end of 1917. Millions of men leaving for military service combined with huge demands for war materials forced armament and other manufacturers of heavy goods to rely on female labor. In June of 1917, *World's Work* had predicted that, during the war, women would not put on "trousers or an unbecoming uniform and try to do something that a man can do better." But by the winter of 1917–1918, the YWCA noted that "avenues of work heretofore unthought of" for women had opened up.

Journals and magazines reported women working in dirigible factories, machine shops, steel mills, oil refineries, railway yards, chemical plants, automobile factories, and iron and steel mills. Newspaper headlines announcing "Steel Mills Want Women" and "Women Print Liberty Bonds in U.S. Bureau of Engraving" became commonplace. A report from Idaho observed; "Women are being employed in considerable numbers in the lumber mills. . . . They wear overalls, do a man's work and receive a man's wages." The dispatch explained that "Employment of the women is declared to be due to shortage of help in preparing the white and yellow pine for airplane use."

By early 1918, women unloaded heavy freight, carried huge shells, painted steel tanks, carried steel parts, and operated welding equipment, all with great proficiency. Because there were so many women working in armament industries, the government created a special division within the Department of Labor to oversee female laborers. This agency later became the Women's Bureau of the Department of Labor. Led by former labor organizer Mary Anderson after 1920, this commission collected data on and studied women workers.

In a report in 1920, the Women's Bureau, newly established in the Department of Labor with Mary Anderson as its head, commented that the war "forced the experiment of woman labor in the craftsmanly occupations." The bureau also reported the surprise of employers when observing the skills and abilities of women workers. According to one manufacturer, "there is hardly a line of work in which a woman cannot adapt herself." Clearly, the war gave women the opportunity not only to enter "inappropriate" jobs but also to show aptitude for them. From surveys and interviews, it also became evident that women war workers enjoyed the challenges presented by their jobs and reveled in high wartime wages.

Women's expectations for employment opportunities and wages began to rise during the war years. Women workers often sought better-paying positions, joined trade unions to protect their jobs, and engaged in widespread militancy when they did not receive what they thought to be just treatment. They were aided in these efforts by middle-class reformers who lobbied local and federal governmental bodies on behalf of female laborers. These "allies" of working women, as they were called, fought for equal pay provisions, decent working conditions, and the right of women to join or organize unions. The National Women's Trade Union League was particularly supportive of working women's causes while encouraging female wage earners' interest in feminist issues.

Men, however, were not highly receptive to female coworkers. The traditional idea of women as wives and mothers persisted and caused many men to believe that women who had to work should be limited to certain "female" occupations and that women who did not have to work should stay at home. Union leaders worried that widespread female labor would lead to a change in working conditions and a dilution of craft skills. And almost all men feared that the introduction of female labor would depress wages for all workers.

Because of their apprehensions, men frequently resisted the hiring of women through protests and strikes, either barred or grudgingly admitted women to their unions, and used protective legislation to block women from a variety of jobs. Afraid of losing their jobs to women, men tended to cooperate with women workers only when jobs were segregated along gender lines. For instance, male laundry drivers in Kansas

City encouraged female laundresses to strike for better wages and working conditions. And male telephone installers and repairmen urged the unionization of female telephone operators.

In 1918, suffrage leader Harriot Stanton Blatch argued in her *Mobilizing Woman-Power* that, in spite of resistance, "American women have begun to go over the top." Although Blatch thought that there was nothing revolutionary about women earning wages, she seemed delighted that women were finally being employed in machine shops and as section hands on railway gangs. She was enthusiastic about women's "quick wits and deft fingers," as well as about their "muscles," which they used "vigorously at three dollars a day." To her, female messengers showed a courage and intelligence that were a definite "improvement upon the manners of the young barbarians of the race." Blatch was exultant that women had "opened up every line of service" and were found in every type of job. "When men go a-warring," she wrote, "women go to work."

The "great industrial and social change" envisioned by Blatch was in reality neither widespread nor smooth. Discriminatory attitudes and practices permeated every industry and business. Even the federal government could not free itself from gender prejudices. In 1917, the United States Civil Service Commission released its usual employment announcement for male stenographers in federal agencies. When a women's committee pursued a grievance, departmental officials trivialized the matter or flatly denied the existence of discriminatory practices. One blithely stated: "It affords me pleasure to state that there is no discrimination against the employment of women in this office, the pay roll for the current month showing that sixty-two per centum of the employees are women." Another official similarly claimed that no bias existed in the Bureau of Mines, because "the number of women stenographers, typewriters, and clerks is 15, and the number of male stenographers, typewriters, and clerks is 17." Others explained that they could not hire women because "certain positions in the public service can not be filled by women" who were unfit for the "strain" of the jobs.

In the express industry, women were accepted more enthusiastically, at first on a gender-limited basis but gradually in "men's work" as well. As a case in point, the Wells Fargo Company welcomed women as agents, cashiers, stenographers, telephone operators, accountants, and auditors. But a special edition of the *Wells Fargo Messenger* published in March 1918, and devoted to the topic "Women in the Express," demonstrated an ambivalence representative of many Americans. One essay spoke of Wells Fargo "girls" as the "weaker sex" who, limited by their physical abilities rather than their enthusiasm for a task, could not participate "in the physical operation of the express." The author explained: "Our highly specialized service, from the collection of shipments of all sizes to their dispatch upon wagons, in depots and on trains, comprises a 'fighting line' which, like train operation, must necessarily be entrusted chiefly to men."

Only a page later, the same writer referred to a female "Wells Fargo man" running a Montana office and to two women investigators who were "shattering the theory" that this was a male task. Some pages later the *Messenger* proclaimed that "woman has come to a new strength in Wells Fargo." Not only did they fill "new" jobs in a "far more capable way than ever mere man" did, but women also performed men's jobs so effectively that "man is fairly certain to have to make a good showing to get the job back again." The *Messenger* went on to assure its readers: "Fargo men everywhere have accepted the changed conditions not only as inevitable, but as a patriotic duty. They everywhere have shown a keen desire to co-operate with and to instruct and help their new companions of the dominant sex." The issue closed with an exhortation to "our girls" to aspire to the same high ideals of individual service that the company expected from its male employees. "Girls," the slogan read, "Let Us All do It the Fargo Way!"

The Wells Fargo Company served as an example of a business that tried valiantly to reconcile traditional attitudes toward women with the reality of the world of work as it stood in 1918. Another area that struggled to accept female laborers was agriculture. Although women had participated in farming as wives and daughters and as migratory workers for centuries, the heavy physical labor of the farm was still thought to be beyond women in 1917. Like industry, agriculture was soon pressed by a shortage of workers. In order to interest women in agricultural labor and to convince farm employers that women were capable of the work, such private women's groups as the New York Woman's Suffrage Party and the New York City Mayor's Committee of Women on National Defense organized agricultural training camps and recruited women for them. Trained recruits were then bussed to nearby farms in squads.

By February 1918, the Department of Labor recognized the potential of female farm labor and began to register women for possible agricultural employment. In that same month, the Women's National Farm and Garden Association, the Garden Clubs of America, the Women's Committee of the Council of National Defense, and a number of women's colleges founded the American Woman's Land Army (WLA). Recruits were guaranteed training and a minimum wage in return for a promise of at least two months of service. The women worked in squads in dairying, livestock, and poultry care, fruit picking, planting, weeding, hoeing, mowing, and the operation of farm equipment.

The demand for women farm laborers soon outstripped the supply. When the summer of 1918 drew to a close, the WLA had placed 15,000 women in 127 units in twenty states. In addition thirty-four women's colleges offered training, while numerous women's clubs offered scholarships to potential recruits. The WLA also published the *Farmerette*, which described various farm jobs, hours, wages, and training camps.

Because the demand for farm labor continued after the war, the WLA did not disband until January 1920. By that time, it had overcome the skepticism of farmers, opened new employment opportunities to women in agriculture, and demonstrated women's capacity for demanding physical labor. Farmers who had been hesitant even to hire women now paid wages willingly. And the women themselves seemed equally pleased with the experiment. As one woman who shocked wheat and cultivated corn wrote in 1919: "Some life! Its great, don't think I shall come back to Omaha until after corn-picking is over."

This acceptance of women workers by business and industry during the war years was not widely extended to native, ethnic, and black women. American Indian women were largely confined to reservations. Mexican-American women continued to be exploited as migrant farm workers in the Southwest. Asian women were offered the most poorly paid and unskilled of jobs, both on the West Coast and in eastern cities. And because employers still generally preferred "American-born" women for anything but the most unremunerative and taxing work, even white, European immigrant women were frequently relegated to domestic labor and piecework in the northern cities.

Black women laborers, too, were still largely segregated. They worked primarily in agriculture in the South and in domestic service in southern and northern urban areas. According to a Women's Bureau bulletin of 1918, however, wartime demands for labor opened a number of industrial jobs to black women for the first time, an opportunity that black women eagerly seized whenever it appeared. And Mary Church Terrell's experiences as a clerk in segregated "colored" sections of the War Risk Insurance Bureau and the Census Bureau suggest that a number of black women filled government jobs.

Despite the discriminatory attitudes and practices endured by black American women, they worked willingly and energetically on behalf of the war effort. They not only responded patriotically to the demands of the war; they also acted on the potential for social reform that it offered. Black women formed a large number of organizations to provide supplies, aided the war effort in such ways as sponsoring bond drives, and improved their own communities through recreational, health-care, and other programs. The Atlanta Colored Women's War Council, for example, established Patriotic Leagues for young black women, initiated food conservation programs, launched a "suppression of liquor campaign," organized community and camp entertainment, offered lodging to soldiers' families, and worked for the improvement of sanitation, police protection, and street lighting.

The Committee on Women's Defense Work of the Council of National Defense exerted a steady pressure on southern states to integrate black women into the civilian war effort. Although many white Southerners resisted this idea, black field representative Anna Dunbar Nelson traveled through the South organizing black women in 1918. Discouraged to learn that "government employment bureaus here recognize in every colored girl who applies for work only a potential scrub woman, no matter how educated and refined the girl may be," Nelson nevertheless pursued her mission. She was received cooly in every state except Florida and Mississippi, where white leaders were eager to include black women in the patriotic war effort. After visiting with black women, Nelson saw that they wanted semi-independent, statewide organizations of their own paralleling white women's groups. This structure developed in Florida but not throughout the South.

Despite problems of organization, the work of Nelson and the Women's Committee opened new opportunities to black women, such as nurses' training, while quietly attacking the caste system of the South. The white state chairperson in Mississippi recognized the potential implications of black women's war work. "I am vitally interested in this, and can see its far reaching effect—not alone now—but after the war, when we will need trained hands and brains, for the great work awaiting." Black women leaders also supported the social change stimulated by the war by encouraging their followers to demonstrate their patriotism and to initiate social reforms on the local level.

During the war years, a large number of southern black women attempted to escape the racial and economic limitations of the South by moving to northern cities. Searching for expanded employment opportunities and a less prejudiced climate in which to live, they were frequently disappointed on both counts.

The high hopes that southern black women held for northward migration were poignantly expressed in the letters they wrote in search of jobs. In early 1917, a Florida woman responded to an employment agent's advertisement in the Chicago *Defender*. "I realey diden no if you can get a good job for me as am a woman and a widowe with two girls," she wrote. "We will do any kind of work," she assured him. Another Florida woman similarly promised that she could perform "any kind of housework laundress nurse good cook who has cooked for northern people." A female respondent from Mississippi described herself as a "willen workin woman" who could serve as a cook or domestic. "I hope that you will help me," she pleaded, "as I want to get out of this land of sufring I no there is som thing that I can do here there is nothing for me to do I may be able to get in some furm where I dont have to stand on my feet all day."

In both the North and the South, black women workers continued to be restricted to, or were expected to return to, domestic service, laundry work, and agricultural employment after the war ended in 1918. By 1920, 75 percent of all employed black women labored in these three fields. In a number of large cities, the proportion of black women in domestic service rose to 85 percent. They were now widely barred from factories and offices by restrictive policies that attempted to attract white workers with the promise of a rigidly segregated workplace. If hired in factories and shops, black women usually worked in separate rooms, lacked such amenities as lunchrooms and clean bathrooms, and were denied privileges commonly extended to white women workers. The menial, dirty, and heavy jobs typically went to black women as well as to non-American-born women of "low grade."

Recognizing the many difficulties created by the mobilization of the war labor force, President Wilson created the National War Labor Board (NWLB) in April 1918. He charged the NWLB to pay special attention to issues concerning female laborers, especially that of equitable pay. In 1918, women workers received only one half to two thirds of the wages earned by men. The claim that women's work was "supplemental" or for "pin money" was used to rationalize the disparity in pay. Yet the introduction of 1,500,000 women into war industries contradicted this argument. The NWLB therefore supported the principle of equal pay for equal work. The NWLB soon found its equal pay stance to be "not so simple as it looks." Confronted with a rapidly changing work world on the one hand and the numerous people who still viewed women primarily as "mothers of the race" on the other, the board often ended up setting women's wages at three fourths of the standard (male) rate. The board did gain, however, shorter workdays and the right to join unions for women.

By the time that the war drew to a close in 1918, the NWLB had failed to devise any consistent policy on working women and to accept the basic equality of women in industry and business. It had barred women from policy making, listening instead to union leaders and employers. As a result, the board was unprepared for demobilization and its attendant difficulties of moving numerous women out of the labor force while moving men back in.

Apparently, the NWLB, like most Americans, assumed that when the war ended women would not hesitate to abandon their wartime jobs in favor of home and family. Believing that the traditional image of the American woman as passive, docile, and homebound must still be attractive to women, people failed to anticipate the resistance of working women expected to surrender their high paying jobs to returning veterans. Many women voiced their preference to continue working and their expectation of equitable wages. Black women resisted leaving industrial jobs to return to domestic and other menial employment. And women who held governmental and relief-agency positions were often loath to return to full-time wife- and motherhood.

In spite of their resistance, protests, and strikes, women workers were indeed phased out of heavy industries in 1918 and 1919. The spirit of the invented American woman was invoked to soften the blow. As women left their jobs, two patterns emerged, according to census data. Female employment remained relatively high in such women-employing sectors as tobacco, leather, and food processing, clerical work, and sales. But in such areas as steel, chemicals, electrical goods, and airplanes and automobiles, women lost their wartime jobs at a rapid rate. The emergency expansion of the American economy and the temporary absence of male workers did not permanently affect patterns of employment beyond the war's conclusion in 1918.

Women in the clerical sector—telephone and telegraph operators, clerks, bookkeepers, stenographers, secretaries, and sales personnel—saw real gains during this period. In 1920, 25.6 percent of women worked in business-related jobs, as opposed to 23.8 percent in manufacturing, 18.2 percent in domestic service, and 12.9 percent in agriculture.

Employment was not the only opportunity opened to women by the First World War; new avenues of reform increased as well. For instance, because they firmly believed in their moral responsibility to give order to a chaotic world, many women entered the movement for world peace. They organized such groups as the Woman's Peace Party (WPP)—a leader of which was Jane Addams—which was dedicated to the principles of pacifism and feminism. Formed in 1915, the WPP denounced the "man-made" war and called for neutral mediation and limitation of armaments. The WPP argued for the "further humanizing of governments by the extension of the franchise to women." During the war years, the WPP conducted educational programs designed to inform the public about the causes of and cures for war. Although women's peace groups did not achieve many of their immediate objectives, they did foster a feeling of sisterhood and feminism among their members.

A similar spirit developed among American women involved in other voluntary organizations and reform activities during 1917 and 1918. Thousands of activist women came to desire reforms for themselves. Consequently, the woman suffrage campaign grew in strength and accelerated its efforts during the war. Incensed that the nation was intent on making the world safe for democracy while denying the rights of a majority of its citizens, woman suffrage leaders continued their crusade despite the war.

The suffrage argument had been developing since the first women's rights convention at Seneca Falls, New York, in 1848. Nineteenth-century suffragists introduced the claims that it was "just" to give women the vote and that it was also "expedient" in that women would use the vote to help clean up society. They expected that admission to the public sphere through the vote would allow them to reform the work-place, education, and eventually the family structure that so severely re-stricted their lives. Between 1904 and 1915, under the presidency of min-ister and doctor Anna Howard Shaw, the National American Woman Suffrage Association (NAWSA) argued that suffrage would produce equal work opportunities.

During the prewar years, the NAWSA underwent an organizational fervor that resulted in the proliferation of local and state equal suffrage associations. The organization experimented with such progressive tac-tics as open-air meetings, silent pickets, leaflet campaigns, and suffrage parades. It acquired aggressive new leaders such as Inez Milholand, an attorney and Socialist who paraded and picketed on behalf of woman suffrage and women workers. And it persuaded educator and suffrage organizer Carrie Chapman Catt, originally from Iowa, to assume its presidency in 1915.

By the time that the United States entered the war in 1917, the NAWSA was well on its way to developing a clear-cut political strategy. Catt combined her dedication to suffrage, years of experience working with the Woman's Suffrage Party of New York City, and a two million dollar bequest to devise what she called her "Winning Plan." She was determined to capitalize on the fact that woman suffrage had become a legitimate concern for many women and men of all social classes. Women could now vote in eleven states; newspapers continually dis-cussed the suffrage issue; and public opinion was beginning to be more positive than it had ever been.

Catt's "Winning Plan" was designed to coordinate state campaigns with massive lobbying in Washington to gain a federal suffrage amend-ment by December 1920. The NAWSA hired such women organizers as Maud Wood Park to travel throughout the country to form woman suf-frage groups. The central office in Washington kept up a steady and huge flow of information and suffrage literature to its workers to help them build pressure on their state's senators and representatives. Park later recalled that, when she joined the NAWSA Congressional Committee, she observed file cases that held "531 portfolios, 96 for the Senate and 435 for the House" that provided "all the known data about a senator or representative." According to Park, these files included printed sketches of his life, and "there were facts supplied by our members in the state about his personal, political, business and religious affiliations; there was everything that could be discovered about his stand on woman suffrage and more or less about his views on other public questions."

State suffrage groups also proved to be highly sophisticated in their organization. Massachusetts suffragists pushed their antisuffrage state into the prosuffrage column in 1919 through dynamic and politically insightful techniques. Three groups—the Massachusetts Woman Suffrage Association, the College Equal Suffrage League, and the Boston Equal Suffrage Association for Good Government—utilized open-air meetings, touring speakers, leaflets, petitions, and "Votes for Women" buttons to persuade Massachusetts citizens to back woman suffrage.

Many western states also developed tightly centralized suffrage clubs. California groups were so effective that the state adopted woman suffrage in 1911 and strongly endorsed the federal amendment afterward. In South Dakota, suffragists battled a strong antisuffrage component of conservative German immigrants and liquor interests who, like national liquor representatives, feared that enfranchised women would vote for prohibition. Beginning in 1910, suffrage leader Mary Shields Pyle pushed the South Dakota Universal Franchise League to copy the NAWSA in style and tactics, a move that resulted in the enfranchisement of South Dakota women in November 1918, and the subsequent support of the federal amendment.

Black women also contributed greatly to the woman suffrage crusade. Although usually overlooked by chroniclers of the suffrage movement, black suffragists were active for many decades. From its inception in 1896, the National Association of Colored Women's Clubs actively supported woman suffrage, as did such black leaders as Mary McLeod Bethune and Mary Church Terrell. Among the individual states, Massachusetts, Illinois, and New York particularly had a number of active black women's suffrage clubs by the first decade of the twentieth century. In New York City, black suffragist Annie K. Lewis was elected vice-chairperson of the largely white New York Woman's Suffrage party in 1917.

Despite their many contributions, black women in New Bedford, Massachusetts, were rebuffed by Charrie Chapman Catt when they attempted to join the NAWSA in 1919. Catt and other white suffrage leaders feared that the admission of black women to membership would alienate white southern members. They purposely decided not to support the enfranchisement of black women in order to gain the support of southern white suffragists and white supremacist Democrats. In southern states, this policy sometimes translated into the actual prevention of black female suffrage in order to gain white backers. By 1919, black suffragists had been snubbed by both the NAWSA and the Woman's party.

This attitude on the part of white suffragists turned many blacks against the suffrage issue. As early as 1917, the *Crisis,* the official newspaper of the National Association for the Advancement of Colored

People, warned against woman suffrage because of the antiblack attitudes of white females who would be casting ballots. Other black leaders feared the introduction of a "grandmother" clause after suffrage that would deny most black women the right to vote.

Yet, large numbers of black women refused to desert the suffrage cause. They organized suffrage clubs, participated in rallies and demonstrations, spoke and lectured on suffrage, and wrote articles on its behalf. Such black women groups as the National Federation of Afro-American Women, the National Association of Colored Women, and the Northeastern Federation of Colored Women's Clubs worked enthusiastically for women's right to vote. Apparently, black women recognized the potential influence that they could wield through the vote, especially in southern states. By 1920, "Colored Women's Voter's Leagues" were common throughout the South.

As a result of the formation of so many different types of energetic groups on local and state levels, the suffrage movement became huge and dynamic during the second decade of the twentieth century. The NAWSA soon became the nation's largest voluntary organization. Through it, two million women across the country voiced their support of state and federal suffrage legislation. In Washington, the central office exerted a steady pressure on President Wilson to endorse woman suffrage. They lobbied, educated, and cajoled Wilson to reverse his conservative view of women in favor of a prosuffrage stance.

At the same time, the Woman's party, formed in 1916 by suffragist Alice Paul, applied militant tactics to President Wilson. First organized as the Congressional Union in 1913, Paul's group had had years of experience with this type of approach. In 1917, the Woman's party initiated twenty-four hour pickets of the White House. When the women were arrested, jailed, and force-fed to avert hunger strikes, they made dramatic headlines. Female picketers persisted in carrying banners reading "Democracy Should Begin at Home"; "How Long Must Women Wait For Liberty!"; and "Kaiser Wilson" outside the White House. The resulting riots, arrests, and hunger strikes of imprisoned women attracted even more publicity and placed greater pressure on the President.

Polish-born Rose Winslow (Ruuza Wenclawska) was one of the Woman's party members arrested during White House demonstrations. Her thoughts while in prison were smuggled out to suffragists and her husband on small scraps of paper. "If this thing is necessary we will naturally go through with it," she wrote early in her prison stay. "Force is so stupid a weapon." In later notes, Winslow described fainting spells and vomiting caused by the irritation of the tube used to force-feed her. One of the most touching missives read: "Alice Paul is in the psychopathic ward. She dreaded forcible feeding frightfully, and I hate to think how she must be feeling. I had a nervous time of it, gasping a long time afterward, and my stomach rejecting during the process. The poor soul who fed me got liberally besprinkled during the process. I heard myself making the most hideous sounds. One feels so forsaken when one lies prone and people shove a pipe down one's stomach."

These hunger strikes and other actions of Woman's party members embarrassed the NAWSA and were often criticized as being counterproductive. But the Woman's party firmly believed that their militancy forced the hands of the President and members of Congress. Perhaps the combined efforts of both groups were what finally persuaded President Wilson, on 9 January 1918, to advise a group of Democrats to vote for the suffrage amendment "as an act of right and justice to the women of the country and of the world."

The next day a stirring drama was witnessed in the House of Representatives. The galleries were packed with women there to watch Representative Jeannette Rankin introduce the "Anthony" amendment, as the suffrage measure was called. One very ill representative was carried in on a stretcher to cast his vote, while another came from the deathbed of his suffragist wife to cast his. When the tally was in, it stood at 274 votes for and 136 against, exactly one vote over the necessary two-thirds majority. As women of the NAWSA and the Woman's party streamed into the hallways they broke into song: "Praise God from whom all blessings flow."

The suffrage amendment moved next to the Senate where it remained mired for a year and a half. The NAWSA worked against the reelection of four antisuffrage senators while the Woman's party again took to the streets in protest. President Wilson took the unprecedented step of personally addressing the Senate on behalf of suffrage. After several negative votes, the Senate finally approved woman suffrage on 4 June 1919, by a vote of sixty-three to thirty.

Next, the suffrage provision needed ratification by three fourths (36) of the states. Eleven ratifications poured in during the first month, and eleven more states approved the amendment during the next five months. But the opposition was tough, well-organized, and needed to hold back only thirteen states. Both the NAWSA and the Woman's party quickly went into action to combat the "antis," as the antisuffrage forces were known.

The tension peaked in August 1920. Thirty-five states had ratified woman suffrage. Only one was needed and only one feasible state existed—Tennessee. Suffragists poured into Nashville to campaign and to lobby. On August 13, the state Senate ratified the measure. When the issue went to the House, the vote was so close that it rested in the hands of Harry Burn, at twenty-four years of age the youngest member of the body. When he cast his decision for suffrage, the amendment carried forty-nine to forty-seven. Reportedly, Burn had just received a message from his mother instructing him: "Vote for suffrage and don't keep them in doubt. . . . Don't forget to be a good boy and help Mrs. Catt put 'Rat' in Ratification."

On 26 August 1920, the Secretary of State proclaimed the ratification of the Nineteenth Amendment. Seventy-two years had passed since the convention at Seneca Falls, where women had first asked for the right of franchise. Suffragists were elated; they believed that the panacea was at hand.

Because they had invested so much emotional energy and hope for the future in the vote, activist women were crushed when they soon learned that it was not "the" answer after all. Within a few years, it became evident that women were not voting in blocs or uniformly for women's reform issues. Like men, female voters responded to their own social class backgrounds, educational levels, race, religious affiliations, and geographical locations.

Another complication developed when the NAWSA, the Woman's party (the National Woman's Party or NWP beginning in 1921), and other women's groups drastically disagreed on how further reforms for women might be activated, or if they were necessary at all. Most Americans seemed to feel that women now had all necessary rights, and that the unending discussion concerning women was finally over. Women's efforts after 1920 were thus fragmented. Anna Howard Shaw foresaw this development when she stated: "I am sorry for you young women who have to carry on the work for the next ten years, for suffrage was a symbol, and now you have lost your symbol."

Just as Shaw prophesied, the suffrage movement soon broke into factions, including social feminists (dedicated to the reform of society), feminists (advocates of enlarged roles for women), pacifists, and women interested in changing the worlds of labor and the professions. Numerous other women devoted their energies to such groups as the Women's Christian Temperance Union, the American Association of University Women, the National Parent Teacher Association, and the National Council of Jewish Women. Yet other women seemed content to turn their attention to themselves and such personal pursuits as bridge, gardening, and current fashions. "We all went back to a hundred different causes and tasks that we'd been putting off all those years," one former suffragist explained. "We just demobilized."

One organization that attracted many women during the 1920s was the newly founded League of Women Voters. Committed to social reform, the elimination of discriminatory laws against women, and the education of women as citizens, the league worked very hard to maintain a nonpartisan and moderate position. It proved to be an effective training ground for women. For instance, Lavinia Engle became director of the Maryland league in 1920, was subsequently elected to the Maryland state legislature, and in 1936, became an officer in the U. S. Social Security Administration. But because league members believed in "the aloof detachment of the scientific method" and in "wooing our legislators in a dignified and league-like manner," they frequently produced more words than action.

Many other issues drew the interest of women. Many joined the Women's Trade Union League and the Consumers' League, still led by Florence Kelley. Carrie Chapman Catt founded the National Conference on the Cause and Cure of War, while Jane Addams joined the Women's International League for Peace and Freedom. A group of teachers and clerical workers formed the National Federation of Business and Professional Women's Clubs to work for equal rights for professional women. Still others became active with the YWCA and its many programs devoted to social reform and the uplift of women.

One group dedicated to further political reform for women was the National Woman's Party (NWP), lead by Alice Paul. Paul and her followers believed that an equal rights amendment to the Constitution was an absolute necessity if women were to be protected from discriminatory laws and practices at the national and state levels. The NWP proposed amendment simply stated that "men and women shall have equal rights throughout the United States and every place subject to its jurisdiction." The NWP campaigned for the Equal Rights Amendment (ERA), their single cause, in their newspaper, *Equal Rights*. In 1923, Paul introduced it to Congress but found both Members of Congress and the American public generally laconic regarding any further "women's" amendments.

The NWP's single-minded commitment to the ERA kept the spirit of feminism alive during the 1920s and pointed the way to future equal rights reforms. But the NWP's stand also made cooperation among women activists difficult. Feminists, such as those in the NWP stood for equality in all areas of life and desired the eradication of protective labor legislation for women because they saw such legislation as unfair and restrictive of their work rights. Social feminists, who desired equality primarily in social and economic areas, thought that the ERA was too extreme a measure, and supported protective labor legislation. As a result of their many differences, feminists and social feminists formed two separate, and often warring, factions, which ultimately hurt the efficacy of both groups.

Black suffragists pursued few feminist activities after 1920. Feeling abandoned by white women activists, black women showed little interest in either the ERA or protective legislation. Concerned about world peace and racial oppression, they joined such groups as the Women's International League for Peace and Freedom and the International Council of Women of the Darker Races. Black leaders such as Mary McLeod Bethune and Jamaican-born nationalist Amy Jacques Garvey turned their attention to racial issues. While Bethune struggled with problems of racial discrimination in education and government, Garvey promoted the argument that blacks had to return to Africa if they were to be happy.

Few black women found membership in the predominantly white League of Women Voters or the National Woman's Party attractive; rather, most black women chose to join the Colored Women Political Group and other similar clubs. In 1922, one black female Socialist exhorted black women to "form clubs, explain the correct use of the ballot, consult among ourselves the best way this particular principle or policy will benefit society, then make a demand and see to it that it is carried out by those whom you have elected into office."

Like many white women, black women seemed more interested in social feminism than in political feminism. Educational reformer Nannie Burroughs organized the National Association of Wage Earners during the early 1920s to publicize the plight of the black working woman. Thousands of others joined church groups, community improvement organizations, and women's clubs of various types.

Black women activists did not always work separately from white women. Black-white interaction occurred in the Commission on Inter-Racial Cooperation of the Women's Council of the Methodist Episcopal Church, South, which in 1920 sponsored a major conference on race relations. Also in 1920, a group of black women appealed to the predominantly white YWCA for black-oriented programs, eventual integration of black women into the organization, and black representation on the national board. In that year, the first black women on the staff of the YWCA, social worker Eva Bowles, patiently explained that "white women do not properly appreciate the strength of our colored women throughout the country." She added: "We must face this job of letting them understand it better." In 1924, the first black woman, social worker Elizabeth Ross Haynes, was elected to the national board of the YWCA.

The most pressing issue to black women during the 1920s, and the one that led to collaboration between black and white women, was lynching. The antilynching movement dated back to 1895, to the one-person crusade of Ida Wells-Barnett. In 1922, black reformer Mary B. Talbert organized the Anti-Lynching Crusade. She hoped to bring together "a million women," both white and black, "to stop lynching."

Studies by Talbert's group revealed that not only black men were lynched: eighty-three women had been lynched since 1892. The impact of these findings was so great that the National Council of Women, representing thirteen million women, voted in 1922 to "endorse the Anti-Lynching Crusade recently launched by colored women of this country." By 1923, Talbert reported that over 700 women leaders in twenty-five states were working hard to stop lynching. Her executive committee outlined further actions: pressuring Congress and state legislatures for antilynching legislation, pursuing suits against lynchers, and widely publicizing episodes of lynching.

White southern women also exerted great efforts to eradicate lynching. They affiliated with black women's groups and formed their own organizations. In 1930, Texas reformer Jessie Daniel Ames founded the Association of Southern Women for the Prevention of Lynching (ASWPL). The organization hoped to devise means to prevent lynching in the South and to mobilize southern white women on behalf of the antilynching cause. Appalled that many lynchings were rationalized as necessary steps to protect white womanhood, Ames's group issued a public statement disclaiming any connection with lynchings: "Women dare no longer allow themselves to be the cloak behind which those bent upon personal revenge and savagery commit acts of violence and lawlessness."

By attacking the dual concepts of paternalism and chivalry, Ames's followers asserted themselves not only as antilynching advocates but as "new women." Southern white women had long been staunch advocates of the suffrage amendment, which they had hoped would bring them a measure of freedom and independence. Such women as Madelina McDowell Breckinridge of Kentucky had worked long and hard to bring woman suffrage to fruition. As the central figure in the Kentucky Equal Rights Association, Breckinridge, and many others like her, had traveled, spoken, and campaigned on behalf of the vote for women. Now, during the 1920s, southern white women wanted to move ahead by promoting social reforms, entering political life, and loosening the bonds on their personal lives.

Southern women intensified their reform activities after suffrage was granted in 1920. Lynching, black women, and child labor were among their many interests. In 1924, the League of Women Voters established a Committee on Negro Problems, while the Southern Council on Women and Children in Industry was organized in 1931. Southern women also moved into politics by becoming active in political parties and by running for the state legislature, as Nellie Nugent Somerville of Mississippi did successfully in 1923. The following year, Miriam "Ma" Ferguson was elected Governor of Texas. The customary image of the Southern Lady, however, was very difficult to combat and change. Crusty with age and heavy with the weight of tradition, stereotypes of the southern female continued to plague women activists throughout the postwar decade.

Overall, American feminists seemed to be pleased with their progress. In 1923, only three years after the granting of the vote to American women, Charlotte Perkins Gilman proclaimed that the "breath of woman's new freedom" was blowing strongly through the land. She cited women's mental and physical development, advances in education, and success in the professions, politics, and independent lifestyles as evidence of "rapid and serious change." In spite of the "new status of women," Gilman assured Americans that they need not be alarmed. "Women are first, last and always mothers," she wrote, "and will so continue." Besides, she added, "in our dread of the 'new woman' we should not lose sight of the fact that we never were satisfied with the old kind."

One area that had experienced change during the years following the granting of the vote to women was childbirth. A short while before, a public health nurse in New York named Margaret Sanger had begun to publicize the issue of birth control. Blocked by federal and state legislation from distributing birth control information, Sanger had purposefully defied the law. She and her colleagues distributed her publication, the *Woman Rebel*, on the streets and through the mails. Facing arrest under the Comstock Law, Sanger fled to Europe in 1914, where she observed family planning clinics.

After Sanger returned to the United States with the help of President Wilson, she and her sister established the first birth control clinic in 1916. They were both arrested and sentenced to the workhouse, where Sanger's sister went on a dramatic hunger strike that almost caused her death. The resulting publicity brought the issue of birth control before the public and created a certain amount of interest in it. The results of the court case and discussions that ensued allowed doctors to dispense a restricted amount of birth control information to women.

Between 1914 and 1921, Sanger published a sixteen-page pamphlet entitled *Family Limitation*, which offered information on preventing pregnancy. She never received a strong endorsement from suffrage leaders, who perhaps considered the vote issue of tantamount importance. Sanger's work did appeal to Socialist women like Crystal Eastman. In 1919, Eastman publicly disparaged the fact that "voluntary motherhood is an ideal unrealized in this country." By 1920, Sanger had turned increasingly to middle-class women and medical doctors for reinforcement and financial subsidies.

In 1921, Sanger founded the American Birth Control League to promote the dissemination of birth control information. Her efforts drew fire from opponents who feared "race suicide," increased promiscuity, and the denial of the respect women gained from being mothers. Sanger responded to these charges: "We want children to be conceived in love, born of parents' conscious desire and born into the world with healthy and sound bodies and sound minds." That some people agreed with her was demonstrated at the American Birth Control Conference in 1921 and the International Birth Control Conference in 1925. By 1937, doctors in all states except Massachusetts and Connecticut were legally permitted to dispense birth control information.

Changes in other areas were not as far-reaching. Many of the women who did become members of Congress were widows of congressmen and had been nominated to take their deceased husbands' places. Quotas determined the number of female students admitted to law and medical schools. Women received one third of all graduate degrees granted but accounted for only 4 percent of full professors. In the workforce, women neither caught up with men in wages nor increased significantly in numbers (23 percent of American women held jobs in 1920; 24 percent in 1930). Women dominated offices but were frustrated by the low pay and lack of opportunity for advancement. They seldom filled executive, managerial or other high-level positions. In business women suceeded by designing and marketing products for other women.

Even areas that seemed to be undergoing drastic revision were often not, upon closer examination, experiencing truly significant change. Women did indeed become pilots, but largely because the airline industry hoped to convince the public that passengers were as safe in the air as at home with mother. Record-breaking pilots Elinor Smith and Amelia Earhart were heroines who fascinated the American public only briefly. Rather then becoming accepted in aviation, female pilots were soon replaced by men. By the end of the decade, women were hired as "hostesses." They were required to have nursing degrees and to care for passengers.

Many significant changes in women's lives during the postsuffrage years were very difficult to assess. In 1927, a special issue of *Current History* devoted to the topic, "The New Woman," asked former suffragists to comment on the impact of these changes. Charlotte Perkins Gilman emphasized once again the progress of women in politics, reform, jobs and professions, and the development of independence. Carrie Chapman Catt reminded readers that suffrage had been the result of a long and difficult struggle dating back to 1848. She added that women wanted the vote to enhance their reform efforts, an ideal that had been partially achieved. Overall, the discussion reflected satisfaction with suffragist and feminist activities and achievements.

Yet, in an issue of *Harper's Magazine* of the same month, journalist Dorothy Dunbar Bromley claimed that "feminism has become a term of opprobrium to the modern young woman" who "freely admits that American women have so far achieved but little in the arts, sciences, and professions as compared with men." Bromley's "Feminist—New Style" was much more interested in individual expression than she was in "women's" issues or women as a group. She did want a career, but without sacrificing or delaying any aspect of marriage and family.

The country in general was in a curious phase, almost antifeminist in tone. It was widely believed that women had achieved all their rights. In her autobiography, playwright Lillian Hellman recalled: "By the time I grew up the fight for the emancipation of women, their rights under the law, in the office, in bed, was stale stuff. My generation didn't think much about the place or the problems of women, were not conscious that the designs we saw around us had so recently been formed or that we were still part of that formation." At the same time, Sigmund Freud told women that they would continue to be incomplete and ridden by "penis envy" until they had fulfilled themselves through childbearing. Other writers and commentators argued that consumerism, fashion, beauty, and sex were all valid female activities. One even warned women that "the return to the home is going to be almost as long and hard a struggle as the struggle for women's rights."

During the 1920s there was a great emphasis on beauty, youth, and thinness for women. Advertisements pictured young, slim women doing their own housework with the vast array of home appliances now available to them. The message was clearly that women should stay home to pursue domestic tasks and to consume commercial goods. This early version of what would later be termed the feminine mystique also emphasized that artificial means—cosmetics—were now necessary for a woman to be attractive.

Silent films, an increasingly popular entertainment, reinforced these values. The pattern of movie heroines first emerged during the war years, when movie vamp Theda Bara popularized the eye makeup developed for her by cosmetic mogul, Helena Rubenstein, and Lillian Gish became the first girl-next-door. During the 1920s, Gloria Swanson played characters who demonstrated women's new sexual freedom. Clara Bow, the "It Girl," personified the kittenish and sexy flapper. And Mary Pickford, "America's Sweetheart," was the eternally youthful, innocent, and forever feminine woman.

By the end of the decade, Joan Crawford was the leading role model for young women in America. According to a study conducted in 1929 of the impact of films on American youth, the chorus girls and dancing flappers whom she portrayed served as a standard of behavior and appearance for a generation of female movie-goers. One sixteen-year-old commented: "These modern pictures give me a feeling to imitate their ways. I believe that nothing will happen to the carefree girl like Joan Crawford but it is the quiet girl who is always getting into trouble and making trouble."

Entrepreneurs and advertisers quickly jumped on the bandwagon of invented femininity. Charles Revson and Elizabeth Arden created new cosmetic products that turned into business empires. Women contributed greatly to the growth of the cosmetic industry from a $17 million business to a $141 million one by 1925. Those who wished to be thin read advertisements that advised them to "Reach for a Lucky instead of a Sweet." And married women who thought about jobs were told by advertisers that their proper role as women was to stay home and consume.

Producers of mass media cranked out novels, magazines, radio shows, and films that gave the American public the type of woman it seemed to want. And in 1921, businesspeople in Atlantic City, interested in extending the tourist season, staged the first Miss America pageant. Soon the concept spread across the nation so that Miss New Yorks, Miss American Rodeos, and Miss Cherry Blossoms abounded.

The decade's seeming obsession with women was also reflected in the work of female writers and artists. Novelist Edith Wharton wrote of New York society, while Ellen Glasgow brought southern women into vivid perspective for the rest of the nation. Others who wrote for women and about women included Fannie Hurst, Gertrude Atherton, and Edna Ferber. Interestingly enough, one of the period's better known art works produced by a woman was Florine Stettheimer's 1924 painting, "Beauty Contest." Painter Georgia O'Keefe, who was just beginning her career during the 1920s, produced unusual work, which her critics dismissed as an expression of extreme female "sensibility" and emotionalism.

The Golden Age of Sports also focused upon women and their achievements. In 1922, Floretta McCutcheon defeated the reigning bowling champion, Jimmy Smith. In 1926, Gertrude Ederle became the first woman to swim the English Channel, with a time that improved on the existing male record by two hours. Glenna Collett was the first woman to break 80 for eighteen holes of golf, while Helen Wills dominated women's tennis.

Marriage also seemed to be changing noticeably during the 1920s. The divorce rate rose rapidly. By 1929, slightly more than one in six marriages ended in divorce. Although this trend was usually attributed to woman suffrage and the emancipation of women, it is more likely that consumerism raised women's expectations of standards of living in marriage to unrealistic levels. At the same time, the media images of romance and everlasting happiness were proving to be untenable to both women and men on a daily basis. Women's attempts to act like "flappers" (the *Ladies Home Journal* described a "flapper" as a morbid woman who smoked, wore short skirts, performed obscene dances, favored one-piece bathing suits, listened to jazz, entered psychoanalysis, practiced birth control, and leaned toward Bolshevism) also did little to contribute to marital satisfaction.

In a sense, the rising divorce rate was paradoxical; the ultimate objective of beauty—sexuality—and consumerism for women was still traditional: to "catch" men. Far from disappearing as a result of woman suffrage and the emergence of the "new woman" during the 1920s, the invented American woman hung on. Despite the many other pursuits now open to her, the American woman's dream continued to focus on romance, a blissful marriage, and a model family.

Of course, this dream was relevant largely to white, native-born women. Non-American-born women had to deal with the realities of urban and often ghetto life. Receiving psychological and financial help from their families, friends, and churches, immigrant women were insulated from their new country. Grouped into ethnic neighborhoods, these women, at least the first generation of them, tolerated family and other practices incompatible with the new American woman. A study in 1930 of Polish families in Chicago showed that wife-beating was acceptable and that the patriarchal family structure was strong. But by the second generation, women of ethnic backgrounds gradually developed expectations similar to native-born women. Those who worked learned American ways, while films indoctrinated thousands into the values and mores of American women.

American Indian women on government reservations also struggled with a traditional, paternalistic system. Forced to fight to retain their status as a result of governmental policies that imposed capitalistic means of production on their society, native women both clung to old ways and tried to develop new ones. For example, when the U. S. Agricultural Extension Service established a program to teach New Mexico women canning techniques, Indian women resisted. Along with their Hispanic neighbors, native women preferred the customary and efficient technique of drying foodstuffs. Throughout the 1920s, these women seldom purchased or used jams, jellies, and canned goods. Clearly, jobs, films, radio, and the image of the flapper could have little impact on and meaning to these isolated women.

Nor did these things seem to speak to black women. Like Indian women, black women embraced traditional ways while developing meaningful new ones. Black female blues singers of the 1920s were an outstanding example of this phenomenon. During what is now referred to as the "classic" blues era, such singers as Bessie Smith, Gertrude "Ma" Rainey, Rosa Hill, Ida Cox, Sippie Wallace, and Georgia White played and sang the blues for black and white Americans. They developed a unique form of artistic expression because of the oppressive conditions imposed on them due to their race. Accordingly, their lyrics reflected the concerns of black women—such as poverty and abandonment by men— rather than those of the dominant white culture.

In literature, black women also contributed their own view of the world. Afro-American poets experimented with the female images important to their people; they wrote of mothers, entertainers, and black women of great beauty and sensuality. Black poets and prose writers, including women, were encouraged to deal with black themes in such black magazines as *Crisis* and the Urban League's *Opportunity*. Some black novelists, particularly Nella Larsen, examined the problems encountered by the "new" black woman. Others, notably Jessie Fauset and Zora Neale Hurston, became important in the Harlem Renaissance, which revealed blacks' literary talents and creative imagination to the nation.

When the era of the First World War and its aftermath was brought to a resounding end by the stock market crash of 1929, numerous changes seemed to have occurred for all American women. In retrospect, they do not appear very significant. White women experienced temporary gains due to the wartime emergency but made only limited progress during the postwar years, while non-American-born, native, and black women continued to be largely segregated. On the other hand, during the war years women did demonstrate without question that they could perform "men's" jobs. In 1920, they did win the right to vote throughout the nation and formally enter the national political arena. And during the 1920s, the "new" women did exercise rights and freedoms not known to women of previous eras.

By 1929, the scene had clearly changed. But were the realities really any different? Although it could no longer be seriously argued that women were passive and docile by nature, it was still maintained that women's lives should be dedicated primarily to wife- and motherhood. The ongoing debate over protective labor legislation manifested this dichotomy. Women were believed to be strong and assertive enough to hold jobs, but only if those jobs were limited and hedged about by laws based on women's presumed weaknesses.

Where would the United States and its women go next? What new onslaughts would the invented American woman confront during the 1930s? Although these questions were impossible to answer specifically, it seemed likely that the economic disaster of 1929 would lead to many changes for the people of the United States.

SUGGESTIONS FOR FURTHER READING

Banner, Lois. *American Beauty.* New York: Alfred A. Knopf, 1983.

Barnet, Evelyn Brooks. "Nannie Burroughs and the Education of Black Women." In *The Afro-american Woman: Struggles and Images,* edited by Sharon Harley and Rosalyn Terborg-Penn, 97–108. Port Washington, New York: Kennikat Press, 1978.

Baxandall, Rosalyn, Linda Gordon, and Susan Reverby, eds. *America's Working Women.* New York: Random House, 1976.

Becker, Susan D. *The Origins of the Equal Rights Amendment: American Feminism between the Wars.* Westport, CT: Greenwood Press, 1981.

Berkin, Carol Ruth, and Mary Beth Norton, eds. *Women of America: A History.* Boston: Houghton Mifflin Company, 1979. Chapters 11–12, 14.

Breen, William J. "Black Women and the Great War: Mobilization and Reform in the South." *Journal of Southern History* XLIV (August 1978): 421–440.

Buhle, Mari Jo, and Paul Buhle, eds. *The Concise History of Woman Suffrage:*

Selections from the Classic Work of Stanton, Anthony, Gage, and Harper. Urbana: University of Illinois Press, 1978.

Conner, Valerie J. "'The Mothers of the Race' in World War I: The National War Labor Board and Women in Industry." *Labor History* 21 (Winter 1979–80): 31–54.

Conway, Jill. "Women Reformers and American Culture, 1870–1930." Journal of Social History 5 (Winter 1971–72): 164–177.

Corn, Joseph J. "Making Flying 'Thinkable': Women Pilots and the Selling of Aviation, 1827–1940." *American Quarterly* 31 (Fall 1979): 556–571.

Cott, Nancy F. "Feminist Politics in the 1920s: The National Woman's Party." *Journal of American History* 71 (June 1984): 43–68.

Diggs, Irene. "Dubois and Women: A Short Story of Black Women, 1910–1934." *A Current Bibliography on African Affairs* 7 (Summer 1974): 260–303.

DuBois, Ellen. "The Radicalism of the Woman Suffrage Movement: Notes Toward the Reconstruction of Nineteenth-Century Feminism." *Feminist Studies* 3 (Fall 1975): 63–71.

Easton, Patricia O'Keefe. "Woman Suffrage in South Dakota: The Final Decade, 1911–1920." *South Dakota History* 13 (Fall 1983): 206–226.

Finn, Barbara R. "Anna Howard Shaw and Women's Work." Frontiers 4 (Fall 1979): 21–25.

Foner, Philip S. *Women and the American Labor Movement: From World War I to the Present.* New York: The Free Press, 1980.

Friedman, Jean E., and William G. Shade, eds. *Our American Sisters: Women in American Life and Thought.* Lexington, MA: D. C. Heath and Company, 1983. Chapters 21–24.

Geidel, Peter. "The National Woman's Party and the Origins of the Equal Rights Amendment, 1920–1923." *The Historian* XLII (August 1980): 557–582.

Gertzog, Irwin N. "The Matrimonial Connection: the Nomination of Congressmen's Widows for the House of Representatives." *Journal of Politics* 42 (August 1980): 820–833.

Gordon, Linda. *Woman's Body, Woman's Right: A Social History of Birth Control in America.* New York: Grossman Publishers, 1976.

Graebner, William. "'Uncle Sam Just Loves the Ladies': Sex Discrimination in the Federal Government, 1917." *Labor History* 21 (Winter 1979–80): 75–85.

Graham, Sally Hunter. "Woodrow Wilson, Alice Paul, and the Woman Suffrage Movement." *Political Science Quarterly* 98 (Winter 1983–84): 665–680.

Greenwald, Maurine Weiner. *Women, War, and Work: The Impact of World War I on Women Workers in the United States.* Westport, CT: Greenwood Press, 1980.

Harrison, Daphne Duval. "Black Women in the Blues Tradition." In *Afro-American Woman: Struggles and Images,* edited by Sharon Harley and Rosalyn Terborg-Penn. 58–73. Port Washington: Kennikat Press, 1978.

James, Edward J. ed. *Notable American Women: A Biographical Dictionary* Cambridge, MA: Belknap Press, 1971.

Jensen, Joan M. "The Evolution of Margaret Sanger's *Family Limitation* Pamphlet, 1914–1921." *Signs* 6 (Spring 1981): 548–555.

———. "Canning Comes to New Mexico: Women and the Agricultural Extension Service, 1914–1919." *New Mexico Historical Review* 57 (October 1982): 361–386.

Kerber, Linda K., and Jane DeHart Mathews, eds. *Women's America: Refocusing the Past.* New York: Oxford University Press, 1982. Part IIb.

Kessler-Harris, Alice. *Out to Work: A History of Wage-earning Women in the United States.* Oxford: Oxford University Press, 1982.

Krause, Corinne Azen. "Urbanization Without Breakdown: Italian, Jewish, and Slavic Immigrant Women in Pittsburgh, 1900–1945." *Journal of Urban History* 4 (May 1978): 291–305.

Lerner, Gerda, ed. *Black Women in White America: A Documentary History.* New York: Vintage Books, 1973.

Lunardini, Christine A., and Thomas J. Knock. "Woodrow Wilson and Woman Suffrage: A New Look." *Political Science Quarterly* 95 (Winter 1980–81): 655–671.

Martelet, Penny. "The Woman's Land Army, World War I." In *Clio Was a Woman: Studies in the History of American Women,* edited by Mabel E. Deutrich and Virginia C. Purdy, 136–146. Washington, D.C.: Howard University Press, 1980.

May, Elaine Tyler. *Great Expectations: Marriage and Divorce in Post-Victorian America.* Chicago: University of Chicago Press, 1981.

May, Lary. *Screening Out the Past: The Birth of Mass Culture and the Motion Picture Industry.* New York: Oxford University Press, 1980.

Pleck, Elizabeth H. "Challenges to Traditional Authority in Immigrant Families." In *The American Family in Social-historical Perspective,* edited by Michael Gordon, 482–503. New York: St. Martin's Press, 1983.

Rosen, Marjorie. *Popcorn Venus: Women, Movies and the American Dream.* New York: Avon Books, 1973.

Rossiter, Margaret W. *Women Scientists in America: Struggles and Strategies to 1940.* Baltimore: Johns Hopkins University Press, 1982.

Rushing, Andrea Benton. "Images of Black Women in Afro-American Poetry." In *The Afro-American Woman: Struggles and Images,* edited by Sharon Harley and Rosalyn Terborg-Penn, 74–86. Port Washington: Kennikat Press, 1978.

Schaffer, Ronald. "The Problem of Consciousness in the Woman Suffrage Movement: A California Perspective." *Pacific Historical Quarterly* 45 (November 1976): 469–493.

Seller, Maxine Schwartz, ed. *Immigrant Women.* Philadelphia: Temple University Press, 1981.

Scott, Anne Firor. *Making the Invisible Woman Visible.* Urbana: University of Illinois Press, 1984.

Steinson, Barbara J. "'The Mother Half of Humanity': American Women in the Peace and Preparedness Movements in World War I." In *Women, War, and Revolution,* edited by Carol R. Berkin and Clara M. Lovett, 259–284. New York: Holmes and Meier Publishers, Inc., 1980.

Stricker, Frank. "Cookbooks and Law Books: The Hidden History of Career Women in Twentieth Century America." *Journal of Social History* 10 (Fall 1976): 1–19.

Strom, Sharon Hartman. "Leadership and Tactics in the American Woman Suffrage Movement: A New Perspective from Massachusetts." *Journal of American History* LXII (September 1975): 296–315.

Tentler, Leslie Woodcock. *Wage-Earning Women: Industrial Work and Family Life in the United States, 1900–1930.* Oxford: Oxford University Press, 1979.

Terborg-Penn, Rosalyn M. "The Historical Treatment of Afro-Americans in the Woman's Movement, 1900–1920: A Bibliographical Essay." *A Current Bibliography on African Affairs* 7 (Summer 1974): 245–259.

———. "Discontented Black Feminists: Prelude and Postscript to the Passage of the Nineteenth Amendment." In *Decades of Discontent: The Women's Movement, 1920–1940,* edited by Joan M. Jensen and Lois Scharf, 262–278. Westport, CT: Greenwood Press, 1983.

Weibel, Kathryn. *Mirror Mirror: Images of Women Reflected in Popular Culture.* New York: Anchor Books, 1977.

Woloch, Nancy. *Women and the American Experience.* New York: Alfred A. Knopf, 1984. Chapters 13–16.

During the 1930s, First Lady Eleanor Roosevelt spent a huge amount of time and energy encouraging New Deal programs. Here she visits the Works Progress Administration black nursery school in Des Moines, Iowa, in 1936. Courtesy of the Franklin Delano Roosevelt Library, Hyde Park, New York.

CHAPTER 8

Making Do and Pitching In:
The Depression and World War II

FTER the stock market collapsed in 1929, the American economy
crumbled. The Great Depression, as it is called, was a disaster so
widespread and drastic that it ushered in a new era of United
States history. Traditional philosophies and institutions were rethought
and often restructured. The controversial New Deal soon emerged. Then,
barely on its feet again, the reconstructed nation became embroiled in
the largest and most destructive war in history.

The years between the beginning of the depression in 1929 and the end
of the Second World War in 1945 were indeed trying ones. Yet there was
no reason for people to give up the hope that better days lay ahead.
Slightly more than three centuries of American history had clearly revealed recurring cycles of economic panic and boom, conservativism and
liberalism, and peace and war.

American women had also experienced cycles. Those who hoped for
eventual liberation from the restriction of the invented American woman
had witnessed reform and reaction, change and backlash, independence
and dependence. Whether the women who struggled against the traditional stereotypes liked it or not, change was often a matter of two steps
forward and one step backward. And so it was for women during the
depression, New Deal, and the war years.

In what direction these steps would lead was difficult to predict in
1929. It seemed likely that some of the trends begun in the 1920s would
continue. When eminent sociologists Robert Lynd and Helen Lynd studied life in "Middletown, USA" (in reality Muncie, Indiana) in the late
1920s, they discovered that the number of children borne by women was
continuing to fall, while divorce rates were still rising. Increasingly, marriage was based on ideals of romantic love and spouses "fulfilling" each
other.

In 1930, evidence also suggested that women's interest in their appearance was rising. Journalist Paul W. White claimed that American women spent $2 billion a year on cosmetics. In their pursuit to appear "feminine," White said that they consumed 52,500 tons of cleansing cream, 6,562 tons of bath powder, and 2,375 tons of rouge each year. The Sears Roebuck catalogue in the autumn of 1930 confirmed women's growing interest in looking "ladylike." The fashion advertisements emphasized long, flowing skirts, defined bustlines, tiny waistlines, and "modern" corsets. The catalogue also said: "The new mode calls for a definitely higher indented waistline, long tapering hips and the molded bust. To wear the new frocks, you must wear the smart, new corsetry."

But was this—divorce, beauty, fashion—what American women were all about by the 1930s? The characters played by trend-setting movie stars certainly made it look that way. Jean Harlow created the blonde temptress by bleaching her hair, while Marlene Dietrich, Bette Davis, and Greta Garbo became models of sensuality. And Mae West not only exuded sexuality but also loved in a "masculine" style; she was neither committed to any single man nor to the idea of marriage.

Yet this picture of women was not an accurate reflection of reality. The Great Depression actually brought the indulgent 1920s flapper to an abrupt end. Most women's lifestyles during the 1930s were dictated by harsh economic times. Women had to learn how to "make do" for their families, seek relief and welfare in spite of their pride, and take whatever jobs they could find to help keep themselves and their families afloat. Both the divorce rate and level of conspicuous consumption of cosmetics and clothes soon fell in the face of the more pressing needs of survival.

Confronted by the depression, women quickly learned how to follow the adage: "Use it up, wear it out, make it do, or do without." Even formerly wealthy women became accustomed to buying day-old bread, relining coats with old blankets, buying meat of a cheaper cut, and moving to smaller living quarters. During the 1930s, over half of American families lived on incomes of between $500 and $1,500 per year. Because women controlled approximately 80 percent of families' spending, it fell to them to stretch out the $20 to $25 allotted each week for food, clothing, and shelter. With careful shopping and deflated prices, a woman could feed a family of six for $5 a week. In northern cities, milk sold for 10 cents a quart, butter for 23 cents per pound, bread for 7 cents a loaf, and hamburger for 12 cents a pound.

On such limited budgets, divorce soon became an expensive luxury for most dissatisfied couples. Also, economic adversity seemed to weld families together. In "Middletown," the divorce rate fell 43 percent between 1929 and 1933, and a similar drop occurred on the national level. The marriage and birth rates also fell because many people felt that they could not afford to get married or have another child and simply postponed these events. By the mid-1930s, the birth rate dropped below replacement level for the first time in the nation's history.

By 1933, over 25 percent of American workers were unemployed, a phenomenon that affected both working and middle-class families. One college-educated, middle-class woman described the terrors faced by those whose "normal" lives were interrupted by the depression. She and her husband both lost their jobs shortly before their first child was to be born in 1933. In desperation, they spent their last $12 on a rat-infested, leaky, cold apartment. Then, completely broke, they turned to the Emergency Home Relief Bureau for help. After numerous investigations and delays, they received woefully small checks. Her baby was born in a public ward, and she returned home weak from inadequate care and poor food. She and her husband devoted all their time to searching for work, begging for relief, and carrying home coal and other necessities, all on one meal a day so that their sickly baby could have milk. "We feel ourselves always on the edge of a precipice," she wrote, "with nothing to save us, sooner or later, from the abyss."

Women who were fortunate enough to get jobs worked to support themselves and to help alleviate their families' financial distress. In 1930, 22 percent of American workers were female; by 1940, this figure had risen to slightly over 25 percent. In 1940, approximately three out of every ten female workers were in clerical and sales positions, two were factory operatives, two were in domestic service, one—a professional— was a teacher or a nurse, and one was a service job. For such labor, women continued to receive low incomes. In 1937, a woman's average yearly wage was $525, while it was $1,027 for men. The average domestic worker earned $312.60 per year. In addition, female workers tolerated long hours, poor conditions, and abusive treatment because they needed employment.

Employed women encountered a general antipathy toward female laborers, particularly if they were married. Public opinion, as well as the leaders of male-dominated unions, especially the American Federation of Labor, favored the idea that jobs should go to men rather than to women. The rationale was that, because men had to support families while women supposedly did not, the jobs should naturally go to men. People still believed that women worked only for "pin-money" rather than to support themselves or to help support their families. Moreover, some people feared the role reversals that were occurring in families in which the man was unemployed or only marginally employed while the woman was able to hold a job and become the primary supporter of the family.

Public hostility to working women manifested itself in laws designed to restrict married female workers. Under the Economy Act of 1933, two members of the same family could no longer be employed in federal governmental service. Although such groups as the League of Women Voters and the National Women's Party protested, workers, three fourths of whom were female, were forced to resign. The policy was not successfully challenged until 1937. State and local governments also refused to hire married women. In 1931, three out of four school boards barred the hiring of married teachers. In that year, one New York official maintained that the employment of married women was reprehensible and that "our federal, state and local governments" must cooperate in removing "these undeserving 'parasites.'" Soon, even women's colleges were encouraging their graduates to avoid paid employment. In 1939, twenty-six states had "married persons" legislation before them.

Despite the opposition to married women workers, their numbers increased during the 1930s. To work, married women had to overcome not only discriminatory policies but also the renewed and widely held belief that women's proper place was in the home with their children. In 1930, 11.7 percent of married women held jobs; by 1940 15.3 percent did so. Women worked because of their husband's inadequate wages or because of raised expectations regarding standards of living. Because necessity was a socially acceptable reason for working they tended to use it as a rationale, thus undermining the feminist stance that women had a right to work if they wanted to.

Some women's groups attempted to protect women's right to work. The Women's Bureau stressed that denial of the right to work posed a potential threat to all citizens, not just to married women. The League of Women Voters actively fought against legislation barring married women from jobs and particularly opposed nepotism rules in the federal civil service. In 1937, the Business and Professional Women's organization argued in its newspaper, *Independent Woman,* that, although married women usually worked out of necessity, they also had to represent "that freedom to seek self-realization that men and women should guard jealously." Despite these efforts, there was little public sympathy for the married woman who worked for any reason except dire want. By the end of the decade, the *Ladies' Home Journal* reflected the sentiment of most Americans in its editorial on behalf of working wives: "No selfish desire for a career prompts them to work, simply the pressure of financial need."

Another major issue concerning working women during the depression years revolved around their employment in the professions. As job opportunities tightened, men expressed interest in entering such female dominated fields as teaching, first displacing married women teachers, then blocking young single women from teaching jobs as well. At the beginning of the 1930s, men accounted for 19 percent of all teachers; at the end of the decade they comprised 24.3 percent of the total. At the same time, the number of men enrolled in teacher training programs increased from 31 percent to 40 percent of the total enrollments.

The negative effect of the depression on female teachers was replicated in other professions. The proportion of women in professions dropped from 14.2 percent of total professionals to 12.3 percent during the 1930s, losses that were not regained with wartime prosperity and post-war recovery. Women lost ground in medicine, law, science, and university teaching. In nursing, social work, and librarianship, the trend toward feminization was reversed. The decline of women in these fields created a multiplier effect; that is, once female role models were less prevalent, fewer women aspired to these positions. Concomitantly, the proportion of women in the nation's college enrollment dropped from 43.7 percent in 1930 to 40.2 percent by 1940. Instead of pursuing professions and careers, women moved into clerical, sales, and other similar jobs lower on the economic and status scale.

The climate of the depression era was not conducive to the blossoming of feminist philosophies and activities. Rather than crusading against the limitations of female images and the resulting restrictive policies, women were forced to turn their attention to the more immediate concerns of food, shelter, and employment. For instance, the Young Women's Christian Association began to offer food, shelter, clothing, medical care, job skills classes, and an employment service as early as November 1930. The YWCA tried to rectify the fact that the plight of unemployed women received much less attention than that of men. It also worked on behalf of single women who were routinely denied relief and tried to alleviate the suffering of thousands of homeless women who lived in city streets and on the open road as hoboes, or "sisters of the road," as they were called.

After the passage of the National Industrial Recovery Act in 1933, which guaranteed labor the right to organize, many women began to see unionization as the answer to some of their problems. In that year, the International Ladies' Garment Workers' Union (ILGWU) mounted a membership drive headed by such organizers as Pauline Newman and Rose Pesotta. The membership of the ILGWU reached 200,000 by late 1934. The Women's Trade Union League also continued its efforts to unionize women. Female members of the Communist party, particularly Ella Reeves "Mother" Bloor, also worked energetically to encourage female workers to join unions. By 1938, an estimated 800,000 women, an increase of 300 percent from 1928, had joined unions. These women worked in such female-dominated industries as clothing, paper products, cigar- and candy-making, restaurants, and laundries.

During the 1930s, the AFL continued to concentrate on organizing skilled workers and craftspeople, despite resulting internal dissension. In

1935, a splinter group called the Committee for Industrial Organization formed to organize workers without regard to gender, race, or skills. In 1938, this group became the Congress of Industrial Organizations (CIO). The CIO focused on all workers in a particular industry. These included automobiles, steel, and textiles, in which 40 percent of the workers were women.

The CIO encouraged women's involvement in strikes as marchers, picketers, and providers of support services. Women also spontaneously formed themselves into groups known as the Women's Emergency Brigade and Women's Auxiliaries which were welcomed by the CIO. These women's groups created diversions to aid pickets, broke windows to prevent strikers from being gassed inside plants, cared for injured picketers, provided food, distributed literature, and joined the marches. When Minnesota writer Miradel La Sueur participated in her first strike during the mid-1930s she heard the guards at the door say "let the women in— we need women."

Still, by the end of the 1930s, women were underrepresented in unions. The idea that women belonged in the home was still prevalent among most male union leaders. Consequently, union-approved contracts often allowed unequal pay scales; women workers were usually expected to join gender-segregated locals, and only a few women served as union organizers and leaders. In addition, fourteen out of every fifteen female laborers remained outside of the union structure. Union leadership overlooked some five million women workers.

Other working women—those working within the home, pieceworkers, and native women on reservations, for example—could not join unions even if they wanted to. Few unions existed for white rural women laborers in the West and the South. In both regions, women continued to serve as unpaid domestic artisans and field workers on family farms. They also worked as day and migrant laborers as well as participating in sharecropping and other tenant farming operations. Poverty, farm mortgages, and hard work characterized these women's lives.

This situation of white southern farm women was particularly desperate. During the depression, the government identified the South as "the nation's economic problem Number 1." The region was plagued by farm tenancy, sharecropping, eroding land, illiteracy, and the highest birth rate in the country. When sociologist Margaret Jarman Hagood studied farm tenant women in North Carolina, Georgia, and Alabama during the late 1930s, she was overwhelmed by the courage and strength of women confronting their own powerlessness in the face of poverty and the demands of raising too many children. Her results, published in 1939 as *Mothers of the South*, showed how harshly cotton, tobacco, children, and the economic hardship of the depression affected southern women.

Numerous other women also lived outside of the pale of labor organizations. Non-American-born women were one such group. Racism barred Japanese women in California, for example, from office and sales jobs. Restricted primarily to domestic service, Japanese women nevertheless used their minimal wages as a lever to achieve small gains in American society as well as in the traditional Japanese family structure.

Mexican women in Texas were another example of non-American-born women who faced a myriad of difficulties without the aid of unions. After the First World War stimulated the economy of the southwest, Mexican women migrated with their families to Texas. By 1930, 15 percent of Chicanos were wage workers. They earned miserable pay as field workers, domestics, and unskilled service and factory workers. Of course, there were few unions for field and domestic laborers. But even when several unions, including the ILGWU, attempted to organize Mexican women workers, the efforts were unsuccessful. Bound by patriarchal family values, the Mexican woman more often than not turned her wages over to her husband, thus giving up any gains that she might have made through her economic contributions. In 1931, a sociologist who studied Chicanos observed that "traditions of feminine subservience" remained strong, while the "supremacy of the male is seldom disputed."

Black women composed another group for which there was little help. They were hit the hardest of all classes of women by the depression. Throughout the 1930s, black women suffered higher rates of unemployment than white women. Over half lost their jobs, while three out of ten white women did so. Black women could not even turn to domestic service, because the number of these jobs declined rapidly or were now taken by white women. Barred from clerical, sales, and factory jobs because of race, many black women soon found themselves with no employment opportunities at all. To make matters worse, they were generally excluded from relief and welfare programs designed to aid males who were assumed to be the "breadwinners."

Black women faced a number of problems relating to unions. In 1930, 90 percent of black women workers were domestic or farm laborers, areas of employment seldom covered by labor organizations. In 1938, only 10 percent of black women worked in industry. When black women workers tried to unionize, they found themselves divided by race from their white coworkers. In the cotton mills of Durham, North Carolina, black women labored in separate areas, earned lower wages, and were considered inferior to white women performing similar tasks. Those national labor leaders who were hesitant to organize women or black men did little to alleviate the problems of black women.

As white women moved down the economic scale, the pressure to survive became intense. In New York, black women responded by gathering into "slave markets" on street corners each morning, where they offered their labor to the highest bidder on an hourly basis, often for as little as ten cents an hour. Observers noted that hundreds of "forlorn and half-starved" girls were lucky to find a few hours work one or two days each week.

Black women responded to economic problems in other ways also. There were several attempts to form unions for domestic workers. In 1934, Dora Jones helped to organize workers in New York into the Domestic Workers' Union. In 1937, the National Negro Congress sponsored a Domestic Workers' Association, also in New York.

Other needy black women entreated the federal government for redress. Throughout the 1930s, black women pleaded with various governmental agencies for help. Their stories were pitiful ones, all revolving around poverty and racial discrimination in hiring. In 1941, a Chicago woman wrote directly to President Franklin D. Roosevelt. "We are citizens just as much or more than the majority of this country," she appealed to him. "This is supposed to be a free country regardless of color, creed or race but still we are slaves. . . . Won't you help us?" The objective of these women was a simple one—to get the President to open jobs to blacks who were willing to work, just as he had done for whites.

In 1932, American voters desperate for relief from economic distress carried Roosevelt into the presidency. After losing faith in President Herbert Hoover's policies, they were willing to take a chance on Roosevelt's ideas. On the eve of the campaign of 1932, journalist Anne O'Hare McCormick wrote: "Now the question is: Where are we? Nobody seems quite sure." According to McCormick, when Americans talked together they went "straight to the new question of America: 'What's the government going to do?'" She noted exasperation, anger, and impatience among voters. "No ordinary political campaign is this on which we now embark," she concluded. "It may be our last chance to prove that there is initiative enough left in democracy to make it worth saving."

After Roosevelt was inaugurated as President in 1933, he set about to meet popular expectations. He crafted a "New Deal" that included such new agencies as the National Industrial Recovery Act (NIRA), the Agricultural Adjustment Act, the Works Progress Administration (WPA), and the Civilian Conservation Corps (CCC). Roosevelt also created a New Deal for women, although there is no evidence that he set out to do so. Much of his legislation aided women. The National Industrial Recovery Act of 1933, for example, established maximum hour and minimum wage guidelines for both men and women workers. When this act was declared unconstitutional by the Supreme Court in 1935, it was replaced by the Fair Labor Standards Act of 1938, which reaffirmed maximum hour and minimum wage standards. But besides New Deal legislation, President Roosevelt helped women to challenge the invented American woman in three additional ways.

The most basic of these was his favorable attitude toward women in public service, gained during his years in New York state government. He was willing to trust women with important policy-making positions. Roosevelt appointed significant numbers of women to high-level jobs. Some of the better known of these were Frances Perkins as secretary of labor, Ellen Sullivan Woodward as head of women's and professional projects for the Works Progress Administration, Josephine Roche as assistant secretary of the treasury, Nellie Tayloe Ross as director of the mint, Marion Glass Banister as assistant treasurer of the United States, and Lucille Foster McMillin as civil service commissioner. In the diplomatic field, Ruth Bryan Owen served as minister to Denmark between 1933 and 1936, while Florence Jaffray Harriman was ambassador to Norway between 1937 and 1941. Many of Roosevelt's appointments of women were "firsts": first cabinet member, first director of the mint, and first ambassador.

A second way that Roosevelt shaped the women's New Deal was his expansion of governmental services and the initiation of a wide variety of social welfare programs that demanded trained social workers to administer them. Since many social workers were female, a large number of official positions went to women. From the Consumer's League, the Women's Trade Union League, and a wide variety of other reform organizations came trained women eager to tackle governmental assignments. Women had decades of experience in being the "moral housekeepers" of society; the New Deal offered them the chance to apply their expertise on a national scope.

A third way that Roosevelt affected the women's New Deal was by introducing his wife, Eleanor—an important presence in her own right—to the Washington scene. A crusader for women's issues, black Americans, and the poor, she soon became the social conscience of America. In addition, she provided access to the president for scores of women. As one of Eleanor Roosevelt's colleagues said, "When I wanted help on some definite point, Mrs. Roosevelt gave me the opportunity to sit by the President at dinner and the matter was settled before we finished our soup." Eleanor Roosevelt's biographer, Joseph P. Lash, described her as truly being "at the center of this growing New Deal sisterhood."

Eleanor Roosevelt was certainly the most active First Lady in the nation's history. She came to this position by a circuitous route. Born to a wealthy and prestigeous New York family in 1884, she had lost both her parents by the time she was ten years old. Raised by her maternal grandmother, she lived a lonely life as an adolescent. When she was eighteen years old, Eleanor joined the National Consumers' League headed by Florence Kelley. As she visited workplaces, she observed firsthand the misery of working women. At the same time, she was active in Junior League and the Rivington Street Settlement House in New York. Her commitment to social reform thus developed early in life.

In 1905, Eleanor Roosevelt married her cousin, Franklin Roosevelt. Franklin's mother, Sara, dominated the household. Eleanor Roosevelt's feelings of inadequacy as a wife and mother duplicated those she had felt as an ungainly, homely young girl. This unhappy woman turned to her husband's political career for fulfillment when he was elected Democratic assemblyman from Dutchess County, New York, in 1910. After his appointment as assistant secretary of the navy in 1913, she became an expert at orchestrating social and political gatherings. But once the war began, Eleanor Roosevelt threw herself back into welfare work.

During the 1920s, Eleanor Roosevelt became active in the League of Women Voters and the Women's Trade Union League. When Franklin was struck by polio in 1921, she became his political representative. At the Democratic National Convention of 1924, she worked for planks in the platform concerning equal pay, child labor, and other women's reform issues. By 1928, Eleanor Roosevelt was a well-known reformer and politician.

When Franklin ran for the presidency in 1932, Eleanor coordinated the activities of the Women's Division of the Democratic National Committee. Along with her friend and Democratic colleague, Molly Dewson, she mobilized huge numbers of women activists as potential administration members. Once she became First Lady, she toured the country observing the conditions of workers, visiting relief projects, and speaking out on behalf of human rights. Beginning in 1936, she also wrote a syndicated newspaper column called "My Day." Through radio programs, she reached millions of other Americans.

Despite the fact that the marriage between Franklin and Eleanor had crumbled in 1918 because of his involvement with Lucy Mercer, the two were able to work together as a political team. Although she had offered to divorce him, the Roosevelts had decided to stay together. Eleanor Roosevelt's emotional energies poured into reform causes and personal attachments to other women activists during the years following the breach between wife and husband.

After Franklin's death in 1945, Eleanor served as a United States delegate to the United Nations General Assembly, where she lobbied for and shaped the Universal Declaration of Human Rights, adopted in 1948. Throughout the 1950s, she continued to be a public figure. Her last major appointment came in 1961, as chairperson of President John F. Kennedy's Commission on the Status of Women. She died of tuberculosis in 1962.

In 1940, Eleanor Roosevelt wrote that women deserved credit for "the government's attitude of concern for the welfare of human beings." She added: "I should say that there has been a tremendous change in the outlook of government, which can be attributed to the fact that women have the ballot." She did not include her own numerous contributions that had led to the humane philosophy practiced by American government by the end of the decade.

Although Eleanor Roosevelt was a conservative feminist who had not believed in suffrage at the time of her marriage and never endorsed the ERA, she did much to advance the cause of women and to break down customary images of them during the New Deal years. She began by initiating press conferences for women only. This gave a tremendous boost to female journalists. Bess Furman, who covered Eleanor Roosevelt for the Associated Press, commented that "No newspaperwoman could have asked for better luck." Many reporters came to be among Roosevelt's closest friends, particularly Lorena Hickok, who was a lifelong companion of Eleanor's.

Among other things, Eleanor Roosevelt also supported the appointment of hundreds of women to official positions, acted as clearing agent of women's project proposals to the WPA, and emphasized the need for numerical guidelines for women's employment in New Deal programs. She helped to organize the White House Conference on the Emergency Needs of Women and pushed for the inclusion of women in the WPA and CCC. She also worked for the establishment of minimum wages and maximum hours for female workers.

In her efforts, Eleanor Roosevelt was assisted by a huge number of other women. One of these was Molly (whose first name was actually Mary) Dewson, a social worker, who had long campaigned for minimum wages for women. When she became a top echelon New Deal politician in 1933—director of the women's division of the Democratic party—Dewson pushed for the equal representation of women in party membership and leadership positions. Partially as a result of her efforts, women campaign workers numbered 73,000 in 1936 and 109,000 in 1940. She also helped to secure an unemployment insurance act in the state of New York in 1935 and minimum wage laws in Illinois and Ohio. She served on the President's Commission on Economic Security and had a hand in shaping the Social Security Act of 1935. As a member of the Social Security Board in 1937 and 1938, she helped to improve federal-state relations in the administration of the Social Security Act.

Another important New Deal woman was Frances Perkins, a social reformer and secretary of labor during the Roosevelt administration. As secretary of labor, Perkins helped to draft such New Deal legislation as the Federal Emergency Relief Act, the Social Security Act, and the National Labor Relations Act. She also helped President Roosevelt to make appointments, maintained harmonious relations with union leaders, and encouraged Roosevelt to bring the United States into the International Labor Organization in 1934. As a woman, her leadership of the Labor Department through the nation's most severe economic crisis helped to establish an image of women as competent, trustworthy individuals. This kind of progress was as important as that achieved by Roosevelt and Dewson.

A lesser-known female figure of the New Deal was Ellen S. Woodward, the director of women's work under the Federal Emergency Relief Administration. She also contributed programs to the Civil Works Administration and, in 1935, became the director of Women's and Professional Projects of the WPA. At the time, Woodward was acclaimed as President Roosevelt's most important noncabinet female appointment. She worked diligently to reeducate the American public to see women as heads of families and to create programs that would train women as mattressmakers, bookbinders, seamstresses, and household workers. Unlike most New Deal officials, Woodward emphasized the importance of reaching both white and black women with federal programs.

Woodward's efforts on behalf of blacks were surpassed by Eleanor Roosevelt, who became the outstanding champion of black rights during the New Deal. She acted as a lobbyist for civil rights and pushed the causes of the National Association for the Advancement of Colored People, particularly the passage of legislation defining lynching as a federal crime. She argued vigorously for the inclusion of blacks in the WPA and the CCC. And she encouraged the work of black writers, artists, and performers. Roosevelt was a significant force in the revival of the principle of racial equality during the New Deal era.

Black women also stood up for themselves and their people during the New Deal. Mary McLeod Bethune was especially significant as the director of the Division of Negro Affairs of the National Youth Administration (NYA) between 1935 and 1943. As a member of President Roosevelt's so-called "black cabinet"—those advisers who assisted in the implementation of black programs in New Deal projects—Bethune exercised great influence. Yet she seldom forcefully challenged segregation, apparently hoping to offend no one while extending her vision of racial equality to all. When necessary, however, she was a strong advocate for black rights. In 1937, she told the director of the National Youth Administration (NYA) in no uncertain terms: "It is about time that white folks recognize that Negroes are human too, and will not much longer stand to be the dregs of the work force."

A more outspoken black woman was Juanita J. Sadler, also an administrator in the Division of Negro Affairs during the organization's formative period. Unlike Bethune, she openly questioned the NYA's and President Roosevelt's stands on desegregation. She argued forcefully for the total integration of blacks into New Deal programs in particular and American society in general.

Bethune and Sadler were only two examples of the strong black women who fought the depression and enlarged their own horizons under the New Deal. Black writer Maya Angelou's autobiographical reflections of the 1930s, *I Know Why the Caged Bird Sings* (1970), praised the endurance of such black women. "The fact that the adult American Negro female emerges as a formidable character is often met with amazement, distaste and even belligerence," Angelou wrote. "It is seldom accepted as an inevitable outcome of the struggle won by survivors and deserves respect if not enthusiastic acceptance."

The assured black woman about whom Angelou wrote worked energetically throughout the 1930s to improve her own lot as well as the condition of her community and race. In 1935, many of these black women activists joined together to form the National Council of Negro Women and elected Bethune as the first president. The council coordinated the efforts of over twenty national and ninety-five local groups that represented almost 850,000 black women. Black women activists also continued to pressure the YWCA to open its doors and its programs to black women. And they maintained their crusade to abolish lynching in the South during the 1930s. Black women retained their vigor and thus achieved some gains during the New Deal years.

American Indian women also gained a little from New Deal legislation. Almost totally invisible now on western reservations, native women and their problems were overlooked by reformers. The general public seemed to believe that Indians as a group had largely disappeared. When the media and popular culture dealt with Indians, it did so either in historic or demeaning, stereotypical terms. In other words, Indians were usually represented as early inhabitants of America or as cigar store figures.

The Indian Reorganization Act of 1934 recognized that American Indians were neither disappearing nor assimilating into American culture. The bill, designed primarily by John Collier, commissioner of Indian Affairs between 1933 and 1945, encouraged a revitalization of Indian culture. It was a blow at the "melting pot" concept, arguing instead that Indians had a right to their Indianness. Collier believed that the dominant group, whites, could live harmoniously with the Indian minority in America. Under his administration, the Bureau of Indian Affairs offered improved education and medical services, religious freedom, and the potential for an artistic and cultural revival to American Indians.

The Indian Reorganization Act and such accompanying legislation as the Indian programs of the CCC were "white" bills devised with very little native input. Still, they provided a major impetus toward self-determination. The Indian New Deal was widely disputed, woefully underfunded, and poorly enforced; yet it sharply broke with the customary belief that Indians should be pseudo-whites. Moreover, the Indian New Deal included a conscious attempt to encourage native women's renewed participation in Indian affairs. John Collier was especially pleased that, of the 135 native constitutions drawn up under the act, not one denied women the right to vote or to hold office. He proudly noted that Indian women were becoming "increasingly interested in tribal affairs, and are being given every opportunity to vote and hold office under the provision of the act."

Collier's policies not only allowed the reentry of many native women into the political arena; they also opened the way for some who had never held such power. In 1936, one Assiniboine woman and one Gros Ventres woman were elected to the Fort Belknap tribal council. Other women, customarily limited to the domestic realm, now moved into leadership positions among the Colorado River tribes—the Oneida and the Blackfeet. Women delegates were also part of the National Congress of American Indians, which met for the first time in 1944.

The Indian New Deal included a number of other programs and activities designed to aid American Indian women. Native women were eligible for relief and social service jobs. They were supervisors and workers in Indian Work Camps of the CCC. They were eligible for extension services that provided training in cooking, sewing, canning, handcrafts, and childcare. They held jobs as clerical workers and seamstresses for the Civil Works Administration. And they held positions as file clerks with the WPA.

Collier also broke with white tradition when he designed educational programs for young native women. In 1942, he explained: "In the earlier days, white teachers refused to recognize Plains Indians customs which assigned work with the farms, gardens or small livestock to the women, and tried without success to make farmers out of the men, who had always been hunters. Today we are recognizing that in many Indian homes there will be no garden, no chickens, and no goats if the woman doesn't provide them—we are training girls to do these things well." The Bureau of Indian Affairs also offered courses in secretarial work and nursing so that native women could support themselves off the reservation.

Overall, it appears that American women lost ground in some areas and gained it in others during the years between 1929 and 1941. The harsh economics of the depression caused a reemphasis on women's domestic roles as wives and mothers as well as an erosion of many of their gains in job and professional areas. On the other hand, the New Deal brought them into prominence in government and created beneficial legislation. Although feminism may not have been active or highly visible during the 1930s, it was present and in a healthier state than is usually thought. The traditional image of women as homebodies may have gained some support, but it also took some telling knocks during the decade.

The changes that took place for women during the 1930s were often reflected in popular culture and the arts. For instance, many movies appeared in which successful businesswomen, reporters, attorneys, detectives, and even spies learned that marriage and family were all that really mattered. In film after film, such stars as Joan Bennett, Rosalind Russell, Ginger Rogers, Claudette Colbert, Joan Crawford, and Katharine Hepburn gave up thriving careers for the man of their dreams. Yet there was a new note in these films as well. They featured characters of wit, intelligence, and sophistication. Dressed in mannish suits with padded shoulders, these women were strong-minded, aggressive, and forceful.

In the popular press, such as the *Saturday Evening Post,* the idealized white woman often had feminist overtones. She was clever, achieving, and assertive. She frequently had to cope with gender prejudice and male chauvinism. But here, too, the modern image of woman was offset by other representations of the vain and silly woman and the married woman who happily sacrificed her career in favor of her husband's. The newly popular comic strips also featured diverse views of women. In 1930, Chic Young's Blondie began to manipulate the inept Dagwood, and, in 1940, female cartoonist Dale Messick (whose real first name was Dalia) created "girl reporter" Brenda Starr. The new radio soap operas, including *Our Gal Sunday, Backstage Wife,* and *Romance of Helen Trent,* similarly vacillated between women who could make their own way in the world and those who found their fulfillment through men.

Even the modest gains made in views of white women did not, however, extend to black women. In the films of the 1930s, black women continued to be represented as artless and affectionate "mammies." Louise Beavers projected the Aunt Jemima image in a number of films, including *Imitation of Life* in 1934, and later went on to become Beulah the maid on television. Hattie McDaniel won an Academy Award for her version of the simple-minded and loyal black servant in *Gone with the Wind.* Meanwhile, talented and beautiful black women like Nina Mae McKinney were signed by MGM but never given leading roles. Black entertainers also gained exposure through radio, records, vaudeville, and nightclubs. The public was presented with the earthy and sometimes ribald blues singers like Ethel Waters and Ella Fitzgerald, who sang songs of pathos, female strength, and tragedy much unlike the love refrains typical of white culture.

Black women were also producing literature and art, but not at the same rate or in the highly visible way that they had done during the 1920s. The Harlem Renaissance had been nearly silenced by the Great Depression, and the arts programs of the New Deal did little to stimulate black writers and artists. Zora Neale Hurston and Ann Petry were two black writers of the 1930s and early 1940s who attempted to explore black lifestyles and oppression in very different ways.

During the 1930s, a number of white women writers made an impact on the public. Pearl Buck's *The Good Earth,* about a Chinese family, was the most widely-read novel of 1932. In that same year, Gertrude Stein published her bestseller, *The Autobiography of Alice B. Toklas*. Martha Gellhorn exposed some of the bleak conditions of the times in *The Trouble I've Seen* in 1936. Margaret Mitchell's Civil War story, *Gone with the Wind*, was a bestseller in 1936 and a movie in 1939. Edna Ferber wrote of modern life in America, while Fannie Hurst described life in contemporary New York.

Although these writers seldom expressed feminist philosophies in their work, they presented images of strong, courageous, and independent women. Two exceptions appeared in the early 1940s. These were Pearl Buck, who wrote, in 1941, *Of Men and Women*, effectively extolling the feminist cause, and Mary McCarthy, whose collection of stories, *The Company That She Keeps* (1942), explored the identity problems of a bright young woman. Most of these writers restricted their feminism to their personal lives and interviews. Often personally supporting women's rights, female authors found themselves bound by cultural expectations of "women's fiction" if they wanted their works to sell.

Women journalists tended to be more outspoken. Freda Kirchwey, Anne O'Hare McCormick, and Dorothy Thompson used their wide-ranging influence to support a number of causes, including women's issues. Meridel Le Sueur, a journalist and Communist reformer, expressed her feminist philosophies in such journals as the *New Masses, Daily Worker,* and *Nation*.

A number of women poets also examined the world from various perspectives during the 1930s. Edna St. Vincent Millay became known for her poem, "Say That We Saw Spain Die," while Genevieve Taggard achieved notice with her collection of poems, *Calling Western Union* (1936). Playwright Lillian Hellman also dealt with a controversial subject in her 1934 Broadway hit, *The Children's Hour*, a story about two teachers accused of lesbianism.

Women's creative endeavors in all fields were stimulated by federal employment projects. The Federal Writers' Project employed writer Tillie Olsen. The Federal Art Project helped to support the work of sculptor Louise Nevelson, and the Federal Theater Project was both formed and administered by playwright and director Hollie Mae Ferguson Flanagan. In addition, the Resettlement Administration and the Farm Security Administration employed photographer Dorothea Lange to document the harsh conditions endured by rural Americans.

The New Deal murals sponsored by the WPA and other agencies were instrumental in displaying women's artistic talents in post offices and other public buildings. Painter Agnes Tait was part of a collaborative team that created a decorative mural in Bellevue Hospital in New York in 1937. Her most well-known mural was *Fruits of the Land,* a freize painted in a North Carolina post office in 1941. These murals were important, not just for women artists, but also for images of women in general; they typically represented strong, courageous women surviving economic reversals, drought, and other hardships.

Folk art was also extremely important during the 1930s. As the home once again became the focal point for American families, there was a remarkable resurgence of quilting among women. Quilts and other textiles reflected new technology in their fabrics, printed patterns, and dyed colors. They also contributed social documentation through their scenes. At the same time, folk artists experienced a revival. A renewed interest in the life of common folk led to an appreciation of the simple and primitive approach of the folk artist. The most famous of these was Anna Mary Robertson Moses, better known as "Grandma Moses," who began her career as a painter in 1933 at the age of seventy-seven, and whose works did much to popularize the genre of "folk" art.

In the fine arts, Romaine Brooks first achieved notice for her paintings of lesbians during the 1920s. Brooks experimented with drawing composed from a single, unbroken line during the 1930s. Undoubtedly, the most important artist of the period was Georgia O'Keefe, whose lucid, colorful works were often labeled "feminine" by the critics because of their use of color, flowing forms, and parts of the female body. O'Keefe's watercolors and other works have also been described as epic, vast, clean-cut, and pristine. She was both a major figure in American art during the twentieth century and a role model for other women artists because of her development of her own unorthodox style.

Other women artists worked through the medium of photography. Margaret Bourke-White traveled across the United States photographing such scenes as the Fort Peck Dam in Montana for *Life, Fortune,* and other major magazines. She collaborated with novelist Erskine Caldwell on *You Have Seen Their Faces,* a study of southern sharecroppers published in 1937. Caldwell's text illustrated by Bourke-White's photographs formed a moving documentary of southern life. Photographer Dorothea Lange was also well known for the keen social documentaries that she created through photography. Lange captured breadlines, the unemployed, and especially migrant workers in the West with her camera. Her best-known work was the *Migrant Mother,* a study in 1936 of a young woman in despair.

Black women artists also gained notice during the 1930s. They produced a good deal of folk art, including quilts, textiles, and handcrafts in the black folk tradition. But black women artists produced more formal works as well. An outstanding case was Minnie Evans, a domestic worker, who began to create pen, ink, and crayon drawings in 1935. She later painted oils and became known as a visionary artist due to her powerful imagery and provocative use of her figures' eyes.

During the 1930s, the musical work of women was prolific and diverse. Already famous composer Amy Beach continued her productive career. Marion Bauer composed symphonies, chamber pieces, and works for piano and voice. Ruth Crawford Seeger became an early leader of avant-garde twentieth-century music. Florence Price was the first black woman to have a composition performed by a major American orchestra. Composer Mary Howe helped to organize the National Symphony Orchestra, and Antonio Brico formed a women's orchestra in New York.

In addition, a widespread interest in ethnomusicology emerged; that is, the collection, writing down, and arrangement of folk music. Women musicians and composers were active in this movement, traveling through the Appalachian Mountains, the South, and the Southwest. They searched out the music of the "hillbilly," the cowboy, the black, the Creole, the Mexican-American, and the American Indian. Ruth Seeger collaborated with her husband Charles in transcribing and arranging more than a thousand folk songs. Other women incorporated folk music into their work. In 1936, composer and pianist Julia Frances Smith presented her first important composition, *American Dance Suite,* based on four folk songs. Smith later wrote several operas based on folk music as well as the *Folkways Symphony,* derived from folk and cowboy tunes.

In addition to the arts, women distinguished themselves in the sports world as well. Alice Marble and Helen Wills became outstanding tennis players. Eleanor Holm and Helen Madison established new swimming records. Floretta McCutcheon predominated in women's bowling. But the most famous woman athlete of the period was Mildred "Babe" Didrickson. She excelled in women's basketball, track, and golf, thus revealing women's athletic potential and providing an ideal for other talented female athletes.

The most popular sports of the decade for women were basketball, swimming, bowling, tennis, golf, and ice-skating. Women's softball and basketball teams, often sponsored by industrial organizations and businesses, flourished. While women's choice of sports was not particularly innovative, their sports clothing was. Lighter tennis dresses, tennis shorts, and satin shorts for basketball players exposed both women's bodies and their athletic skills.

Clearly, women had continued to be achievement-oriented despite the difficulties posed by the depression. They took full advantage of the New Deal and its programs throughout the 1930s. By 1940, the direction that the new decade would take could not be predicted, but most women, like most Americans, hoped that it would offer more economic opportunities than the 1930s had done. They could not foresee that international events would soon take command of the destiny of the American nation.

On 7 December 1941, the Japanese bombing of the U. S. fleet in Pearl Harbor drew the United States into the Second World War. The war did introduce prosperity into the 1940s, but it brought many problems with it as well. One of the first of these was the mobilization of manpower for the front lines and womanpower for home production. Under the leadership of President Roosevelt, now in his third term, the government turned its attention to these tasks.

The War Manpower Commission was faced with a real challenge in mobilizing women workers. The course of American history had made it obvious that women were regarded as a flexible labor supply to be pulled out of the home when needed and pushed back in when not. But the difficulty in 1941 was that women had been lectured for better than a decade on their responsibilities as wives and mothers. Women had been told repeatedly not even to think about employment unless it was an absolute necessity. Now the government had to recast the image of women as potential workers.

To pull women out of their homes and into wartime industries, the War Manpower Commission created the character of "Rosie the Riveter." Much like the famous "Uncle Sam Wants You" poster, Rosie the Riveter posters soon plastered walls and sides of buildings everywhere. Rosie also appeared in newspapers, magazines, and advertisements. Dressed in overalls, her hair covered by a bandana, Rosie called out to housewives across the land to join the army of the employed.

Rosie quickly fired the public's imagination. Movies appeared with such titles as *Swing Shift Maisie*. Songs called "We're the Janes Who Make the Planes" and "Rosie the Riveter" became instant hits. Magazines ran articles proclaiming, "I Take Part in the War Effort." And advertisements declared, "There's a new woman today doing a man's job so that he may fight and help finish this war sooner."

No possibilities were overlooked in persuading American women to take jobs. The Office of War Information believed that the most effective propaganda would be that based "on a highly emotional, patriotic appeal." Accordingly, its campaign compared machines and acetylene torches to vacuum cleaners and argued that women could handle any kind of machinery. The agency encouraged the design of special fashions to guarantee "vain" women the ability to be glamorous while working. It distributed war recruitment literature and posters that stressed a woman's patriotic duty to her country: "The More Women at Work—The Sooner We'll Win." It emphasized a woman's duty to her man: "Longing Won't Bring Him Back Sooner—Get A War Job!" And it appealed to women's spouses by putting the sentiment, "I'm Proud—My Husband *Wants* Me to Do My Part," in Rosie's mouth.

The wartime propaganda directed at women had two major effects; it created an image of women as dynamic citizens, and it helped to persuade millions of them to go to work. Acting on the new view of themselves and lured by high wages, American women poured into the labor force. Between 1940 and 1945, female workers increased by slightly more than 50 percent. In 1940, 11,970,000 women worked outside of their homes; in 1945, 18,610,000 did so. The proportion of women so employed rose from 17.6 to 37 percent in this period, three fourths of whom were married.

Women moved primarily into industrial jobs, where they replaced male workers in ordnance plants, shipyards, aircraft factories, and steel mills. But they also seized newly opened opportunities as musicians, scientists, doctors, attorneys, university professors, governmental officials, athletes, and teachers. The federal government itself hired a huge number of women. In 1939, less than 200,000 women worked in civil service jobs; in 1940 they numbered more than one million—an increase of 540 percent.

For their labor, women were rewarded with high wartime wages, regulated hours, decent working conditions, and support services, including daycare centers beginning in 1942. From the beginning of the war, the Women's Bureau, the War Production Board, and the War Manpower Commission all endorsed the principle of equal pay. In 1942, the one agency that had the power to actually enforce equal pay—the National War Labor Board—ordered equal wages for women who performed "work of the same quality and quantity" as male laborers. Although actual gains in the enforcement of equal pay standards were modest, the ideal had been established.

For black women, the war brought a welcome respite. As jobs long closed to them suddenly opened, black women inched up the economic ladder. Approximately 600,000 entered the labor force between 1941 and 1945, while many of those already employed bettered their positions. Twenty percent of domestic servants and 50 percent of farm laborers moved into the laundry and other jobs vacated by white women in favor of factory employment. Aided by the Fair Employment Practices Committee, created in 1941, the National Council of Negro Women, and the NAACP, the number of black factory operatives more than doubled, while black clerical, sales, and professional workers increased substantially by 1945.

Black women workers continued, however, to face a number of difficulties in the workplace. In Detroit, where many defense plants were located, they had to resort to demonstrations to gain access to factory jobs. In St. Louis, they worked in segregated plants and workshops. In the federal civil service, they not only labored in separate offices but were denied opportunities for advancement. And everywhere they were the very first to be laid off at the war's end.

Many black women looked to labor unions to protect them and their gains. In 1941, black union organizer Sabina Martinez encouraged black women workers to have confidence in "the principles of organized labor" and to join the union appropriate to their field of employment. Martinez organized for the Amalgamated Clothing Workers of America, while other black union women worked to organize the southern to-bacco industry, domestic laborers, and black factory operatives.

White women workers also sought union affiliation in large numbers. Although many male workers were still wary of working next to women, some union leaders began to be more accepting of female laborers. From its inception in 1935, the CIO admitted all workers. The AFL had long included the ILGWU as an affiliate, but now it began to open member-ship in craft-oriented affiliates to women as well. By the end of the war, there were 3 to 3.5 million women union members (including black women), an increase of over 12 percent since 1940. Yet the struggle for access to unions was not over for women; they still faced restrictions on their membership, the prejudice of male members, and exclusion from positions of leadership.

Although the story of working women between 1941 and 1945 is a fascinating one, it must be remembered that two thirds of the adult fe-male population were not gainfully employed. A large number of these women worked as volunteers for the war effort. They gave their time and energy to the Red Cross and the Office of Civil Defense. They provided entertainment for military men and women at USO canteens. And they sold war bonds, raised victory gardens, canned their own foods, col-lected tin cans and newspapers for recycling, and stretched their families' food and gasoline rationing stamps as far as they would go.

Another large group of women chose to combine employment and patriotic support of the war effort by joining the armed services. For the first time, women engaged in every military activity except combat. Furthermore, they achieved regular status in women's military units. The Women's Army Corps enrolled 140,000 women; the Navy's WAVES had 100,000; the Marine Corps Women's Reserve, 23,000; the coast guard's SPARS, 13,000; the Army Nurse Corps, 60,000; and the Navy Nurse Corps, 14,000.

Because of racial discrimination throughout the services, these military women were primarily white. The black women who were admitted to WAC detachments were segregated in barracks, mess halls, and recrea-tional areas. In 1941, the fifty-six black nurses admitted to the Army Nurse Corps were restricted to caring for black patients only. In 1944, President Roosevelt finally ordered the admission of black women to the WAVES, but it was so late in the war that less than one hundred black WAVES actually served.

Women's military units were plagued by sexism, predictions of failure, stories of sexual liaisons with military men, and rumors of lesbianism. Yet, despite the stiff opposition, women proved themselves to be effective and efficient military personnel who handled a wide variety of duties. According to a WAC publication, "Wacs do every job—little or big—with a thrilling competence that awakens respect in the eyes of even the ablest G.I. For wherever they serve—around the world and back—Wacs are doing a job. A gallant, soldier's job. Making a glorious war record!" Women's military record, combined with the authoritative and masculine uniforms that they wore, created a new image of women in the public eye. Also, the overall success of women's military units opened a new option for women.

By the time that the war came to a welcome end in 1945, American women had experienced many modifications in their images, roles, and lifestyles. At first glance, these seem to have been almost strong enough to destroy the invented American woman at long last. But on closer examination, it becomes clear that most of the changes affecting women were temporary, war-related measures. At the war's close, Americans returned for the most part to their conventional attitudes concerning women.

Many women participated in this revival of traditionalism. A study of women workers in Michigan defense plants revealed that most of them did not desire basic alterations in their lives. Consequently, they neither saw nor seized the opportunities presented by the war to create long-term changes for themselves. They did not interpret the war as a chance for emancipation, but, like men, saw it as a temporary emergency.

The majority of women, however, did not want to surrender their jobs. In 1945, the Women's Bureau reported that 80 percent of working women wanted to keep working after the war. Of these, 57 percent were single, 34 percent married, and 15 percent widowed or divorced. The government did little to encourage these women in their aspirations for postwar employment. Rather, efforts were made to reverse Rosie's image, to show her abandoning her torch as she retreated to the suburbs. The media cooperated in this effort. Demobilization literature encouraged women to marry and to bear the children that they had delayed until after the war, to create the warm home life that the national emergency had interrupted, and to be sweet, supportive, and motherly to their returning veterans.

Layoffs of women workers came quickly and day-care centers closed abruptly. In early 1946, a *New York Times* reporter commented, "The courtship of women workers has ended." After losing their wartime jobs, women often sought others—in department stores, offices, or service industries. One million of them withdrew from the labor pool, but of these 500,000 listed themselves as unemployed—that is, wanting to work and actively seeking employment. By 1950, the number of women working climbed almost to its wartime peak, suggesting that women, including a high proportion of married women, wanted to continue to work after the war's end.

By 1945, American attitudes concerning women had experienced many changes. The flapper of the 1920s had given way to the strong woman of the depression and New Deal years, who had in turn yielded to Rosie the Riveter. Women had been through a number of accelerated cycles between 1929 and 1945; reform and reaction, change and backlash, independence and dependence.

The key question now was, what would happen next? For what was the demise of Rosie making way? Maybe the invented American woman had finally sustained so many blows that she would disintegrate. Or perhaps she would once again demonstrate her durability and strength in the face of adversity. More likely yet, she would experience more cycles; she would take more steps forward and backward in the agonizingly slow dance of change during the era that emerged after 1945.

SUGGESTIONS FOR FURTHER READING

Ammer, Christine. *Unsung: A History of Women in American Music.* Westport, CT: Greenwood Press, 1980.

Anderson, Karen Tucker. *Wartime Women: Sex Roles, Family Relations, and the Status of Women during World War II.* Westport, CT: Greenwood Press, 1981.

————. "Last Hired, First Fired: Black Women during World War II." *Journal of American History* 69 (June 1982): 82–97.

Banner, Lois W. *Women in Modern America: A Brief History.* San Diego: Harcourt Brace Jovanovich, Publishers, 1984.

Baxandall, Rosalyn, Linda Gordon, and Susan Reverby, eds. *America's Working Women.* New York: Random House, 1976.

Berger, Jason. *A New Deal for the World: Eleanor Roosevelt and American Foreign Policy, 1920–1962.* New York: Columbia University Press, 1982.

Berkin, Carol Ruth, and Mary Beth Norton, eds. *Women of America: A History.* Boston: Houghton Mifflin Company, 1979. Part IV.

Bernstein, Alison. "A Mixed Record: The Political Enfranchisement of American Indian Women during the Indian New Deal." *Journal of the West* 23 (July 1984): 13–20.

Blackwelder, Julia Kirk. "Women in the Work Force: Atlanta, New Orleans, and San Antonio, 1930 to 1940." *Journal of Urban History* 4 (May 1978): 331–353.

Bogle, Donald. *Brown Sugar: Eighty Years of America's Black Superstars.* New York: Harmond, 1980.

Bolin, Winifred D. Wandersee. "The Economics of Middle-Income Family Life: Working Women during the Great Depression." *Journal of American History* 65 (June 1978): 60–74.

Campbell, D'Ann. *Women at War with America: Private Lives in a Patriotic Era.* Cambridge, MA: Harvard University Press, 1984.

Christian, Barbara. *Black Women Novelists: The Development of a Tradition, 1892–1976.* Westport, CT: Greenwood Press, 1980.

Clive, Alan. "Women Workers in World War II: Michigan as a Test Case." *Labor History* 20 (Winter 1979: 44–72.

Dewhurst, C. Kurt, Betty MacDowell, and Marsha MacDowell. *Artists in Aprons: Folk Art by American Women*. New York: E. P. Dutton, 1979.

Glenn, Evelyn Nakano. "The Dialectics of Wage Work: Japanese-American Women and Domestic Service, 1905–1940." *Feminist Studies* 6 (Fall 1980): 432–471.

Gonzalez, Rosalinda M. "Chicanas and Mexican Immigrant Families 1920–1940: Women's Subordination and Family Exploitation." In *Decades of Discontent: The Women's Movement, 1920–1940*, edited by Joan M. Jensen and Lois Scharf, 59–84. Westport, CT: Greenwood Press, 1983.

Green, George N. "ILGWU in Texas, 1930–1970." *The Journal of Mexican American History* I (Spring 1971): 144–169.

Harris, Ann Sutherland, and Linda Nochlin. *Women Artists 1550–1950*. New York: Alfred A. Knopf, 1979.

Hartmann, Susan M. *American Women in the 1940s: The Home Front and Beyond*. Boston: Twayne Publishers, 1982.

Honey, Maureen. "Images of Women in *The Saturday Evening Post*, 1931–1936." *Journal of Popular Culture* 10 (Fall 1976): 352–358.

———. *Creating Rosie the Riveter: Class, Gender, and Propaganda during World War II*. Amherst: University of Massachusetts Press, 1984.

James, Edward T., ed. *Notable American Women: A Biographical Dictionary*. Cambridge, MA: Belknap Press, 1971.

Janiewski, Dolores. "Flawed Victories: The Experiences of Black and White Women Workers in Durham during the 1930s." In *Decades of Discontent*, edited by Jensen and Scharf, 85–109.

Kennedy, Susan Estabrook. *If All We Did Was to Weep at Home: A History of White Working Class Women*. Bloomington: Indiana University Press, 1979.

Kerber, Linda K., and Jane DeHart Mathews, eds. *Women's America: Refocusing the Past*. New York: Oxford University Press, 1982. Part III.

Kessler-Harris, Alice. *Out to Work: A History of Wage-Earning Women in the United States*. Oxford: Oxford University Press, 1982.

Lash, Joseph P. *Eleanor: The Years Alone*. New York: W. W. Norton & Company, Inc., 1972.

Lerner, Gerda, ed. *Black Women in White America: A Documentary History*. New York: Vintage Books, 1973.

Marzolf, Marion. *Up from the Footnote: A History of Women Journalists*. New York: Hastings House, 1977.

Morgan, Kathryn L. *Children of Strangers: The Stories of a Black Family*. Philadelphia: Temple University Press, 1980.

Patterson, James T. "Mary Dewson and the American Minimum Wage Movement." *Labor History* 5 (Spring 1964): 134–152.

Rosen, Marjorie. *Popcorn Venus: Women, Movies and the American Dream*. New York: Avon Books, 1973.

Ross, B. Joyce. "Mary McLeod Bethune and the National Youth Administration: A Case Study of Power Relationships in the Black Cabinet of Franklin D. Roosevelt." *The Journal of Negro History* LX (January 1975): 1–28.

Rupp, Leila J. *Mobilizing Women for War: German and American Propaganda, 1939–1945*. Princeton: Princeton University Press, 1978.

Sicherman, Barbara, and Carol Hurd Green, eds. *Notable American Women: The Modern Period*. Cambridge, MA: Belknap Press, 1980.

Sochen, June. "*Mildred Pierce* and Women in Film." *American Quarterly* 30 (Spring 1978): 3–20.

Swain, Martha H. "'The Forgotten Woman': Ellen S. Woodward and Women's Relief in the New Deal." *Prologue* 15 (Winter 1983): 200–213.

Scharf, Lois. *To Work and to Wed: Female Employment, Feminism, and the Great Depression*. Westport, CT: Greenwood Press, 1980.

Wandersee, Winifred D. *Women's Work and Family Values, 1920–1940*. Cambridge: Harvard University Press, 1981.

Ware, Susan. *Beyond Suffrage: Women and the New Deal*. Cambridge: Harvard University Press, 1981.

———. *American Women in the 1930s: Holding Their Own*. Boston: Twayne Publishers, 1982.

Westin, Jeanne. *Making Do: How Women Survived the Depression*. Chicago: Follett Publishing Company, 1976.

Weibel, Kathryn. *Mirror Mirror: Images of Women Reflected in Popular Culture*. New York: Anchor Books, 1977.

Woloch, Nancy. *Women and the American Experience*. New York: Alfred A. Knopf, 1984. Chapters 17–18.

After the publication of The Feminine Mystique *in 1963, Betty Friedan spent a good deal of time lecturing to interested groups of American women and men. Here, the name plate identifies the feminist author by her marital title, "Mrs."* Courtesy of the Schlesinger Library, Radcliffe College.

CHAPTER 9

The Feminine Mystique:
The Modern Era
1945 to the Present

I N 1945, most Americans were determined to enjoy the peace and prosperity that they hoped would characterize the immediate future. Many also expressed a desire to "get back to normal," by which they seemed to mean a return to a happy, industrious lifestyle in an idyllic country. Of course, such a time had never really existed in the nation's history, but a war-weary generation clung to such illusions. Only gradually did such events as the Cold War, military conflict in Korea and Vietnam, and widespread protest movements convince Americans that they had to abandon their unrealizable dreams and cope with the realities of the modern world.

While it lasted, this idealized postwar America had definite plans for the nation's women. The belief that women would return to the home, where they would contentedly bear children and keep house, was widespread. Newspaper articles, political speeches, sermons, and casual conversations indicated that many Americans felt that the invented American woman would now become the norm for all women. Passive and domestic, the "true" woman would limit her activities to her home and leave the activities of the "outside" world to men. This kind of thinking has been labeled the "cult of domesticity" when applied to mid-nineteenth century women. During the latter half of the twentieth century, it became known as the "feminine mystique."

Like postwar America itself, this conception of women was eventually challenged by numerous events. The model American woman, sweet and docile, proved to be as illusory a part of America's past as the dream of pervasive cheerfulness and prosperity. Just as Americans found it necessary to cope with the modern world, they had to deal with the modern woman. This involved recognizing the fact that larger proportions of women than ever before were rejecting confinement to the "domestic sphere." Early in the modern period, many women who maintained that they were motivated largely by economic need combined home and work. By the mid-1960s, increasing numbers of women began to argue that they had a right to participate in both the private and public worlds if they so desired. Thus, instead of becoming the dominant model, the invented American woman came under attack from a variety of forces after 1945.

Initially, however, it did appear that women were accepting the return to domestic life with joy. The late 1940s and 1950s were characterized by early marriage and a dramatically rising birth rate known as the "baby boom." In the years immediately following the war, the average age of marriage for women fell to twenty. By 1951, one out of every three women married by age nineteen. And by 1958, more women married between the ages of fifteen and nineteen than of any other age category. Childbearing occurred most often in the teens and early twenties, with the average woman bearing her last child by age twenty-six. In 1957, the birth rate reached a high of 25.3 per thousand people. At the same time, the La Maze method of natural childbirth and the La Leche League, an organization dedicated to helping mothers nurse their babies, attained great popularity.

These developments were accompanied by a tremendous expansion of suburbs. The exodus to the suburbs involved a commitment to home, family, house and childcare on the part of women. One million new homes a year demanded decoration, furnishing, and upkeep. House-wives, now making 75 percent of all family purchases, formed a signifi-cant market. As one advertising expert recognized, "the buying of things could provide a sense of identity, purpose, creativity, and self-reali-zation" for women. Madison Avenue soon excelled in convincing the American woman that domestic consumption offered her fulfillment. Thus, technology freed women from heavy labor only to create the need to devote their time to the choice of appliances, products, and household services. By the end of the 1950s, women's household work actually in-creased slightly from fifty-two to fifty-four hours per week.

The message of domesticity was also preached by a variety of "ex-perts." In 1946, psychoanalyst Helen Deutsch emphasized that the fem-inine woman "leaves the initiative to the man and out of her own needs, renounces originality and experiences her own self through identifica-tion." The following year sociologist Marynia Farnham and historian Ferdinand Lundberg published *Modern Woman: The Lost Sex*. They ar-gued that such problems of modern society as war and depression stemmed from women leaving their homes and families. In 1952, Ashley Montagu's *Natural Superiority of Women* stressed the importance of "mother love" to human development and progress. Meanwhile, Dr.

Benjamin Spock, whose *Baby and Child Care* reached one million readers per year between 1945 and 1960, created the image of the ideal mother who neither worked nor left her child for extended periods of time. Should a mother consider paid employment, Spock advised her to seek psychological counseling and to consider the deprivation and potential delinquency of her abandoned children.

There were a few dissenting voices to such views of women. In 1952, Simone de Beauvoir's *Second Sex* was published in the United States. Although it gained only a limited audience, it effectively revealed the great prejudice directed at women. In 1953, Alfred C. Kinsey also attacked prevailing notions of womanhood by arguing that women were actually highly sexual. In his *Sexual Behavior of the Human Female,* he maintained that, despite long-held beliefs to the contrary, the possibility of a vaginal orgasm was doubtful. He also emphasized the great range of female sexuality.

Other critics were less confident in their opposition to the model American woman. In 1953, sociologist Mirra Komarovsky argued in *Women in the Modern World: Their Education and Dilemmas* that women's lack of accomplishments relative to men resulted from their cultural conditioning rather than from any inherent inferiority. Yet, Komarovsky also indicated that women bore the primary responsibility for home and children. To her, the evidence seemed to point to the father as a secondary figure in the development of a child. Even anthropologist Margaret Mead glorified women's roles as wives, mothers, and homemakers. Although Mead criticized the rigid sex roles in American society in her study, *Male and Female* (1955), she idealized women's domestic functions.

Given these views, it is not surprising that in 1956 a special issue of *Life Magazine* chose a thirty-two-year-old mother of four as the ideal American woman. She was described as a wife, hostess, volunteer, and "home manager." But, above all, she was lauded as a "conscientious mother" who spent "lots of time with her children, helping with their homework and listening to their stories or problems." Other popular media and personalities also portrayed women as sweet and innocent homebodies. The very popular television shows, "I Love Lucy" and "Father Knows Best," were two examples. Film stars Debbie Reynolds and Doris Day were others. Even Marilyn Monroe and Elizabeth Taylor combined their aggressive sexuality with an artlessness and dependence that made them more sex objects than threats.

Women's fashions reflected a similar "feminine" image. The mannish styles of the war years were replaced by Christian Dior's "New Look" in 1947. Dior's creations focused on long, full skirts, defined bustlines, and tiny waists. During the 1950s, the "baby doll" style introduced cinchbelted waists, padded brassieres, and full skirts over crinoline petticoats. Shoes featured extremely pointed toes and heels so high and spindly that they had to be made of steel to avoid breakage. These confining styles reinforced the idea of women's passivity and helplessness.

Not surprisingly, many women's organizations declined in strength during the postwar years. The League of Women Voters and the Consumers' League lost members at an alarming rate. The Women's Trade Union League disbanded in 1947. The Woman's party, the National Federation of Business and Professional Women's Clubs, and the National Federation of Women's Clubs continued to support the Equal Rights Amendment, but when it was passed by the Senate in 1950 and 1953, these groups were unable to push the bill through to ratification. Apparently, women's efforts were now directed more toward their local parent teachers associations, churches, and schools than toward national reform or women's rights.

Of course, the widely accepted notion that the "typical" American woman was a simple, cheerful, and financially secure suburban housewife ignored reality in many ways. Thousands of women lived in cities, slums, and ghettoes. Others lived on farms, in depressed rural areas, and on reservations. Many suffered from poor health, unemployment, and poverty. Still others worked to help support their families or supported themselves and their children without the aid of a male partner. As a case in point, during the 1950s, discriminatory housing practices and low income levels excluded black women from suburban life. Over 40 percent of black mothers with small children worked outside their homes, while approximately one quarter of them headed their own households. As had always been the case, the domestic ideal lacked meaning for many black women.

But, in truth, the model of the home-bound American woman was not even valid for women in general. Although the invented American woman seemed to prevail, closer examination reveals numerous instances in which its dominance was merely apparent. Many women fell into line with the back-to-the-home movement for only a while; others, not at all. Increasing numbers of women chose paid employment for some period or the entirety of their lives, despite their marital status.

During the 1950s, the number of salary and wage-earning women crept steadily upward, and the level of female employment grew at a rate four times faster than that of men. In 1950, women accounted for 29 percent of the total work force. By 1960, this figure had jumped to nearly 35 percent. In that year, 40 percent of all women over sixteen held a job, while 30 percent of married women worked. The number of working mothers rose 400 percent. According to historian William H. Chafe, this trend contributed to a form of "cultural schizophrenia" during the postwar years, with "attitudes going one way and behavior the other." While business leaders, politicians, and social commentators insisted that women return to the home, women themselves were moving into the job market in huge numbers.

That many women chose to work did not automatically indicate a rejection of domestic values. In fact, most women claimed that they were simply supplementing the family income in order to purchase a second car or to finance a child's college education. They maintained that it was now necessary for middle-class families to have two incomes in order to live according to their rising expectations. Thus, many women accelerated their participation in the work force. By 1960, increasing numbers of women worked fulltime, continued to work after marriage, and returned to work after their youngest child entered school.

Yet women's motives for working were not merely financial. In 1946, a *Fortune* poll discovered that a startling 25 percent of American women would have preferred to have been born male. And in 1947, *Life* magazine addressed the "American Woman's Dilemma": the fact that women now faced two options—a husband and paid work. *Life* puzzled over how this could have happened in a society that discouraged independence and autonomy for women, urging them to stay docilely at home.

Other indications of women's discontent appeared during the 1950s. Alcoholism and divorce rates rose alarmingly. The consumption of tranquilizers jumped from 0 pounds in 1955 to 1.15 million pounds in 1959. Female college graduates publicly admitted that they were restive in their domestic roles. As one Barnard graduate put it: "We stagger through our first years of childrearing wondering what our values are in struggling to find some compromise between our intellectual ambition and the reality of everyday living." And many women continued to work even though their family incomes were more than adequate.

Evidently, there was trouble of some sort in surburbia. Yet there is no evidence that women purposely escaped their problems by entering the work world. Working to "help their families," a traditional female function, women sought such gender-defined jobs as clerical and sales work. They accepted poor pay and the lack of opportunity for promotion. Union hostility continued, and the notion of women as "pin-money" workers was perpetuated. And they did not gain access to the professional, technical, and managerial fields.

Rather than to struggle for justice and equality in employment, women entering the labor force tended to accept conditions and help perpetuate stereotypes that would plague later generations of female laborers. For example, women's acceptance of low wages caused the median income of female workers to drop from 63.9 percent of those earned by men in 1955 to nearly 60 percent by 1960. Also, their dissatisfaction with low-level jobs caused many women to leave and reenter the job market repeatedly, a phenomenon which was identified as a "naturally" high attrition rate among women.

Although women workers seldom viewed themselves as reformers or crusaders, they still effected change. As Chafe notes, this transformation of the American labor force "eventually undercut the social basis for traditional assumptions about women's proper place." By 1960, it was apparent that most women would no longer spend most of their lives taking care of homes and children. Despite the back-to-the-home movement, the life-time devoted exclusively to home and family was now an exception rather than a rule for American women.

The patterns of employment of black women also changed during this period. The majority still tended to work at domestic and service jobs in the North, while in the South they were tenant farmers, tobacco strippers, and textile workers. Black female workers did make gains in white-collar work, however, for less than one fifth of black female workers held such jobs in 1940, and over one third did so in 1960. Black women also made substantial advances in the disparity of income between themselves and white women. In 1940, black women earned only 38 percent of the median wage of white women; in 1960, they earned 70 percent. But black women workers failed to make strides against the discrimination of white male-dominated unions.

The plight of the black women workers in particular and black women in general was captured by some contemporary black authors. The author of many short stories and several novels, including *The Street* (1946) and *Country Place* (1947), Ann Petry offered insights into how the lives of black women differed from those of their white counterparts. In *The Street*, Petry was especially effective in detailing the destruction of hardworking, earnest, and honest Lutie Johnson of Harlem. Poet Gwendolyn Brooks, winner of a Pulitzer Prize in 1950, also presented brave, hopeful women who endured the difficulties of being black in postwar America.

Since there was a great deal of confusion over whether women in general should work, it is little wonder that so few people outside of contemporary literature got around to considering the role of the black working woman. Mexican-American, Asian, rural, poor southern, and American Indian women were also overlooked in public discussions. During the 1950s, the Women's Bureau was the only organization that represented the interests of working women. The bureau had its hands more than full with complaints of sex discrimination and demands for equal-pay legislation, the establishment of day-care facilities, and protective legislation.

By 1955, however, the cause of working women was brought to the American public through the White House Conference on Effective Uses of Woman-Power, sponsored by the Women's Bureau. Here, a bureau speaker urged acceptance of women in all occupations. She also emphasized that women were "achievement-oriented" individuals who had the right to work. Other speakers argued the value of significantly increasing the effectiveness of the nation's "woman power." Although the conference concluded that "The structure and the substance of the lives of most women are fundamentally determined by their functions as wives, mothers, and homemakers," it also marked a subtle shift in governmental policy, insisting on women's ability and right to hold other jobs. Perhaps the most significant change this conference marked was that women were now seen as a permanent part of the labor force, rather than as a temporary resource to be utilized during a time of emergency.

By 1960, American attitudes toward working women were beginning to change. Rather than encouraging women to stay at home, a variety of commentators now discussed the ways in which women could combine home and work. Esther Peterson, head of the Women's Bureau, remarked that "today's homemaking chores are no great challenge" to competent women whose "sense of frustration is likely to heighten after children go to school and there is even less need for her in the home." Researchers and sociologists, too, began to argue that women should work because employed women exercised a greater role in family decision-making and fostered self-reliance in their children. Research showed that working mothers were also less protective and more confident with their children than were nonworking women. By 1965, sociologist Robert O. Blood asserted that "employment emancipates women from domination by their husbands, and secondarily, raises their daughters from inferiority to their brothers." To him, "the male-dominated, female-serviced family is being replaced by a new symmetry."

At the same time, attitudes toward women in general were undergoing change. For one thing, the backlash against women's progress, which had characterized the years between 1945 and 1960, was abating. In addition, the discontent of women—especially educated, middle-class women—with the limitations placed on their lives was growing. Also, social critics and reform efforts concerning numerous issues, ranging from the environment to minority group relations, were beginning to shake traditional American attitudes to their very foundations.

As early as 1961—several years before a revitalized feminist movement erupted in America—President John F. Kennedy created the President's Commission on the Status of Women. At the urging of Esther Peterson of the Women's Bureau and Democratic party women, Kennedy appointed commission members and Eleanor Roosevelt as chairperson. The commission presented a sixty-page report on its deliberations in 1963 that included its endorsement of women's access to education, aid to working mothers, child-care services, equal employment opportunities, equality of rights under the law (preferably under the Fifth and Fourteenth Amendments rather than under the ERA), and a wider role for women in government. The report also asked for continuing governmental action on behalf of women, a recommendation that led President Kennedy to establish the Interdepartmental Committee on the Status of Women and the Citizens' Advisory Council on the Status of Women.

Although the commission's findings were fairly conservative, they had wide impact. The deliberations of the commission initiated a national debate on women's issues. Every state formed commissions on the status of women. And the government committed itself to a more comprehensive policy of reform for women rather than simply appointing a few to office, as the Truman and Eisenhower administrations had done. This commitment was further demonstrated in the Equal Pay Act of 1963 and the prohibition of discrimination against women in the federal civil service.

In 1963, the year of the commission's report, a seminal book gave focus to the growing discussion concerning women. Betty Friedan's *Feminine Mystique* exposed the triviality and frustrations of domesticity that was unrelieved by other activities or employment. She described "The Problem That Has No Name" as "a strange stirring, a sense of dissatisfaction, a yearning that women suffered in the middle of the twentieth century in the United States." She observed that wives and mothers across the nation were gnawed at by a vague discontent with their "happy" and "fulfilled" lives. Moreover, they felt guilty and ill at ease about their feelings. "What kind of a woman was she if she did not feel this mysterious fulfillment waxing the kitchen floor?" Friedan wrote. "She was so ashamed to admit her dissatisfaction that she never knew how many other women shared it." She concluded that women had to add other pursuits to "occupation housewife" and the "comfortable concentration camp" of the home as soon as possible.

The following year, sociologist Alice Rossi expanded Friedan's plea with her call for equality between the sexes. Rossi insisted that equality was a social good that needed concrete measures to effect it. Day-care centers and freedom from sexual stereotyping in education were two of her recommendations. She declared that sexual equality would not exist "until women participate on an equal basis with men, in politics, occupations, and the family." Like Charlotte Perkins Gilman during the 1920s, Rossi emphasized the need to reorder society and its institutions to achieve the larger goal of sexual equality.

In the same year that Rossi called for social reform, Title VII of the Civil Rights Act of 1964 emerged. This provision attempted to outlaw discrimination by employers and trade unions against both blacks and women. It also created the Equal Employment Opportunity Commission (EEOC) as the enforcing body of the equal-employment opportunity clause. A few years later, Senator Everett Dirksen of Illinois commented that Title VII was Congress's attempt to "remake the social pattern of this country."

During these years, a number of women were directly confronting the issues of both racial and sexual equality by contributing their energies to the civil rights movement. When southern blacks began to revolt in the late 1950s and 1960s, groups of black and white southern women were drawn into the movement, many of them into the Southern Christian Leadership Conference (SCLC) and the Student Nonviolent Coordinating Committee (SNCC). They acquired a language that described oppression and advocated revolt, experienced the strategy and techniques of organization, and started to see themselves collectively as objects of discrimination. They also experienced great frustration that, while the civil rights movement offered them a heightened sense of self-worth, it also replicated traditional sex roles. They were frequently expected to make the coffee and provide other services, rather than to write pamphlets, make speeches, and march in protest.

During the "freedom summers" of 1964 and 1965, 650 northern white women went south to work on behalf of civil rights. They were confronted with a movement that defined oppression and quality in terms of race and class rather than gender. Consequently, these northern white women, too, encountered discriminatory treatment. Working within the Congress of Racial Equality (CORE), the SCLC, and the SNCC, they soon came to resent sexist definitions of their roles in the movement. Sexual stereotyping, rather than their interests and abilities, determined their job assignments. They were seldom asked to participate in policy decisions. And they were often the unwilling recipients of sexual advances.

Both black and white women civil rights workers gradually began to develop a feminist viewpoint. In 1964, the first formal analysis of sexism in the civil rights movement by Casey Hayden charged SNCC with rampant paternalism: "Assumptions of male superiority are as widespread and deep rooted and every much as crippling to the woman as the assumptions of white supremacy are to the Negro." Other indictments that followed served as further catalysts for the emergence of vehement feminism among these disgruntled women.

Similarly, in new-left community organizing projects in northern cities, women volunteers learned about oppression and inequality firsthand. While such groups as the Students for a Democratic Society (SDS) encouraged women to believe in a participatory democracy, they denied them a full role in it. In addition, the student movement's commitment to social action and equality pushed these women to question all the customary social rules and roles. Thus, new-left politics in the North also spawned feminism among its female members. Women emerged from the experience with a dedication to egalitarianism and to the need to change the quality of human relationships.

At the same time, Latin women in the Los Angeles area and in New York City began to raise other civil rights issues. They soon asked for the representation of Latin peoples on school boards, town councils, and police forces; bilingual education in the schools they attended; and access to food stamps. One California Chicano who urged her friends and co-workers to speak up informed them that times had changed: "You know, we're not back in the 20s. We can stand up! We can talk back! Its not like when I was a little kid and my grandmother used to say, 'You have to especially respect the Anglos.'" She added that the time had come also for women to reject their customary deference to men.

While community organizations on behalf of increased civil rights were offering young women the opportunity to recognize oppression directed at themselves, to stand up for themselves, and to break through patterns of passivity in the process, another group of women was also moving toward feminism. These were educated, middle-class women, often professionals with career-orientations that were not consistent with the domestic ideology of the feminine mystique. Like the women of the civil rights movement, these women were increasingly upset with the discrepancy between the promise of American democracy and the reality of their limited share in it. By the mid-1960s, they too were ready to begin working for the revision of a restrictive system.

Formal organization of the contemporary feminist movement came in 1966, during the Third National Conference of the Commissions on the Status of Women. Tired of the ponderous discussion concerning women's issues that seemed to lack concrete results, twenty-eight women met in Betty Friedan's hotel room in Washington, D.C., to contribute ideas and five dollars each to the founding of the National Organization for Women (NOW). This initial gathering was followed by an organizational meeting several months later. Here, 300 women and men adopted by-laws, elected officers, and named Friedan president.

This assembly issued a statement of purpose that attacked "the traditional assumption that a woman has to choose between marriage and motherhood on the one hand and serious participation in industry or the professions on the other." NOW's goal was to bring women into "full participation in the mainstream of American society NOW, exercising all the privileges and responsibilities thereof in truly equal partnership with men." To achieve this end, NOW advocated such reforms as legal abortion, maternity leaves, tax deductions for child-care expenses, day-care centers, reform of the welfare system, job-training programs for women, and in 1967, the passage of the equal rights amendment. NOW pressed its case for these issues through literature, speeches, public protests, lobbying, and litigation.

NOW was soon joined in its reform efforts by other newly organized women's groups, including the Women's Equity Action League (WEAL) in 1968, the Professional Women's Caucus (PWC) in 1970, and the National Women's Political Caucus (NWPC) in 1971. These organizations attempted to raise women's consciousness regarding oppression, sexism, and discrimination through "rap" groups and consciousness-raising (c-r) sessions. They also tried to hammer out a feminist ideology designed to restructure society in a way that would grant equal opportunities to women, men, blacks, American Indians, Chicanos, homosexuals, and other minority and special interest groups.

The feminist message was carried in a number of publications. One of these was *MS.* magazine, founded by the Women's Action Alliance and Gloria Steinem in 1971. Individual authors also advocated feminist reforms. In *Sexual Politics* (1969), Kate Millet indicted American society as a patriarchy and asked for immediate revision. In the *Dialectic of Sex: The Case for Feminist Revolution* (1970), Shulamith Firestone envisioned a nation in which class and gender would play no role. Robin Morgan's *Sisterhood Is Powerful* (1970) and Germaine Greer's *Female Eunuch* (1971) also were feminist polemics. Other kinds of writers also focused on feminist issues. Novelists Sue Kaufman, Alix Kates Shulman, and Marilyn French, among others, used fiction to build the case against male chauvinism, while poets Sylvia Plath and Adrienne Rich mobilized verse on behalf of the feminist cause.

The academic world also began to recognize the significance of women's issues. Such journals as *Feminist Studies, Women's Studies,* and *Signs: A Journal of Women in Culture and Society* developed to publish research about women. By 1972, over 600 courses in women's history, psychology, and sociology were offered in American colleges and universities. By 1974, 500 schools offered over 2,000 women's studies courses; by 1982, they had grown to 30,000 courses. These were followed by the proliferation of women's studies programs across the nation which, by the early 1980s, began to attempt to "mainstream" women's materials into general courses.

Meanwhile, scholars in individual fields of study began to do research and to teach about women. In history, for example, women's history courses emerged. To work for reform in the practice and teaching of history, women historians formed into such groups as the Coordinating Committee for Women in the Historical Profession, and Women Historians of the Midwest.

In 1977, the feminist movement demonstrated its growing strength and maturity at the International Women's Year Conference in Houston, Texas. Here 15,000 women gathered to devise a plan for the liberation of womankind. The delegates represented white, black, Hispanic, Asian, Oriental, and American Indian women, all of whom presented their views and outlined their needs. The wants of rich and poor, young and old, worker and fulltime housewife, heterosexual and homosexual were also considered. The National Plan of Action, drafted in Houston, spoke to inequities faced by women in the home, on the job, and in government.

Of course, these varied attempts at feminist reform did not go unopposed. The ERA was one explosive issue. Phyllis Schlafly of Illinois organized STOP ERA in 1972; she argued that "ERA offers absolutely no benefit to women, no new right, no new opportunity that we do not have now." In 1982, the ERA failed to achieve the requisite number of states for final ratification. Abortion was another key concern that generated continued controversy, even after the Supreme Court, in 1973, supported women's right to choose it. Efforts to reverse this proabortion stance resulted in the Right to Life movement and finally in the eruption of violence against abortion clinics in 1985.

Other setbacks came from several Presidents. One curb to the feminist momentum of the 1970s was President Richard M. Nixon's veto of the Comprehensive Child Development bill in 1972. This act would have provided nationwide day-care centers for employed mothers, a move that Nixon believed to be a "communal approach to child-rearing" that had "family-weakening implications." A similar presidential roadblock appeared with the inaugurations of President Ronald Reagan in 1981 and 1985. The Reagan administration was slow to enforce affirmative action laws and quick to cut back social welfare programs that affected women. It also opposed abortion and the ERA.

Furthermore, feminism and the women's liberation movement of the 1960s and 1970s developed only gradually among minority women. For instance, the American Jewish community responded slowly and cautiously to feminist demands. Yet, since 1971, when groups of Jewish women began to attempt to synthesize American feminism and American Judaism, some significant modifications did occur. A partial reconciliation between feminism and Judaism resulted in greater female participation in communal prayer, limited acceptance of innovative liturgy and life cycle rituals, and the entry of women into positions of communal authority and status. These changes encouraged Jewish women to criticize Jewish religious texts, propose changes in Jewish pedagogy, and pursue such professions as the rabbinate and cantorial work, customarily monopolized by men.

The relationship of feminism and black Americans is even more involved. As has been noted in this and earlier chapters, neither the model of American womanhood nor attempts to modify it had had a great deal of meaning to the cultural values and needs of black women. For one thing, the emphasis on women's participation in the labor force in black society created notions of womanhood contradictory to those held by white society. The black woman tended to be a laborer in a country that stressed domesticity for women. For another, the black family structure offered women a degree of equality with men, which the white family structure did not. Black women expected to assume a strong role in their families and already possessed some of the autonomy that white feminism was demanding.

Moreover, black women's daily lives were shaped more by racism than by sexism. Because black women tended to see racism as a more direct cause of their subordination than sexism, they often viewed the feminist movement with disdain or even distrust. The alienation of black women was exacerbated by the prejudicial attitudes of many white feminists, who did little to reach out to black women or to understand their needs and concerns. Such issues as domesticity, the feminine mystique, and inequality in the family and society were much more the issues of white women than of black women.

This historic division between white and black women was well demonstrated within the ranks of the civil rights movement. Here black women sometimes assumed leadership roles with little opposition, while white women were restricted to performing support services as a result of gender stereotyping. As a case in point, Cynthia Washington, an engineering student who became a member of SNCC in 1963, rose to leadership positions and the direction of her own freedom project in Mississippi. She observed the limitations placed on white women workers and listened to their complaints about them. Washington explained that black women were in a different position because they "were respected and admired for their strength and endurance. . . . They worked hard in the cotton fields or white folks' houses and raised and supported their children." Washington added that black women were "raised to function independently. . . . The notion of retiring to housewifery someday is not even a reasonable fantasy." To her, black and white women started "from opposite ends of the spectrum" and lacked a "program or tactic to begin building sisterhood."

In 1965, when white activists Mary King and Casey Hayden left the civil rights movement, they addressed a memorandum to black women workers. It expressed the hope that "perhaps we can start to talk with each other more openly than in the past and create a community of support for each other so we can deal with ourselves and others with integrity and can therefore keep working." The memorandum revealed King and Hayden's discomfort and isolation as white women in the movement, but it also recognized that black women followed a different path. Black women clearly needed to fight racism first and sexism second.

Ella Baker, one of the foremost freedom workers, also commented on the number of black women within the movement in 1970 as she looked back over her five decades of work with the NAACP, the SCLC, the

SNCC, and the Mississippi Freedom Democratic party. She recognized black women's dedication to eradicating racism when she wrote that "the movement of the '50s and '60s" involved many black women. She lamented the lack of recognition of these women but noted that many of the younger women workers were becoming increasingly insistent on "an equal footing" with black male freedom fighters.

Other black women reformers remarked on the distance between black and white women. In 1970, Dara Abuakari (also known as Virginia E. Y. Collins), vice-president of the so-called Republic of New Africa, directed the following remarks to the women's liberation movement: "You cannot separate men from women when you are black. The black woman is not undergoing the same kind of oppression that white women have gone through in the homes. The black woman is independent. The struggle of black women and white women is not the same. White women have to look at their problem and it is their husbands. He is the oppressor, because he is the system. It's a white male system." In that same year, Renee Ferguson of the *Washington Post*, also emphasized that, although "the women's liberation movement touches some sensitive nerves among black women, . . . they are not always the nerves the movement seems to touch among so many whites." To Ferguson, "the first priority of virtually all black people is the elimination of racial prejudice in America." Once that was accomplished, then perhaps black women would turn to "the elimination of oppression because of sex."

Given the differences in black and white women's needs, why did a black feminist movement eventually develop? A number of black leaders concluded that many of the reforms aimed at by the women's liberation movement would be of value to black women. The right to have abortions, child-care centers, equal pay, and equal access to employment and the destruction of degrading stereotypes were some of the changes that would benefit all women. In 1964, attorney and poet Pauli Murray pointed out that black and white women shared "a common burden because of traditional discriminations based upon sex." Dr. Anna Hedgeman of Harlem and Dorothy Height, president of the National Council of Negro Women, also pointed out that such problems as job discrimination, false stereotypes, and sexual exploitation transcended race.

In addition, a growing number of black women became more responsive to feminist issues as they moved into the mainstream of American life and began to encounter blatant sexism. As they increasingly pursued college educations, entered white collar jobs and the professions, and attempted to enlarge their political participation, they faced gender discrimination. In politics, for example, black women were denied the political access given to black men. In 1974, 2,293 black men were elected to office, as opposed to only 337 black women.

As a consequence of their encounters with sexism, black women began to espouse feminist causes and to form organizations dedicated to erad-icating both evils. In 1973, the Black Women Organized for Action (BWOA) was founded in San Francisco. Later that year, the first confer-ence of the National Black Feminist Organization (NBFO) met in New York. Although these groups recognized the distance between black and white women's issues, they also asserted that such goals of the women's liberation movement as day care, abortion, equal pay, and maternity leaves were critically important to black women. In fact, they suggested that some of these were of greater importance to black women because of their poverty.

Gradually, the feminist movement began to include many special groups of women. It integrated black, American Indian, Third World, and white working class women into its ranks. A concern developed for lesbian women and, more recently; for the special difficulties faced by older women. It also elicited the support of such women's organizations as the Girl Scouts of America, the League of Women Voters, and the UWCA for its causes.

This strong and diverse feminist movement achieved a wide variety of gains. In 1967, for instance, President Lyndon B. Johnson issued an ex-ecutive order prohibiting gender discrimination by federal contractors. Johnson also recruited more women to high administrative office in Washington than any other president before or since. The federal govern-ment was also active in other ways on behalf of feminist issues. In 1970, the Labor Department issued affirmative action guidelines to all federal contractors. In 1972, Congress passed both the ERA and Title IX of the Education Amendments Act, which forbade discrimination against stu-dents and employees in federally assisted educational programs. During the next few years, Congress enacted a virtual barrage of equity laws, including the Women's Equity Act, which supported training programs for women.

Perhaps one of the most important achievements of feminism was a widespread awareness of discrimination. A Gallup poll in 1962 revealed that less than one out of three women felt discriminated against. In 1970, 50 percent of the women questioned said that they had experienced dis-crimination. In 1974, two out of three said that they were victims of discrimination. In 1979, another study showed that the beliefs of women of all classes and ages had undergone a significant shift toward egalitar-ianism between 1962 and 1977. Although they might not count them-selves as members of the feminist movement, the majority did espouse feminist positions on day care, abortion, and equal access to job and professional opportunities. Yet another study indicated that many Amer-ican men also dramatically revised their attitudes toward women during the early 1970s, a result of raised awareness of the status of women in American society.

Clearly, many modifications took place in the lives of American women after 1960. The invented American woman, with her passivity and docility, survived more as an unrealized myth than as a functional model. But whether these alterations can be directly attributed to the feminist movement itself is unclear. In all probability, the feminist movement was both a cause and an effect of the changing social climate. That is, feminism probably resulted from some developments and accelerated others. The only certainty was that between 1960 and the present, American women began to function in a society that had at least begun to recognize the existence of gender discrimination and its high cost to the nation.

The role of employment in women's lives radically altered during this era. Between 1960 and 1980, the female work force almost doubled. During the 1970s, it grew at a rate almost twice that of the 1950s. By 1980, over half of all married women worked, and approximately three out of five women with children held jobs. By 1985, more than three out of five women worked. Because women could no longer be considered a temporary or marginal labor force, they began to receive a number of benefits, including maternity leave, equal-pay provisions, and day-care and training programs.

Not all problems were solved, however. The majority of women continued to be segregated into clerical, sales, and office jobs at low wages. In 1985, they earned between 55 to 57 cents of every dollar men made. Furthermore, women's work frequently called for few skills and offered little opportunity for advancement. And, contrary to popular belief, rather than improving the position of women in the labor market, mechanization (from the typewriter to the computer) contributed to their subordination.

A number of historians and economists believe that the 1970s were a watershed for the employment of women. Their research encourages them to be hopeful that revised cultural values will support a variety of social forms that will help to equalize employment opportunities for women and men. They note that more women are working in such formerly male areas as steel production and mining. Furthermore, they point to governmental intervention on behalf of working women as a particularly promising sign.

There has also been a growing willingness of working women to organize. Between 1956 and 1976, women workers, a large number of whom were teachers and public employees, accounted for nearly half of the growth in total union membership. Between 1976 and 1978, Department of Labor statistics indicated that women trade union members increased by 455,000, bringing women to approximately 28 percent of union membership. In 1974, 3,500 union women launched a new organization, the Coalition of Labor Union Women (CLUW). This group committed itself to increasing affirmative action on the job, pressing for passage of legislation affecting female laborers, supporting women's involvement in politics, and bringing unorganized women into unions.

At the same time, unions began to understand that their survival could be affected by their willingness to consider the needs of the ever-increasing numbers of women in the work force. In 1980, the new president of the AFL-CIO announced his intention to bring women into top leadership positions. During the 1980s, unions began to reach out to unorganized women workers, to add women to their leadership structures, to introduce coverage of women's issues and activities into their newsletters and other publications, and to include women's causes in their lobbying efforts.

The place of black women in the labor force altered as well. Black women workers moved in great numbers into areas customarily dominated by white female workers. In 1965, only 24 percent of employed black women were white-collar workers, a figure that rose to 46 percent in 1981. They also abandoned domestic service in impressive numbers and were replaced by immigrants from Mexico, Puerto Rico, and other areas of Latin America. In 1965, 30 percent of all working black women were in domestic service; by 1977 this figure had dropped to 9 percent.

In addition, black women moved into the organized labor movement. In 1970, black garment worker Lillian Rice complained that unions were of little use to black workers because they discriminated against minorities. This situation improved somewhat during the 1970s. Trade union activist Lillian Roberts is an outstanding example of the change. A public employee, Roberts climbed up the union hierarchy in the American Federation of State, County, and Municipal Employees until she achieved the position of associate director for organization in New York by the end of the 1970s.

The lot of rural women workers underwent less modification. In the rural South, both black and white women labored in their homes and in the fields for long hours for wages often below the poverty level. A study of tobacco farms in 1980 indicated that a significant number of women contributed their labor as sisters, wives, and daughters. According to one researcher, this family system of survival functioned "under the leadership of the male head" and "blended patriarchal forms with the market economy."

Because of the growing economic pressures on family farms during the 1970s and 1980s, many farm women across the nation also "helped out" by working off the farm or running the farm while the men of the family held outside jobs. A study of Kentucky farm women in 1980 revealed that 38 percent worked off the farm. Another researcher noted that farm women were caught in a "triple squeeze," for "not only do they have to fill in for their part-time farming husbands on the land, but they themselves are increasingly entering the nonfarm labor force ... and must moonlight their own farm work."

By 1985, a sizable number of women were employed as laborers on farms or as farm managers. Another significant group acted as farmers themselves. In 1978, census figures indicated that 5 percent of all farmers, or 128,170 of them, were female. A Department of Agriculture survey in 1981 discovered that 55 percent of all farm women considered themselves the main operators. These results suggested that the census data underestimated the number of female farmers. In 1983, rural sociologist Carolyn Sachs interviewed a large number of these women farmers and laborers. She learned that, although their labor and other contributions were substantial, they remained invisible in terms of power. Banks tended to refuse their applications for loans, male farmers excluded them from information sessions, and even tractor producers ignored their needs for equipment modified to a smaller scale.

The lives of women migrant farm workers were also fraught with difficulties. Largely Mexican American, they endured terrible working conditions, poor wages, wretched housing, patriarchal family structures, and lack of opportunities to improve their situations. Elizabeth Loza Newby described the anguish that she felt when, in 1966, her migrant worker father forced her to sacrifice her family ties in order to pursue the education that was her only escape from the migrant life and an arranged marriage. Jessie Lopez de la Cruz chose a different path of resistance by becoming the first female farmworkers union organizer in 1962. She then became a Chicano spokesperson and a member of the California Commission on the Status of Women.

Another group who continued to struggle with problems were American Indian women. Confined to reservations or ghettoes in urban areas, they faced prejudice in housing, education, and employment. The reemergence of the movement for Indian self-determination during the 1960s brought a few gains, including more native control over Indian schools and some public recognition of the degrading stereotyping of American Indians in the media. By the 1980s, the American Indian Movement (AIM) had brought national attention to the desperate conditions of such reservations as Rose Bud and Pine Ridge in South Dakota. Social problems, including alcoholism and unemployment, were also widely discussed. And by 1985, a number of colleges and universities offered Indian studies courses and programs. Still, as a native, female director of one Montana Indian studies program noted, the discrimination and personal problems encountered by Indian women were staggering.

Although rural, migrant, and native women's lives saw little reform, other women encountered and seized the many new opportunities. One of the areas of greatest alteration and gain for American women after

1960 was education. Programs designed to eradicate women's "fear of success" and "math anxiety" attempted to offset the negative effects of gender stereotyping. Women's athletic programs expanded and became more equitable with men's in some respects. The number of female college students rose noticeably. West Point and Anapolis graduated their first women in 1980. And by 1985, affirmative action programs were in place in a large number of the nation's schools, colleges, and universities.

As a consequence of expanded educational opportunities and the growing acceptance of well-educated women by Americans, women in the professions increased. Between 1971 and 1981, the percent of lawyers and judges who were female jumped from 4 to 14; of doctors, from 9 to 22; and of engineers, from 1 to 4. In medicine, women moved into a wide variety of roles, including nurse, nurse-midwife, general practitioner, and surgeon. Women also entered graduate schools at an unprecedented rate. After 1970, the number of women receiving doctorates grew more than 1 percent each year; by 1985, women earned nearly 30 percent of all Ph.D. degrees granted.

Black women participated in these gains to some extent. Teaching, nursing, and the social sciences continued to be attractive fields for black women, but they also entered law and medicine in growing numbers. Although they benefited from affirmative action and economic opportunity programs, the actual number of black women in the professions remained small. Also, while white women were rushed into highly visible positions as anchorpersons, news reporters, executives, and governmental officials, the number of black women in these positions grew more slowly.

The sports world also exhibited some marked changes relating to women after 1960. Track and field stars Wilma Rudolph and Wyomia Tyus dramatically lowered women's record times in Olympic competition. The Women's Professional Basketball League formed in 1978, and in golf, Nancy Lopez was winning purses whose amounts approached those of male golf. Althea Gibson smashed through the color barrier in tennis, while tennis star Billie Jean King was among the first nine women inducted into the Women's Sports Hall of Fame in 1980. Jockeys Mary Bacon and Robyn Smith not only rode against male jockeys, but also frequently won. And race-car driver Janet Guthrie drove in the renowned Indianapolis 500.

Women also made gains in the media. Not only did sexual stereotyping come under widespread attack, but the number of women's roles and themes also increased in both the movies and television. Sally Field portrayed a labor organizer in southern cotton mills in the film *Norma Rae;* Barbara Streisand raised serious questions about women's roles in the film *Yentl,* and Jessica Lange demonstrated the strength of women faced by adversity in *Country.* Professional, single-parent, and minority women gained more visibility on television. Barbara Walters became an outstanding and highly paid television journalist. And in 1985, the show "Cagney and Lacy" featuring two female detectives received high ratings.

In the arts, impressive numbers of women produced works ranging from folk art to surrealism. The works of black folk artists Minnie Evans, Ethel Mohamed, Inez Nathaniel, and Queena Stovall were popular. Two other folk artists of the period were Theordora Hamblett and Gertrude Rogers, who began painting late in their lives and were known for their autobiographical scenes. Malcah Zeldis, who began painting in her late thirties, focused on historical events, Jewish religious themes, and personal memories. This outburst of production of female folk art was accompanied by a resurgence of interest in quilting, which led to the formation of quilting clubs and conferences. Of special note is Judy Chicago's massive work, *The Birth Project*. Other very interesting and more traditional artistic compositions were produced by feminist artist Alice Neel and the painter of women, Isabel Bishop.

In the field of classical music, women were also creative and productive. Female composers began to work with innovative modes of expression. Annea Lockwood's 1976 composition, *World Rhythms,* combined natural sounds from rivers, earthquakes, and human breathing with the playing of a gong. Another creative and frequently performed composer was Barbara Kolb, who wrote many pieces for chamber ensembles. Joyce Mekiel gained critical acclaim for her experiments with unusual ways of using the human voice and traditional instruments. Meanwhile, women musicians gained some stature. The first regular female player with the New York Philharmonic was a double bassist hired in 1966. During the 1960s, the number of employed women musicians increased. Women began to be hired as section heads, if not yet as conductors. The appointment of Beverly Sills as artistic director of the New York City Opera Company in 1983 marked another advance.

Women also enjoyed success in other types of music. In jazz, pianist Marian McPartland and black singers Ella Fitzgerald, Sarah Vaughn, and Nancy Wilson enjoyed great popularity. In popular music, black singers Aretha Franklin and Diana Ross and white singers Helen Reddy, Janis Joplin, and Bette Midler were a few of the many outstanding female vocalists.

Women writers were also prolific and imaginative. Erica Jong's *Fear of Flying* (1973) examined sexual themes in a way not expected from a female author. In a wide variety of works, Joan Didion and Joyce Carol Oates dealt with topics relating to the struggle of women to understand modern society. Black writer Toni Morrison attracted favorable attention with such works as *Sula* (1975) and *Song of Solomon* (1978), while black feminist writer Alice Walker explored relationships among women and within families in *The Color Purple* (1982).

Women also became more visible in the political realm in the decades after 1960. Between 1969 and 1981, the number of women holding office as state legislators grew from 301 to 908. Between 1975 and 1981, the number of female elected officials increased from 5,765 to 14,225. In 1968, Democrat Shirley Chisholm became the first black woman elected to the U. S. House of Representatives, and in 1972, she ran in the Democratic presidential primaries. In that same year, Representative Barbara Jordan, a black Democrat from Texas, delivered the nominating speech at the Democratic convention, while Representative Martha Griffith, a Democrat from Michigan, distinguished herself in fighting for the ERA. During the Watergate scandals, Representative Elizabeth Holtzman, a Democrat from New York, proved herself to be a forceful interrogator as part of the House Judiciary Committee's investigative team, and Barbara Jordan also was one of the persons who voted articles of impeachment against President Richard M. Nixon.

By the decade of the 1980s, women's competence and effectiveness as politicians were recognized and rewarded with top level positions. In 1981, President Reagan appointed Sandra Day O'Connor as the first woman justice on the U. S. Supreme Court. In 1983, he appointed Elizabeth Dole as Secretary of Transportation and Margaret Heckler as Secretary of Health and Human Services. In 1984, the Democratic party chose New York congressperson Geraldine Ferraro as its candidate for the vice-presidency of the United States.

The family, however, was perhaps the most dramatic area of change for women. By 1980, only 15 percent of American families were composed of a father who worked and a mother who stayed at home to care for the children, a figure that had stood at over 70 percent in the early 1950s. With the assistance of the birth-control pill, the average family size fell to 1.6 children. At the same time, roughly 50 percent of marriages ended in divorce, and 23 percent of adults chose to live in single-person households. As a result, the definition of family expanded to accomodate two employed adults, spouses who lived in separate households, a single-parent household, a "reconstituted" family made up of two remarried adults and their children from previous marriages, a group of unmarried people representing several generations living together, and an unmarried person living alone. Dual-career marriage, single-parent family, commuter marriage, super-mom, singlehood, and latch-key child all became catchwords.

These shifts in family composition were accompanied by new attitudes toward sex, self-fulfillment, and gender roles. Many men learned to do more than "help" around the house, to enjoy child care, and to share decision-making with their wives. Many women began to function effectively in the world outside the home, to develop interests beyond their families, and to contribute regularly to the family finances. Many children recognized that a variety of choices of lifestyles were open to them, adapted to divorce and other revisions in family structure, and participated in the care of themselves and their homes.

A number of other changes accompanied these modifications in the American family. The proportion of Americans who chose to remain single, to bear children without marrying, and to terminate their marriages increased significantly. As a result, there was an ongoing public concern for the future of marriage, the family, and gender roles.

A particularly notable development was the "feminization" of poverty. The rise of the female-headed household due to divorce, combined with the segregation of women into low paying jobs, created a huge group of American women who lived near or under the poverty level. In 1980, two thirds of female-headed families received child welfare, while over 80 percent of welfare recipients were female. Moreover, two thirds of the poor were women.

The growth of female poverty particularly affected black women. By 1980, 55 percent of black children were born outside of marriage, 85 percent of black teenage mothers were unmarried, and 47 percent of black families had female heads. Lacking skills and still discriminated against in employment, most of these women turned to welfare, or to such organizations as the National Council of Negro Women for aid. Other minority group women were similarly affected. One example was Innocencia Flores, a Puerto Rican woman living in Harlem. A mother of four, separated from her husband and living on relief, Flores waged a daily battle with rats, junkies, the indifference of landlords, and the exhaustion of overloaded welfare caseworkers.

Since social change always brings difficulties and disruptions, many people and organizations studied the problems and offered possible solutions. Feminist groups, governmental agencies, researchers and scholars, social workers, sociologists, and private individuals suggested various strategies for dealing with the many alterations in American society. Workshops and other public programs offering to aid individuals in their adjustment to the changing world proliferated, while a large self-help literature developed and often enjoyed "best-seller" status. Affirmative action programs, the passage of the ERA, litigation equalizing wages of female and male workers, job training programs, paid maternity leaves, a remodeling of outdated notions of femininity and masculinity, crisis intervention programs, nonsexist education, and equal political representation were among the ideas considered and frequently implemented.

During the 1980s, public debates over these and other issues were widespread and often heated. Some Americans still longed for the idyllic past and the "normality" fabricated by the escapist needs of the postwar society of 1945. They still envisioned the possibility that the invented American woman would become the ideal for all women. They resented the demands of feminists and other reformers. In 1985, for example, one male public figure commented: "So cry not for the Ferraro candidacy. Nobody lost by it. The women were in the kitchen when the thing started, and they're in the kitchen where they belong at the end of it."

Other Americans seemed more than willing to explore new sexual and social roles and to back the extension of equality to women. A Gallup poll in 1980 revealed widespread support for women's reproductive freedom and their right to hold political office. A survey in 1983 showed that the majority of respondents believed that wives and husbands should share not only household chores and childcare but financial and other decision-making as well. In 1985, yet another poll revealed a growing willingness on the part of both women and men to destroy the traditional double standard and erect new social roles and expectations in its place.

Apparently, the model American woman had not yet vanished from the scene. But she was caught in a terrific tug of war. If and how she was to be restructured was a question that eluded prophets and analysts alike. It could only be answered by the future.

SUGGESTIONS FOR FURTHER READING

Ammer, Christine. Unsung: *A History of Women in American Music*. Westport, Ct: Greenwood Press, 1980.

Bataille, Gretchen M., and Charles L. P. Silet, eds. *The Pretend Indians: Images of Native Americans in the Movies*. Ames: Iowa State University Press, 1980.

Banner, Lois W. *Women in Modern America: A Brief History*. San Diego: Harcourt Brace Jovanovich, Publishers, 1984.

Berkin, Carol R., and Mary Beth Norton, eds. *Women of America: A History*. Boston: Houghton Mifflin Company, 1979. Part IV.

Berch, Bettina. *The Endless Day: The Political Economy of Women and Work*. New York: Harcourt Brace Jovanovich, Inc., 1982.

Chafe, William H. *The American Woman: Her Changing Social, Economic, and Political Roles, 1920–1970*. London: Oxford University Press, 1972.

Christian, Barbara. *Black Women Novelists: The Development of A Tradition, 1892–1976*. Westport, Ct: Greenwood Press, 1980.

Cohen, Steve Martin. "American Jewish Feminism: A Study in Conflicts and Compromises." *American Behavioral Scientist* 23 (March/April 1980): 519–558.

Cowan, Ruth Schwartz. "From Virginia Dare to Virginia Slims: Women and Technology in American Life." *Technology and Culture* 20 (January 1979): 51–63.

Degler, Carl N. *At Odds: Women and the Family in America from the Revolution to the Present*. Oxford: Oxford University Press, 1980.

Dill, Bonnie Thornton. "The Dialectics of Black Womanhood." *Signs* 4 (Spring 1979): 543–555.

Epstein, Cynthia Fuchs. "Positive Effects of the Multiple Negative: Explaining the Success of Black Professional Women." *American Journal of Sociology* 78 (January 1973): 912–935.

———. "Ten Years Later: Perspectives on the Woman's Movement." *Dissent* 22 (Spring 1975): 169–176.

Estep, Rhoda. "Women's Roles in Crime as Depicted by Television and Newspapers." *Journal of Popular Culture* 16 (Winter 1982): 151–156.

Evans, Sara. "Women's Consciousness and the Southern Black Movement." *Southern Exposure* 4 (Winter 1977), 10–14.

———. *Personal Politics: The Roots of Women's Liberation in the Civil Rights Movement and the New Left*. New York: Alfred A. Knopf, 1979.

Ferree, Myra Marx. "A Woman for President? Changing Responses: 1958–1972." *Public Opinion Quarterly* 38 (Fall 1974): 390–399.

Foner, Philip S. *Women and the American Labor Movement: From World War I to the Present*. New York: The Free Press, 1980.

Friedman, Jean E., and William G. Shade., eds. *Our American Sisters: Women in American Life and Thought*. Lexington, MA: D. C. Heath and Company, 1982. Part IV.

Gabin, Nancy. "Women Workers and the UAW in the Post-World War II Period: 1945–1954." *Labor History* 21 (Winter 1979–80): 5–30.

Gill, Gerald R. "'WIN OR LOSE—WE WIN': The 1952 Vice-Presidential Campaign of Charlotta A. Bass." In *The Afro-American Woman: Struggles and Images*, edited by Sharon Harley and Rosalyn M. Terborg-Penn, 109–118. Port Washington, NY: Kennikat Press, 1978.

Goldin, Claudia. "Female Labor Force Participation: The Origin of Black and White Differences, 1870 and 1880." *Journal of Economic History* 37 (March 1977): 87–108.

Harrison, Cynthia E. "A 'New Frontier' for Women: The Public Policy of the Kennedy Administration." *Journal of American History* 67 (December 1980): 630–646.

Howe, Louise Kapp. *Pink Collar Workers: Inside the World of Women's Work*. NY: G. P. Putnam's Sons, 1977.

Katzenstein, Mary Fainsod. "Feminism and the Meaning of the Vote." *Signs* 10 (Autumn 1984): 4–26.

Kennedy, Susan Estabrook. *If All We Did Was to Weep at Home: A History of White Working-class Women in America*. Bloomington: Indiana University Press, 1979.

Keohane, Nannerl O., Michelle Rosaldo, and Barbara Gelpi, eds. *Feminist Theory: A Critique of Ideology*. Chicago: University of Chicago Press, 1982.

Kerber, Linda K., and Jane DeHart Mathews, eds. *Women's America: Refocusing the Past*. New York: Oxford University Press, 1982. Part III.

Kessler-Harris, Alice. *Out to Work: A History of Wage-Earning Women in the United States*. Oxford: Oxford University Press, 1982.

Klein, Ethel. *Gender Politics.* Cambridge: Harvard University Press, 1984.

Kobrin, Frances E. "The Fall in Household Size and the Rise of the Primary Individual in the United States." *Demography* 13 (February 1976): 127–138.

Lerner, Gerda, ed. *Black Women in White America: A Documentary History.* New York: Vintage Books, 1973.

——. *The Majority Finds Its Past: Placing Women in History.* Oxford: Oxford University Press, 1979. Chapters 3, 4, and 9.

Lewis, Diane K. "A Response to Inequality: Black Women, Racism, and Sexism." *Signs* 3 (Winter 1977): 339–361.

Litoff, Judy Barrett. *American Midwives: 1860 to the Present.* Westport, Ct: Greenwood Press, 1978.

Margolis, Maxine L. *Mothers and Such: Views of American Women and Why They Changed.* Berkeley and Los Angeles: University of California Press, 1984.

Morantz, Regina Markell. "The Scientist as Sex Crusader: Alfred C. Kinsey and American Culture." In *Procreation or Pleasure? Sexual Attitudes in American History,* edited by Thomas L. Altherr, 145–166. Malabar, FL: Robert E. Kreiger Publishing Company, 1983.

Melosh, Barbara. *"The Physicians Hand": Work, Culture, and Conflict in American Nursing.* Philadelphia: Temple University Press, 1982.

Painter, Diann Holland. "The Black Woman in American Society." *Current History* 70 (May 1976): 224–227, 234.

Robinson, Donald Allen. "Two Movements in Pursuit of Equal Employment Opportunity." *Signs* 4 (Spring 1979): 413–433.

Rothschild, Mary Aickin. "White Women Volunteers in the Freedom Summers: Their Life and Work in a Movement for Social Change." *Feminist Studies* 5 (Fall 1979): 466–495.

Rupp, Leila J. "The Survival of American Feminism: The Women's Movement in the Postwar Period." In *Reshaping America: Society and Institutions, 1945–1960,* edited by Robert H. Bremner and Gary W. Reichard, 33–65. Columbus: Ohio State University Press, 1982.

Ryan, Mary P. *Womanhood in America: From Colonial Times to The Present.* New York: New Viewpoints, 1979. Chapters 6–7.

Sachs, Carolyn E. *The Invisible Farmers: Women in Agricultural Production.* Totowa, NJ: Rowman & Allanheld, 1983.

Scott, Anne Firor. *Making the Invisible Woman Visible.* Urbana: University of Illinois Press, 1984.

Scott, Joan Wallach. "The Mechanization of Women's Work." *Scientific American* 247 (September 1982): 166–187.

Seller, Maxine Schwartz, ed. *Immigrant Women.* Philadelphia: Temple University Press, 1981.

Senese, Guy. "Promise and Practice: Important Developments in Wartime and Post-War Indian Education Policy: 1940–1975." *Journal of Thought* 19 (Fall 1984): 11–30.

Sexton, Patricia Cayo. *The New Nightingales: Hospital Workers, Unions, New Women's Issues.* New York: Inquiry Press, 1982.

Sicherman, Barbara, and Carol Hurd Green, eds. *Notable American Women: The Modern Period.* Cambridge, MA: Belknap Press, 1980.

Strasser, Susan. *Never Done: A History of American Housework* New York: Pantheon, 1981.

Thornton, Arland, and Deborah Freedman. "Changes in the Sex Role Attitudes of Women, 1962–1977: Evidence from a Panel Study." *American Sociological Review* 44 (October 1979): 831–842.

Wallace, Michele. *Black Macho and the Myth of the Superwoman*. New York: The Dial Press, 1979.

Walsh, Mary Roth. *"Doctors Wanted: No Women Need Apply": Sexual Barriers in the Medical Profession, 1835–1975*. New Haven: Yale University Press, 1977.

Weibel, Kathryn. *Mirror Mirror: Images of Women Reflected in Popular Culture*. New York: Anchor Press, 1977.

Weiss, Nancy Pottishman. "Mother, the Invention of Necessity: Dr. Benjamin Spock's *Baby and Child Care*." *American Quarterly* 24 (Winter 1977): 519–546.

Wells, Robert V. "Demographic Change and the Life Cycle of American Families." *Journal of Interdisciplinary History* 2 (Autumn 1971): 273–282.

Wertheimer, Barbara Mayer. *We Were There: The Story of Working Women in America*. New York: Pantheon Books, 1977.

Woloch, Nancy. *Women and the American Experience*. New York: Alfred A. Knopf, 1984. Chapters 19–20.

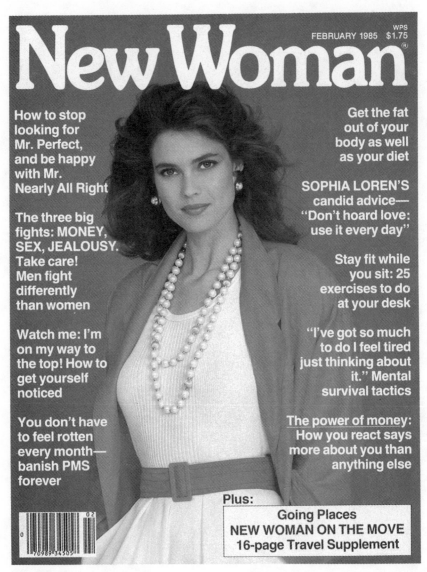

New Woman *was one of the most popular women's magazines by the mid-1980s. Its articles, special features, and cartoons recognized the growing diversity of women's pursuits and interests.* Courtesy of *New Woman* magazine. Photograph by Bill Connors.

The Resiliency and the
Future of the Model

B ETWEEN 1607 and the mid-1800s, the model of what an American woman should be changed in many ways, yet its overall configuration stayed much the same. According to the ideal during these years, a "true" woman was a wife and mother. She was domestic, physically weak, and morally strong. She was too virtuous to participate in politics and too maternal to take paid employment. She could exercise, but only moderately. She could read if the subject matter were morally improving. And, of course, she was fair of skin, with rosy cheeks and flowing brown tresses down her back.

Between the mid-nineteenth century and the 1980s, the model of what an American woman should be came under attack from every side yet did not succumb to destruction. In fact, the image of women as domestic, docile, cheerful, simple, and submissive enjoyed periods of rejuvenation, especially during the back-to-the-home movement that followed the conclusion of the Second World War. Apparently, many Americans were hesitant to surrender the traditional view of women as properly relegated to, and fulfilled by, the world of home and family.

Clearly, the model did not fit many American women. Although there is no way to quantify the number of women who did not conform to the ideal, they were probably in the majority. The fact that the employed, professional, reform, suffrage, immigrant, black, and American Indian women certainly did not fit the model or accept its dictates suggests that thousands of American women lived outside the bounds of the prescribed image. Yet the stereotype was so prevalent that even women who rejected the ideal in their minds often tried to meet at least part of its teachings in their lives. As a result, such women as Anne Bradstreet and Lucretia Mott set the pattern for later generations of "Super Moms" who would try to care for their homes and families in the "proper" way while attempting to pursue their own personal interests as well.

Many events encouraged close scrutiny of the efficacy of the customary model of women. War, industrialization, urbanization, economic depression, and the development of reform movements all led to a general rethinking of women's roles and responsibilities. Were women to be limited only to wife- and motherhood? Or was there another part that they might happily and effectively play in addition to these roles? Was the nation squandering a crucial resource in restricting women to customary, domestic lifestyles?

Numerous people argued for the expansion of women's participation in American society. For instance, both female and male reformers exerted pressure on all levels of society to become more egalitarian. Through voluntary associations, these people worked for social and gender reforms. Those who were also suffragists argued particularly for women's right to the ballot. Although these people believed that the country would benefit greatly as a result, they found it difficult to convince their fellow citizens.

When the right of suffrage was finally granted to American women in 1920, it became clear that the vote was not a panacea. Years earlier, Elizabeth Cady Stanton had dismissed the right to vote as "not even half a load . . . only a crust, a crumb." During the decades following the achievement of suffrage, women's-rights advocates realized that the surface had barely been scratched. The vote had not, as once had been hoped, given women the tool they needed to bring about other changes.

By the 1960s, the need for a renewed feminist movement seemed apparent to numbers of women from a variety of backgrounds. Throughout American history, feminism had ebbed and flowed in harmony with the exigencies of the time. But each time that it reasserted itself, it did so with renewed vigor. Consequently, its contemporary manifestation—the feminist movement of the 1960s and afterward—was the largest ever in membership and the most widely based in constituencies, platforms, and programs. It appealed to all races, classes, and types of women and men.

The contemporary feminist movement attacked domesticity, or what it called the feminine mystique. Domesticity had exhibited amazing tenacity through wars, depression, and various other crises. Yet at the same time, its very fiber was being weakened. Change was at least as powerful a trend as was continuity.

In the years after 1960, the model American woman was altered beyond recognition by basic and pervasive modifications in the structure of American institutions, in the fabric of American culture, and in interpersonal relations. By the 1980s, backlash and resistance to feminist trends had developed. Whether conservative factions would be able to reinstate the invented American woman in future decades was uncertain. It seemed probable, however, that social changes and pervasive feminism would continue to reshape the traditional female model into a fresh image, a figure who might suggest new ways of living to both women and men.

The struggle between the model of womanhood and the reality of women's lives exhibited more complexity than ever before, a development that can partially be understood and dealt with through the study of women's issues and women's history. Fortunately for scholars and others who are curious about the historical heritage of Americans, research in the field of women's history is proliferating at an impressive rate. As one can see from the lists of suggested readings, women's history is a vital pursuit that attracts both female and male scholars and involves a wide variety of journals, topics, and perspectives.

Such creativity and growth demand notice. Thus, neither the vitality nor the significance of women's history can be overlooked any longer. It is an undertaking that is well pursued by women and men alike, since it stands to benefit both groups in their future dealings with the modern world. The current climate may be uncertain, but the 1980s and 1990s offer American women and men an unprecedented opportunity to effect change in their lives and in American society.

Index

New York Woman's Suffrage Party, 187, 193
"Nigger Ellen," 139
Nineteenth Amendment, 195–196
Nixon, Richard M., 248, 257
Normae Rae, 255
Normal and Industrial School for Women, 146
North Carolina, University of, at Greensboro, 146
North Carolina Federation of Women's Clubs, 160
Northeastern Federation of Colored Women's Clubs, 194
Norton, Mary Beth, 14, 45
Nurses. *See also* Medicine
  army and navy, 166, 231
  black women as, 165–166
  during American Revolution, 40, 41
  during Civil War, 122–123
  during early industrial period, 70
  during Gilded Age, 145–146

Oates, Joyce Carol, 256
Oberlin College, 98, 115, 165
O'Brien, Charlotte Smith, 148
Observations on the Real Rights of Women (Crocker), 74
O'Connor, Sandra Day, 257
"Ode to General Washington" (Wheatley), 41
Office of Civil Defense, 231
Office of War Information, 229
Of Men and Women (Buck), 226
O'Hare, Kate Richards, 158
O'Keefe, Georgia, 203, 227
Oneida Indian women, 224
Oneida, New York, 97–98
O Pioneers (Cather), 68
Opportunity, 204
Oregon Trail, opening of, 140
O'Reilly, Leonora, 173
Organization of American Historians, 5
Ornaments for the Daughters of Zion, 15
Orphism, 167–168
Osborn, Sarah, 26
Our Gal Sunday, 225
Our Lady of the Rosary Center (New York), 148
Outerbridge, Mary E., 131
Owen, Ruth Bryan, 219

Paine, Thomas, 38
Paiutes, 142–143
Palmer, Alice Freeman, 163
Palmer, Frances Flora, 168

Panic of 1937, 63, 101
Park, Maud Wood, 192
Parke, Mary, 49
Partridge, Mary, 159
Patapsco Female Institute (Baltimore), 93–94
Patent medicine, 99, 131
Patents, issuance of, to women, 133
Patriotic Leagues, 188
Paul, Alice, 194, 197
Pauline doctrine of silence, 21, 75–76
Peale, Charles Wilson, 34, 49
Peale, Sarah Miriam, 49–50
Pember, Phoebe Yates, 123
Pennington, Patience, 139
Pennsylvania Hospital, 47
Pennsylvania Magazine, 41
Peoples' party. *See* Populist party
Perkins, Frances, 219, 221
Perkins, Sarah, 49
Perry, Lilla Cabot, 168
Pesotta, Rose, 215
Peterson, Esther, 243
Petry, Ann, 225, 242
Phelps, Almira Lincoln, 93–94
Philadelphia Female Anti-slavery Society, 79, 108, 110
Philipse, Margaret, 17
Photography, during New Deal, 226, 227
Pickford, Mary, 202
Pinckney, Charles Cotesworth, 23
Pinckney, Thomas, 23
Pine Ridge reservation (South Dakota), 254
Pinkham, Lydia E., Vegetable Compound, 131
Pinney, Eunice, 73
Pioneers. *See* Westward expansion
Pitcher, Molly (McCauley, Mary), 40
Place, Sarah Steins, 25
Plains Indians, 142
Plath, Sylvia, 247
Pleasant, Mary Ellen "Mammy," 141
Pocahontas, 10, 28, 29
Pocasset women, lives of, 30
Polish Women's Alliance, 174
Politics, women in, 183, 200–201, 221–224, 250, 257, 259
Polygamy, 141
Populist party, involvement of women in, 158–159
Pound, Louise, 164–165
Poverty, feminization of, 258
Powderly, Terence V., 144
Powhatan, Chief, 28
Powhatan Indians, lives of native women among, 28

Glenda Riley is professor of history and director of the Women's Studies Program at the University of Northern Iowa. She is the author of *Frontierswomen: The Iowa Experience* (1981), *Women and Indians on the Frontier, 1825–1915* (1984) and over sixty articles on the early feminist movement in America, women in the American West, and the teaching of women's and public history. She has taught women's history since 1972.

Inventing the American Woman was copyedited by Susannah H. Jones and Lori Elizabeth Winters. Production editor was Brad Barrett. Susan Nagel and Carolee Lipsey proofread the copy; Schroeder Editorial Services compiled the index. The text was typeset by Graphic Composition, Inc., and printed and bound by Edwards Brothers, Inc.

The cover and text were designed by Roger Eggers. Cover illustration: Madonna of the Prairie by W. H. D. Koerner. Courtesy Buffalo Bill Historical Center, Cody, Wyoming.